# The Executive, Congress, and Foreign Policy

# John Lehman

The Praeger Special Studies program—utilizing the most modern and efficient book production techniques and a selective worldwide distribution network—makes available to the academic, government, and business communities significant, timely research in U.S. and international economic, social, and political development.

# The Executive, Congress, and Foreign Policy
## Studies of the Nixon Administration

PRAEGER SPECIAL STUDIES IN U.S. ECONOMIC, SOCIAL, AND POLITICAL ISSUES

**Praeger Publishers**   New York   Washington   London

Library of Congress Cataloging in Publication Data

Lehman, John F
   The Executive, Congress, and foreign policy.

   (Praeger special studies in U.S. economic,
social, and political issues)
   Bibliography: p.
   Includes index.
   1.  United States—Foreign relations—1969–1974.
I.  Title.
JX1417.L387      353.008'92      76–13835
ISBN 0–275–56490–8

PRAEGER PUBLISHERS
111 Fourth Avenue, New York, N.Y. 10003, U.S.A.

Published in the United States of America in 1976
by Praeger Publishers, Inc.

Printed in the United States of America

for Constance

The period upon which this work focuses, the first term of the Nixon administration, appears from the perspective of present post-Watergate enervation to have been one of unbridled executive license and domination of foreign affairs. In fact, it was not so. Those years instead were transitional and very contentious, with Congress playing an increasingly determinate role.

Massive struggle began almost at once between the Nixon administration and Congress over foreign and defense policy. The legislative reaction against Vietnam that forced Lyndon Johnson from office erupted in some 30 legislative battles between 1969 and 1973, with the Executive losing ground with each one. The anti-ballistic missile battle was bitterly fought three times, the first winning by one vote only, and attempts to cut defense programs and withdraw U.S. forces from overseas were perennially lengthy conflicts. But through this disintegration of the Cold War consensus, there were those in both branches who like Henry Kissinger, patiently but successfully were promulgating an intellectual order to the new realities facing the U.S. and the outlines of a new consensus began clearly to be seen.

But events decreed that instead of a transition from the 30 years of Presidential dominance of bipartisan consensus borne of war, hot and cold, to a more normal shared distribution of foreign policy powers, those years led to annihilation of bipartisan consensus and violent reinstitution of Congressional domination that seems likely to endure for some time.

The seeds of this tumultuous revolution are clearly to be discerned in the events recounted here. Indeed as we shall see in Chapter 1, the cycle of Congressional reassertion after wars is historic and reliable. But one will also find in these chapters that it need not have been so. The seeds may also be found in a newly emerging consensus between the branches of government and among the people: A new view of the proper role of the U.S. in the world—no longer a world policeman but still vigorously encouraging democratic development and providing support to those resisting subjugation.

Watergate, however, destroyed that promising emergence, and set in motion events that have produced instead a rather brutish, even at times anarchic, confrontation between the Executive and Congress, rendering the U.S. government incapable of coherent policy abroad.

"The great ordinances of the Constitution," wrote Mr. Justice Holmes, "do not establish and divide fields of black and white. Even the more specific of them are found to terminate in a penumbra shading gradually from one extreme to another." Because of the lack of clearly affirmative grants of specific powers, and the especial vagueness of those actions bearing upon foreign affairs, the United States Constitution has been described as an invitation to the Executive, the Congress jointly, and the Senate to struggle for the privilege of directing American foreign policy.

The foreign policy powers are distributed between the branches of government in a manner purposely unspecific. The process by which this power sharing is carried out between the branches is a dynamic, ever-changing one. If it is not constantly attended to it can swiftly go awry. It has done so often in the republic's history. The tending must be done by all three branches and by the people. Watergate has demonstrated what every scholar of the presidency knows well—that the office of President is the focal point of virtually limitless, awesome power. Such power is a dazzling and volatile substance in the hands of any man. The office and the man need constant policing, and it is to that objective that the United States Constitution is addressed throughout. In foreign policy this is achieved by setting against the Executive a legislative department that is in Madison's words "everywhere extending the sphere of its activity and drawing all power into its impetuous vortex."

The approach in the present work seeks to order the almost infinite number of actions, events, and interactions constituting the relationship between the branches in foreign policy into functional components. It is based on the proposition that there are four important patterns of interaction in which the foreign policy process between the branches takes place. They are the war process, the treaty process, the investigative process, and the authorization/appropriation process. Of course there is overlapping and intertwining between these processes as in all human affairs, but that is a manageable problem of analysis. Each of them is discrete and identifiable. The functioning of each process will be seen through an examination of a contentious issue of the recent past. As Justice Holmes put it, "The life of the law has not been logic; it has been experience."

Chapter 1 examines the fundamental question of dominance. That basic issue simply was not established in the Constitution, and remains, intellectually at least, unresolved to this day. Should the executive branch be dominant in foreign policy formulation and execution, or should Congress have at least an equal role? By exploring the constitutional basis of these two opposing theories, this chapter provides a historical and theoretic context for the events in subsequent chapters.

Chapter 2 discusses the operation of checks and balances in a system of executive dominance of foreign policy, and the functioning, and dysfunctioning, of the processes involved.

In Chapter 3 the war power process is analyzed through a case study of the first Cooper-Church amendment. In May 1970, in response to the President's decision to attack the Cambodian sanctuaries, Senators John Sherman Cooper and Frank Church introduced an amendment to the Foreign Military Sales Bill, which sought to set sharp restrictions upon the President's freedom of action in Indochina. There followed seven weeks of intense debate, accompanied by considerable maneuvering by the executive branch. The actual participation of Congress in the exercise of war powers and decision making may be seen in this chapter.

Chapter 4 examines the treaty process through a case study of the renewal of the base rights agreement with Spain. In August 1970, the executive branch signed an agreement of friendship and cooperation with Spain which provided for a five-year extension of the right to use the four U.S. built military bases in Spain. The interaction between the Senate and the executive branch during the nine months preceding final signature, and the unexpected refusal of the executive branch to submit the agreement to the Senate as a treaty raised fundamental issues of the treaty power of the Senate and of the powers of the Commander in Chief. These issues have risen once again with the impending expiration of that agreement, and were settled in a quite different fashion with the signature of a treaty by Secretary Kissinger during January 1976 in Madrid.

Chapter 5 presents the investigative process through a case study of the Symington Subcommittee on Commitments Abroad. The Symington Subcommittee on Security Agreements and Commitments Abroad began hearings in September 1969, on United States relations with the Philippines. During the subsequent 12-month period, hearings were conducted on Laos, Thailand, Korea, Taiwan, Japan-Okinawa, NATO, nuclear weapons deployment, Spain, Greece, Turkey, Morocco, Libya, and Ethiopia. It provides an excellent opportunity to examine the investigative powers of Congress and the issues of executive privilege and secrecy, in circumstances free of the drama and demagoguery that later attended the Senate and House investigations of the intelligence community in 1975-76.

In Chapter 6 the authorization and appropriation process is examined through a case study of the Cambodia Supplemental. In November 1970, the administration submitted the Supplemental Foreign Assistance Bill to authorize a substantial military assistance program for Cambodia. There followed an unusually intense period of debate and of behind-the-scenes bargaining between the branches, culminating in the passage of the bill after a revised Cooper-Church amendment was attached and accepted by the administration. Here we see the power of the purse operate in surprising ways.

Chapter 7 attempts to abstract regularities and patterns of interaction between the two branches in each of the four components of the analytical framework described above, and to draw some conclusions. The conclusions offered are not astonishing, and address, not surprisingly, the elemental requirement for consensus.

We witness today the effects of non-consensus between Congress, the Executive, and the American people. As a recent member of the U.S. delegation to the Mutual Balanced Force Reduction negotiations in Vienna, I found myself repeatedly explaining U.S. policy intentions to both NATO and Eastern diplomats, all too often to be answered by, "Ah yes, no doubt that is your government's intention, but what will Congress do?" And of course I could not tell them.

Allies and potential adversaries alike deserve to know what to expect from the United States, the costs of opposing its interest, the value of its commitments and the rewards of cooperation. After the Congressional initiatives repudiating executive policy in Southeast Asia, Turkey, and Angola, a seriously destabilizing uncertainty has been established in the world.

There are things seriously wrong with the present state of U.S. foreign policy formulation and conduct. It is hoped that serious readers of these pages may gain some insights into the abuses and dysfunctions that have recently afflicted our ability to pursue wise and rational foreign policy. As Secretary of State Kissinger has said, "Our government is in danger of progressively losing the ability to shape events, and a great nation that does not shape history eventually becomes its victim."

# ACKNOWLEDGMENTS

I am much indebted to the patient and incisive counsel of a number of my friends who read early drafts of this work—Bryce Harlow, David Abshire, Dan McMichael, Bud McFarlane, and Tom Korologos. I am indebted also to Robert E. Osgood, dean of the School of Advanced International Studies, Johns Hopkins University, where I had the privilege of spending a most intellectually satisfying term as a Visiting Fellow. I am especially grateful to Covey T. Oliver for his intellectual guidance and wisdom drawn from a unique blend of accomplishment as professor of international law at the University of Pennsylvania and assistant secretary of state. He shares with Senator Gale McGee of Wyoming a special place in my pantheon for a vigorous defense of academic freedom at a time when the present work came under attack. I acknowledge with gratitude the invaluable contribution of Constance Frydenlund who combined substantive criticism and superb technical competence in preparation of the manuscript. My wife Barbara, of course, merits bouquets for her help in all aspects. Let me assure all of these worthy people that they are to be held blameless for the heresy and error that despite their efforts may yet endure in the text.

# CONTENTS

# The Executive, Congress, and Foreign Policy

# EXECUTIVE DOMINANCE
# OR CONGRESSIONAL EQUALITY
# IN FOREIGN POLICY

*Il faut que le pouvoir arrête le pouvoir.*[1] With this simple axiom Montesquieu launched a persistently vexing debate in modern political theory. In a statement translating roughly as "One should set a thief to catch a thief," Montesquieu wisely perceived that governments of future corporate states would constitute engines with a power of a magnitude wholly unknown in his time and for the control of which wholly new mechanisms would have to be devised if tyranny were to be avoided.

Montesquieu believed the answer to this future challenge could be found in the mechanisms evolved under the British constitutional monarchy. He thought that the growth of democracy and stability in England was the result of the separation within its government of the major elements of sovereignty, the vesting in different branches of the essential functions of sovereignty—legislative, executive, and judicial—and the keeping of each wholly separate.[2]

In fact, Montesquieu quite wrongly perceived the British system. As Walter Bagehot, A.V. Dicey, Sir Ivor Jennings and others have well demonstrated, the real virtues of the British Constitution in Montesquieu's time—as well as in the present—lay in the centralizing of the three functions, as Hobbes had admonished, under one supreme authority wherein "the supreme determining power is upon all points the same."[3]

When in due course Montesquieu became a leading light of the founding fathers of the United States, from among his many brilliant insights his one great misperception seemed to have greatest inspirational power.

While the intent of the framers on many points in the Constitution is subject to dispute, it is safe to say there was a clear consensus on the need to separate legislative, judicial, and executive powers. Having suffered the tyranny of George III, they sought to avoid creating the seeds of another tyranny by insuring that sovereignty would not reside in a single place. As Bagehot put it, they adopted instead the principle of having many sovereign authorities, hoping that their multitude might atone for their inferiority.[4]

It is equally safe to say that there was no clear consensus with regard to the actual distribution of powers, especially those involving the conduct of foreign policy. The excessive vagueness of the sections of the Constitution dealing with these powers—Article I, sections 8 and 9; Article II, sections 1, 2, and 3—reflects that lack of consensus.

Especially difficult to plumb is the intent regarding the question at hand: should the Executive be in a dominant position vis-à-vis Congress in foreign policy, or should Congress be on a footing of equality? There were strong advocates of both views among the framers, but the fragmentary records of the Constitutional Convention, and the often contradictory arguments found in *The Federalist* and in speeches and commentaries during the formative years, lend conclusive support to neither view.* (For further discussion of the intentions of the framers see beginning pages of Chapters 3, 4, 5, and 6.)

Much of the bitter ratification debate of 1789 focused on excessive power in the presidency. "How easy is it for him to render himself absolute!" said Patrick Henry.[5] Yet even such critics of executive power as John Marshall spoke of the President as "the sole organ of the nation in its external relations, and its sole representative with foreign nations."[6]

The more vigorous Federalists, such as Hamilton, Madison, Marshall, and Jay, at times argued forcefully for executive primacy as in "Federalist Nos. 23 and 48," "First Letter of 'Pacificus.'"[7] At other times, however, they responded to Whig criticism by implying support of Congressional equality ("Federalist Nos. 69-75," "First Letter of 'Helvidius'"). [8]

Active Whigs such as Thomas Jefferson who believed in the firm subordination of the Executive to "the supreme legislative power" were not without a certain dualism on the issue. "The transaction of business with foreign nations," wrote Jefferson, "is Executive altogether."[9]

---

*"As one historian of the Presidency who followed the tortuous progress of the incipient Presidency through Madison's *Notes* several times has frankly conceded: 'I am still not sure' how a formal consensus on the Executive power was reached...As a summation of all the labyrinthine debates of the Convention, this did not define: it deferred. With a truly 'peculiar' restraint—of spectacular shrewdness—the Founding Fathers thus left the Presidency, their most special creation, to be shaped by the live touch of history. And this could fairly be called their forever memorable gamble." Emmet John Hughes, *The Living Presidency: The Resources and Dilemmas of the American Presidential Office* (New York: Coward, McCann and Geoghegan, 1972), pp. 34, 40.

The frequently renewed struggles between the two branches that have appeared since ratification owe their vigor in no small measure to the failure in the earliest years to reconcile the contending views on primacy. Thus the document and the conventions of the Constitution contain two fundamentally inconsistent conceptions. There is one conception of the presidency as existing for the most part to serve the legislative power, wherein resides the will of the people, and another conception of the Executive's power as being subject only to specific and limited qualifications.[10]

In strict constitutional terms, therefore, the President is conferred with certain powers capable of affecting our foreign relations, and other powers of the same nature are conferred upon Congress; but which of the two branches shall have dominant or final voice in determining the course of foreign relations is not established.[11]

## DOMINANCE IN PRACTICE

History has failed to establish by convention the issue of dominance left unreconciled by the framers. The interaction of widely different personalities in the presidency with the events of their times has given us periods of unchallenged executive dominance and periods of Congressional dominance of foreign policy. While the period from the end of World War II until Watergate was clearly in the former category, since Watergate we have embarked just as clearly upon a period of Congressional ascendency.

While the views of the first occupant of the presidency toward his office seem to have been in the Whig tradition, the issue of dominance proved less than settled in his practice. When President Washington traveled for the first time to the Congress for the purpose of consultation, he found the advice so abusive that he strode from the Senate chamber swearing that he would "be damned if he ever went there again!" And of course he never did.[12] In 1793 he sparked a vigorous debate on the issue of dominance when he asserted the Presidential prerogative by proclaiming American neutrality in the war between France and Britain without obtaining the advice and consent of the Congress.[13] The precedent stood, although Congress recovered ground by passing a neutrality act of its own the following year.[14]

John Adams, exercising the prerogative in the same manner, sent commissioners to France to end the undeclared war with that country without any reference to Congress.[15]

Thomas Jefferson, in theory a strict Whig, inaugurated the war with the Barbary pirates without obtaining prior Congressional consent. In the accompanying debate Alexander Hamilton squarely joined the issue of dominance by advocating that Congress' prerogative in the war powers was exclusive only when it came to putting the country into a state of war ab initio. Jefferson, however, viewed his relationship to "the supreme legislative power" differently and went to Congress requesting its formal assent, which was then granted ex post facto.[16]

Even ex post facto approval was not thought appropriate by President Monroe when he promulgated his famous doctrine with regard to the Americas; but when its execution came to the test in the form of Colombia requesting United States protection, Monroe's Secretary of State, John Quincy Adams, replied that the Constitution provided "the ultimate decision...to the legislative department."[17]

Although hardly a strict Hamiltonian, John Quincy Adams seems clearly to have accepted executive dominance when, in his eulogy on Madison, he said: "However startled we may be at the idea that the Executive Chief Magistrate has the power of involving the nation in war, even without consulting Congress, an experience of fifty years has proved that in numberless cases he has and must have exercised the power."[18]

Andrew Jackson is often regarded as a strong advocate of the dominant presidency, and it is no doubt true that his view of the President's authority was at times rather sanguine, as in his famous challenge to Chief Justice Marshall and his unauthorized incursion into Florida. Nevertheless, in 1831, after ordering an armed vessel to South America to protect American shipping, he felt compelled to submit his action to the consideration of Congress, "to the end that they may clothe the Executive with such authority and means as they deem necessary...."[19]

Franklin Pierce is generally considered a weak President; yet in 1854 he felt justified in ordering an American squadron to bombard Nicaragua. Though the legality of the action was hotly debated and ultimately brought before the Supreme Court, its validity was sustained.*

The ground lost by Congress on the issue of dominance in the first half-century was largely regained in the decade preceding the Civil War. Congress took special pleasure, for example, in rejecting a half-dozen requests for authorization to use the armed forces made by President Buchanan, who believed that "without the authority of Congress the President cannot fire a hostile gun in any case except to repel the attack of an enemy."[20] In his annual message to Congress in 1858 he went further, saying, "The Executive...of this country in

---

*"Now as respects the interposition of the Executive abroad for the protection of the lives or property of the citizen, the duty must, of necessity, rest in the discretion of the President...." Justice Nelson as quoted in Commager, "Does the President Have too Much Power?," pp. 23-24.

its intercourse with foreign nations is limited to the employment of diplomacy alone. When this fails it can proceed no further. It cannot legitimately resort to force without the direct authority of Congress...."[21]

The relationship between the presidency and Congress during Lincoln's term, just as in the wartime terms of Wilson and Franklin Roosevelt, really stands apart from the evolution being surveyed. While we have seen that the dominance of the Executive over the Congress is far from a settled issue in peacetime, in times of clear national emergency the dominance—and, in Lincoln's case, even dictatorship—of the presidency has never seriously been challenged. Lincoln's conception of executive power went far beyond that of any of his predecessors and, indeed, has not been equalled since.[22] His rule during the early months of the war was absolute, and his reference to Congress throughout its duration was minimal.* It cannot be said, however, that Congress accepted Presidential dominance even in such perilous times. The infamous Joint Committee on the Conduct of the War never approached a coequal voice with Lincoln, but it nevertheless provided considerable distraction to his direction of the war effort.[23] (Also see Chapter 5.)

While the precedents of power established by Lincoln no doubt provided the basis for subsequent expansion by strong Presidents, the effects upon his immediate successors and their relationship to the Congress were little short of calamitous.[24] The fate of Andrew Johnson provides the most dramatic example of the rejection by Congress of executive dominance in foreign as well as domestic affairs that followed the war and endured until the end of the century.

The new century was begun with an event that proved a prelude of things to come. President McKinley sent 5,000 troops to China to put down the Boxer Rebellion. This was done without any reference to Congress and without any objection from it.[25]

Even less troubled by the need to gain authorization from Congress for what he felt had to be done such as "taking" the Panama Canal, was Theodore Roosevelt: "I took the Canal Zone and let Congress debate, and while the debate goes on the canal does also."[26] In him we find the true flowering of the Hamiltonian concept of executive dominance in foreign affairs, justified by Roosevelt in his "stewardship theory." His belief was "...that it was not only the President's right but his duty to do anything that the needs of the nation demanded unless such action was forbidden by the Constitution or by the laws...the

---

*"I felt that measures, otherwise unconstitutional, might become lawful by becoming indispensable to the preservation of the Constitution, through the preservation of the nation." John Nicolay and John Jay, eds., *The Complete Works of Abraham Lincoln* (New York: Francis D. Tandy Co., 1894),10: 65-68.

Executive power was limited only by specific restrictions and prohibitions appearing in the Constitution or imposed by the Congress under its constitutional powers."[27]

An opposite view was held by Roosevelt's hand-picked successor, William Howard Taft. In contrast with his very restricted view of the powers of the presidency while he occupied the office, however, as Chief Justice, Taft wrote in 1916 that the President as Commander in Chief "can order the Army and Navy anywhere he will if the Appropriations furnish the means of transportation."[28]

Though far more circumspect than Roosevelt, President Wilson brought a return to the Hamiltonian concept. In 1914 he sent United States troops into Mexico without prior authorization, although he received ex post facto approval, and then advance approval for another intervention in 1916. In 1917 he sought advance authority from Congress to arm American merchantmen. He added that he had the power to do this "even without special warrant of law, by the plain implications of my constitutional duties and powers." When "a little group of willful men" in the Senate filibustered this request to death, Wilson had the merchantmen armed by executive order. He did not even bother to seek Congressional authorization when he sent troops into Siberia in 1918. Congressional attempts to limit his actions perished in committee.[29]

The final defeat of the Versailles Treaty, however, began two decades during which the dominance of the Executive disappeared in foreign policy. Congress, regarding World War I as the malign consequence of Presidential dominance, imposed a rigid isolationism on U.S. policy, so complete that strict neutrality policies were imposed on the Executive in the face of German and Japanese expansionism. So thoroughly deplored and universally considered a failure was this period of Congressional assertion in foreign policy that it provoked an intellectual reaction against Congressional equality and provided the basis for the tremendous resurgence of executive dominance after World War II.*

The culmination of this era of the Nye Committee and "America First" was reached with the Selective Service Act of 1940, in which the Senate came within one vote of denying the Executive the very substance of an army. Nevertheless, the act contained an amendment stipulating that draftees could not be used outside the Western Hemisphere. Notwithstanding this provision, President Franklin Roosevelt sent troops to Iceland shortly thereafter with no authorization from Congress. Although Senator Robert Taft and others protested that the

---

*"Particularly in the crucial period of the thirties it was a serious handicap to the conduct of American foreign policy that the President was not permitted to be the responsible initiator, even if not the sole director, of foreign policy. The Constitution certainly intended him to be the former, at least." William Yandell Elliott, *United States Foreign Policy: Its Organization and Control* (New York: Columbia University Press, 1952), p. 6. Also see Schlesinger, "Making of Foreign Policy," p. 93.

President had "no legal or constitutional right to send American troops to Iceland,"[30] the growing threat of war had worked its effect in the Senate and this action and the subsequent destroyers-for-bases deal was sustained by Congress.* Thus began the wartime presidency of Roosevelt and, as with Lincoln and Wilson, his dominance of foreign policy became unchallenged if not unquestioned. While the relationship between the Executive and Congress in times of national emergency raises many interesting questions, it is nevertheless a subject beyond the scope of the present study.

Students of the presidency have noted that it has been a recurrent pattern for the suppressed frustrations of a Congress dominated during a national emergency such as World War II to erupt with great intensity once the crisis has passed, reasserting the prerogatives of the Congressional leadership and the jurisdictions of its committees. The inevitable result is that maintaining a co-ordinated and disciplined policy lead from the Executive becomes a near impossibility.[31] The history of the immediate postwar period bears out the validity of this thesis. But reassertion, even in the five-year period following the end of the war, cannot be said to have fully overcome the clear executive dominance and initiative that had developed during the war. It is significant that the United Nations Participation Act of 1945, for instance, bases United States implementation of the charter not on Presidential prerogative but on the national legislative power, the theory being that American participation in the United Nations is a matter for Congressional collaboration, not Presidential execution.[32] It is no less significant to note that three years later, with the tide of Congressional reassertion having abated considerably, the Atlantic Pact abandoned this theory completely and adopted instead the controversial Article V implementation clause.†

---

*"Tom Connally, the Chairman of the Senate Foreign Relations Committee, responded with a stirring assertion of high prerogative. 'The authority of the President as Commander in Chief to send the Armed Forces to any place required by the security interests of the United States,' he said, 'has often been questioned, but never denied by authoritative opinion.'" Schlesinger, "Making of Foreign Policy," p. 95.

†Article V, *The North Atlantic Treaty* reads in part: "The Parties agree that an armed attack against one or more of them in Europe or North America shall be considered an attack against them all and consequently they agree that, if such an armed attack occurs, each of them, in exercise of the right of individual or collective self-defense recognized by Article 51 of the Charter of the United Nations, will assist the Party or Parties so attacked by taking forthwith, individually and in concert with the other parties, such action as it deems necessary, including the use of armed force, to restore and maintain the security of the North Atlantic Area...."

The treaty thus stipulates immediate executive action with no prior reference to Congress.

Congressional assertion during this period was evidenced in many ways. In 1948 Congress forced an additional $400 million in aid to China, and it imposed a mandatory loan to Spain against executive objections. There were bills like the Hoffman Bill that attempted to assert a clear dominance of the Congress over the presidency, and the resolution passed by the House of Representatives demanding "full and complete information" on any agreements, commitments, or understandings reached during discussions held between the President and other heads of state.[33]

One of the more interesting confrontations in the struggle for dominance during this period was the so-called "Great Debate" that followed President Truman's ordering four divisions to Europe pursuant to the implementation of the NATO Treaty without specific authorization from Congress. For months the debate raged in the Senate and in the press on the question of the President's constitutional right to act as he did. Ultimately the stationing of the troops in Europe was approved, but a ceiling was enacted beyond which the Executive was told it could not go without prior authorization from Congress. The challenge thus set up has never been tested, since United States force levels in Europe have never exceeded that ceiling.

The great showdown of the postwar effort by Congress to overcome executive dominance was of course the Bricker Amendment. Strongly pushed by a majority of the members of Congress and by the American Bar Association, the Bricker Amendment in its various forms was introduced in Congress several times over a period of years. Although the versions varied in detail, they provided that a treaty could become effective as internal law in the United States only through the enactment of enabling legislation by Congress; and that executive and other agreements with foreign nations should be made only in the manner and to the extent prescribed by law. The high-water mark occurred on February 26, 1954. The final vote on passage in the Senate was 60 ayes and 31 nays with 5 not voting. Two-thirds being required for passage, it thus failed by only one vote.[34]

The Executive was not cowed by this assertiveness. The Truman Doctrine, the Berlin Airlift, the Atlantic Pact, and the Marshall Plan are well-known initiatives originated by the Executive, in some cases with little prior consultation of Congress, although their successful implementation was achieved only by leading and educating Congress into a partnership in the policy. While demanding—albeit sometimes unsuccessfully—a role of equality on most foreign policy issues during this period, Congress was almost completely silent (with the exception of Senator John W. Bricker) in its acceptance of the President's bold assertion that it was for him alone to decide whether the H-bomb should be built.[35]

Congressional reaction, however, could hardly be termed acquiescence in the case of President Truman's commitment of United States forces to Korea without consulting Congress or seeking its approval. Senator Taft and other critics contended that the President usurped Congressional powers and also breached section 6 of the Act to Implement the United Nations Charter by not consulting Congress or asking for its sanction.[36] The executive branch reacted vigorously, asserting that the President had authority to use armed forces to carry out the broad foreign policy of the United States without Congressional interference.

Dwight Eisenhower's conception of the presidency drew its inspiration more from the Jeffersonian than from the Hamiltonian view. His statements and his writings reveal an approach to decision- and policy-making in which consultation and consensus with his staff, his Cabinet, and above all with Congress were paramount in matters of national policy.[37] Opponents of Presidential dominance in foreign policy point out that in the two major crisis areas of his administration, the Far East and the Middle East, Eisenhower formally requested authority from Congress before undertaking policy initiatives. They note also that Eisenhower ran on a platform charging "That they [the Truman administration] have plunged us into war with Korea without the consent of our citizens through their authorized representatives in Congress...."[38]

Advocates of Presidential dominance, however, argue that Eisenhower did not believe he required authorization in either case but was motivated by the political desire to deny the Democrats a partisan issue and the strategic desire to present a dramatic show of national unity abroad.[39]

It is interesting to note the views of two contemporary Congressional leaders. In 1957, the Senate Foreign Relations Committee actually deleted the idea of Congressional authorization from the draft Middle East Resolution, with Senator J. William Fulbright expressing the fear that such a resolution might limit the President's power as Commander in Chief.[40] The Speaker of the House, Sam Rayburn, had gone further with regard to the Formosa Resolution, saying that the President had the unilateral power to do what he proposed without consulting Congress.[41]

The Hamiltonian conception of Presidential power was renewed in John F. Kennedy's view of the office. Even as the issue of Presidential dominance had been used to advantage by Eisenhower in the 1952 campaign, so was it used in an opposite way by candidate Kennedy in 1960. In an address early in the campaign he stated: "...Congress must not surrender its responsibilities. But neither should it dominate. However large its share in the formulation of domestic programs, it is the President alone who must make the major decisions in our foreign policy.[42] He believed that the modern presidency had suffered a steady constriction of its powers vis-à-vis Congress.[43] His experience in the presidency apparently did nothing to change his views on the subject. In a press conference shortly before his assassination, he remarked with some bitterness that while he remained responsible for protecting the national interests, Congress threatened to deny him the means to do so.[44]

Lyndon Johnson brought to the presidency an experience of Congressional leadership unmatched since James Madison. One might have expected such conditioning to have predisposed Johnson to deal with his former branch as an equal in foreign affairs. It is true that he did consult with and solicit the advice of Congressional leaders more than any of his modern predecessors. It is also true that Johnson decided to go to Congress for a resolution authorizing action following the Tonkin Gulf incident.[45]

It must be remembered, however, that Johnson's Congressional experience began in the darkest days of "mossback" isolationism and matured amid the universal repudiation of that view after 1941, and the flowering of Presidential dominance and Congressional acquiescence that marked the next 25 years.*

The motivation for requesting the Tonkin Gulf Resolution may be hinted by the remarks of the resolution's Senate floor leader, J. William Fulbright, when he said during its consideration: "Why, this resolution doesn't mean a damn thing. Lyndon wants it. He's got a tough campaign coming up. Goldwater's being rough on him. Lyndon just wants this to show he can be decisive and firm with the communists too."[46]

It must be noted also that the most far-reaching claim to executive dominance over foreign affairs since Hamilton was made by Johnson's Undersecretary of State, Nicholas Katzenbach, before the Senate Foreign Relations Committee in 1967.[47]

Wide acceptance of the view that Congressional isolationism helped to bring about World War II provided a kind of legitimacy to executive assertiveness after the war. Twenty-five years of unremitting crisis, war, and cold war added the virtue of necessity to executive dominance. Except for "mossbacks" like Robert Taft, Bricker, and Watkins (the reputations of whom are now undergoing considerable rehabilitation), Congressional leaders not only acquiesced but were the principal apologists and defenders of that dominance. Arthur Vandenberg and Tom Connally defended the President's war powers; Fulbright repeatedly criticized the meddling of Congress, with its "localism and parochialism," and as late as 1961 called for more powers over foreign affairs to be transferred from Congress to the President.[48] Senator Everett Dirksen, himself a firm constitutional conservative, could find no basis for constitutional limitations on the President's power as Commander in Chief.[49] Richard Russell, perhaps the most influential member of the Senate in the postwar era, was completely opposed to Senate interference in strategic matters.[50] John Stennis, successor to Russell as chairman of the Armed Services Committee, came to the Senate a believer in the preeminence of Congress in foreign affairs, but by 1970 had come to accept a secondary role for Congress in military affairs at least.[51]

---

*"There are many, many, who can recommend, advise and sometimes a few of them consent. But there is only one that has been chosen by the American people to decide." President Johnson in 1966, as quoted by Schlesinger, "Making of Foreign Policy," p. 101.

Senator Barry Goldwater, a frequent critic of Presidents Kennedy and Johnson, believed nevertheless that "There is no question that the President can take military action at any time he feels danger for the country or, stretching a point, for its position in the world."[52]

Clinton Rossiter has noted that the primacy of the Executive comes under attack from time to time, usually from those who oppose a specific policy more than the way a President happens to be pursuing it.[53] This certainly was true in the origin of the vigorous attempts in the Ninety-first and Ninety-second Congresses to abrogate executive primacy and reassert a claim to Congressional equality in foreign affairs. The growth of opposition to the Indochina policies of the Executive in 1966-68 transformed the Senate Foreign Relations Committee and its chairman from champion and legitimizer of Presidential primacy into relentless constitutional critics of Presidential power, first in Indochina and then throughout the world.

Members of the committee, J. William Fulbright, Jacob Javits, Clifford Case, Stuart Symington, and Frank Church were joined by nonmembers Thomas Eagleton, George McGovern, Mike Gravel, Mark Hatfield, and others in building their policy criticism increasingly during the period 1969-72 around the theme of the unconstitutionality of executive "despotism" in foreign affairs. In summary, these members have articulated a reassertion of the Whig conception of Congressional equality in foreign affairs policy formulation and initiative. The collective judgment of Congress in this view is claimed superior to that of a single man in the presidency. Lesislation is urged to end executive dominance by specifying war powers, ending executive privilege and the use of executive agreements, and making executive agencies and officials answer to Congress as well as to the President.

## JUDICIAL VIEWS ON DOMINANCE

It has been said that the law is no more and no less than what the courts will enforce. The courts, specifically the Supreme Court, have been singularly reluctant to intrude, however gingerly, upon matters involving allocation of powers between the branches. This has been true in special measure with regard to powers over foreign affairs. Hard law, therefore, is necessarily sparse. The Court will not adjudicate "questions of a political nature," and such law as involves separation of powers has come before the Court only because private rights have been involved. Even when private litigation brings the Court face to face with an issue of constitutional powers, it usually has avoided decision, or decided the case on grounds enabling evasion of the constitutional issue. It has taken pains to limit the effect even of such cases by using the most cautious, qualified, and ambiguous language. This judicial reluctance to apply its judgment of constitutionality in matters of foreign relations was reflected by Justice Robert Jackson in the *Korematsu* case, when he pointed out that the final arbiters of the validity of the actions of those who exercise constitutional powers are "the political judgments of their contemporaries and...the moral judgments of history."[54]

One major issue involved in the question of primacy, however, does seem to have received legitimacy from the Court. The view of Hamilton and Theodore Roosevelt that in the absence of restrictive legislation, the Executive possesses a residual power to act in those gray areas of shared powers involving national security"...in the sense that the Executive may move within them until they shall have been occupied by legislative action," received explicit support from a majority of the Court in the *Youngstown Steel* case.[55] This case, combined with two earlier cases, establishes a clear judicial position.

In the case of *Little* v. *Barreme*, Chief Justice John Marshall, speaking with reference to a vessel seizure under an Act of Congress, said: "...that since Congress had acted in the matter the President was bound to follow its directions and that the seizure had been illegal,"[56] clearly implying that if Congress had not acted, the President could have.

In the case of *In re Neagle*, Justice Samuel Miller held that the constitutional phrase "to take care that the laws be faithfully executed" was not limited to the enforcement of Congressional legislation but included "rights, duties, and obligations growing out of the Constitution and our international relations...."[57]

In a judgment that has lately become somewhat controversial, *The Prize Cases*, the Court legitimized a broad exercise of Presidential powers in emergency. It accepted the view that the President, without reference to Congress, can determine the existence of an emergency and act to meet it. It accepted also the view that the President may commit the nation to military action without Congressional approval.[58]

The great landmark case in the substance of primacy in foreign policy is *U.S.* v. *Curtiss-Wright Export Corporation*. The opinion was written by Justice George Sutherland, whom Rossiter describes as no friend of executive power, and even less of Franklin D. Roosevelt.[59] He was, interestingly, also former chairman of the Senate Foreign Relations Committee. In what amounted to a clear affirmation of executive primacy, the Court held that "the powers of external sovereignty did not depend upon the affirmative grants of the Constitution," and endorsed the existence of "the very delicate plenary and exclusive power of the President as the sole organ of the federal government in the field of international relations—a power which does not require as a basis for its exercise an act of Congress." The Court pointed out the special status of foreign affairs:

...with its important, complicated, delicate, and manifold problems, the President alone has the power to speak or listen as a representative of the nation....

Congressional legislation must often accord to the President a degree of discretion and freedom from statutory restriction which would not be admissible were domestic affairs alone involved. Moreover he, not Congress, has the better opportunity of knowing the conditions which prevail in foreign countries....[60]

During World War II, again speaking through Justice Sutherland, the Court, in *U.S.* v. *Belmont*, held that the conduct of foreign relations, including the recognizing of foreign governments and concluding of international agreement, belongs to the Executive alone.[61]

*Youngstown Sheet and Tube Co.* v. *Sawyer* remains the most important example of the Court-invalidating actions taken by the Executive pursuant to his inherent power to act in emergency. While it is significant that none of his concurring colleagues agreed with his view of the source of Presidential power, the opinion of the Court rendered by Justice Hugo Black declares: "The President's power...must stem either from an act of Congress or from the Constitution itself."[62]

But in a more recent case, *Orlando* v. *Laird*, the President's power to conduct operations in Indochina in the absence of formal authorization from Congress was upheld. The United States District Court held that "the reality of the collaborative action of the executive and legislative required by the Constitution has been present from the earliest stages," through Congress "appropriating the nation's treasure and conscripting its manpower."[63] (See discussion of this and subsequent cases in Chapters 3, 6, and 7.)

It must be concluded, from a review of the meager body of the relevant cases, that the question of executive dominance or Congressional equality in foreign affairs has not been, and will not be, resolved by the third branch of the government.

## DOMINANCE IN SCHOLARLY AND EXPERT COMMENTARY

We have seen that history, precedent, and judicial opinion provide an abundance of argument in support of both sides of the dominance issue. The opinion of scholars and expert commentators yields much less diversity but brings us little closer to a definitive answer.

Until the Vietnam conflict produced an intellectual reaction against the Executive, it was very difficult to find a defender of Congressional equality in foreign affairs anywhere in the intellectual community. Even today, with the conversion of a number of "strong Executive" men, it is hard to identify a coherent school of theory in defense of Congressional equality.

Observing the balance in the early nineteenth century, Alexis de Tocqueville found the presidency without power compared with Congress. It was his view that the Constitution had created an Executive essentially at the mercy of Congress.[64] Walter Bagehot, writing later in the century, believed the Constitution sought to establish Congressional control over the Executive just as under a parliamentary system.[65] He observed elsewhere that in practice, that relationship was not established. This theme—that equality in making foreign and military policy was embodied in the theory of the Constitution, but had failed in practice—has been held in varying degrees by such modern strong Executive men as Corwin, Rossiter, Huntington, Francis Wilcox, and Elliott.

Others have recently taken that observation and developed prosposals to regain functional equality for Congress. James A. Robinson argues that "the old equilibrium" is preferable and recommends action to regain lost initiative for Congress.[66]

Professors Alexander Bickel and Ruhl Bartlett have been consistent constitutional critics of executive dominance, laying the blame on Congress for acquiescence in the unconstitutional usurpation of the Executive. Bickel makes the constitutional argument that it is Congress' right to set foreign and war policy when it chooses. He goes so far as to suggest that Congress has the right "...to prescribe the mission of our troops in the field."[67] Raoul Berger expands Congressional supremacy to cover all foreign affairs powers, dismissing executive privilege as a myth and executive agreements as usurpation.[68]

Many of the prominent intellectual apologists for the growth of executive dominance in the 1940s and 1960s have lately argued for curbing the Executive and strengthening Congress. MacGregor Burns, Emmet John Hughes, Henry Commager, Richard Neustadt, Arthur Schlesinger, Jr., and others, however, have yet explicitly to reverse positions on the issue of executive primacy.

Without question, the overwhelming consensus of the intellectual community in this century has accepted the legitimacy of executive dominance in foreign affairs. Beginning with the writings of Woodrow Wilson and Edward Corwin, the Hamiltonian, Jacksonian, and stewardship justifications for executive dominance were synthesized into a comprehensive theory justifying Presidential control "...which is very absolute, of the foreign relations of the nation." "The initiative in foreign affairs, which the President possesses without any restriction whatever, is virtually the power to control them absolutely." This power "cannot be substantially curtailed."[69] Clinton Rossiter believed that the "Constitution, laws, custom, the practice of other nations, and the logic of history" made the President's position in international affairs "...necessarily dominant, but not necessarily absolute...."[70]

Arguing that Congress was structurally incapable of leadership in foreign affairs, writers such as Samuel P. Huntington, Adolf Berle, J.W. Fulbright, Walter

Lippmann, George Kennan, Sidney Hyman, and Arthur Krock described Congress' role as merely that of a "prodder," its judgment ill-informed and "lagging behind the facts...a decentralized, independent-minded, and largely parochial-minded body of legislators."

"As a general proposition," wrote MacGregor Burns, "the stronger we make the Presidency, the more we strengthen democratic procedure and can hope to realize modern liberal democratic goals."[71] This view was endorsed and elaborated by Henry Steele Commager, Richard Neustadt, Arthur Schlesinger, Jr., and Kenneth Waltz.

Standard textbooks written by scholars such as Burton Sapin, James Robinson, Louis Koenig, E.A. Kolodziej, and others have treated executive dominance as axiomatic in foreign policy.

## CONCLUSION

We have seen in the discussion above that the intention of the framers cannot be relied upon to settle the issue of dominance. Still less useful are the bare provisions of the Constitution itself or the *travaux préparatoires*, such as they are.

We have seen that actual practice and historical precedent have failed to establish the legitimacy of executive dominance. The presidency under Jackson, Polk, Lincoln, Theodore Roosevelt, Wilson, Franklin Roosevelt, Truman, Johnson, and Nixon was clearly dominant in foreign affairs. Yet most of those administrations were followed by periods of Congressional resurgence and, in some cases, dominance.

We have seen that no settlement of this issue can be expected from the judicial branch, though it dealt Congressional equality a heavy blow in the *Curtiss-Wright* decision.

We have seen, finally, that opinion of scholars and experts clearly favors executive dominance. This view is by no means unanimous, however, and there is a considerable revisionism now under way that could conceivably evolve a new intellectual consensus against executive dominance.

The purpose of this chapter has not been to make a case for or against executive dominance but, rather, to explore the issues involved so that the events examined in subsequent chapters can be placed in context. Executive dominance was, until Watergate, a fact of life.

## NOTES

1. Raymond Williams, ed., *Political Ideas*, "New Thinker's Library" (London: C. A. Watts, 1966), p. 89.

2. George H. Sabine, *A History of Political Theory* (3rd ed.; New York: Holt, Rinehart & Winston, 1961), p. 558.

3. Walter Bagehot, *The English Constitution* (London: Fontana Library, 1963), p. 215; A. V. Dicey, *An Introduction to the Study of the Law of the Constitution* (London: Macmillan, 1965); Sir Ivor Jennings, *The Law and the Constitution* (London: University of London Press, 1959).

4. Bagehot, *The English Constitution*, p. 220.

5. Patrick Henry, "Speech Against Ratification," June 5, 1788, as cited by Robert S. Hirschfield in *The Power of the Presidency—Concepts and Controversy* (New York: Atherton Press, 1968), p. 22. Hereinafter referred to as *Power of the Presidency*.

6. Clinton Rossiter, *The American Presidency* (New York: Mentor, 1956), p. 14.

7. Alexander Hamilton, James Madison, and John Jay, *The Federalist Papers* (New York: New American Library, 1961), "Federalist No. 23," p. 152; "Federalist No. 48," p. 308; "First Letter of 'Pacificus' by Alexander Hamilton," cited by Hirschfield in *Power of the Presidency, p. 51.*

8. Hamilton, Madison and Jay, *The Federalist Papers*, "Federalist Nos. 69-75," pp. 415-54; "First Letter of 'Helvidius' by James Madison," cited by Hirschfield in *Power of the Presidency*, p. 57.

9. Rossiter, *American Presidency*, p. 16.

10. Edward S. Corwin, "Some Aspects of the Presidency," *Annals of the American Academy of Political and Social Science*, November 1941, pp. 122-31.

11. Edward S. Corwin, *The Constitution and What It Means Today* (New York: Atheneum, 1967). Hereinafter referred to as *The Constitution*. Also see Senator John C. Stennis and Senator J. W. Fulbright, *The Role of Congress in Foreign Policy* (Washington, D.C.: American Enterprise Institute for Public Policy Research, 1971), pp. 23-24. Hereinafter referred to as *Role of Congress*.

12. Emmet John Hughes, *The Living Presidency: The Resources and Dilemmas of the American Presidential Office* (New York: Coward, McCann and Geoghegan, 1972), p. 49.

13. Wilfred E. Binkley, *President anc Gongress* (3rd ed.; New York: Vintage, 1962), p. 51; Hirschfield, *Power of the Presidency*, pp. 216-20.

14. Arthur Schlesinger, Jr., "Congress and the Making of American Foreign Policy," *Foreign Affairs Quarterly* 51, no. 1 (1972): 82. Hereafter referred to as "Making of Foreign Policy."

15. U.S. Congress, Senate, reprint of Henry Steele Commager, "Does the President Have too Much Power?," 82nd Cong., 1st sess., April 2, 1951, *Congressional Record* 97: 3101.

16. Corwin, *The Constitution*, p. 125.

17. Schlesinger, "Making of Foreign Policy," p. 85.

18. Commager, "Does the President Have too Much Power?," pp. 23-24.

19. Schlesinger, "Making of Foreign Policy," p. 85.

20. Schlesinger, "Making of Foreign Policy," p. 88.

21. Stennis and Fulbright, *Role of Congress*, p. 42.

22. Hirschfield, *Power of the Presidency*, p. 45.

23. Binkley, *President and Congress*, pp. 140-41.

24. Hirschfield, *Power of the Presidency*, pp. 216-20.

25. Schlesinger, "Making of Foreign Policy," p. 91.

26. Commager, "Does the President Have too Much Power?," pp. 24-25.

27. Wayne Andrews, ed., *The Autobiography of Theodore Roosevelt* (New York: Scribners, 1958), pp. 197-220.

28. Schlesinger, "Making of Foreign Policy," p. 105.

29. Commager, "Does the President Have too Much Power?," pp. 23-24; Hirschfield, *Power of the Presidency*, pp. 313-14; Schlesinger, "Making of Foreign Policy," p. 92.

30. Schlesinger, "Making of Foreign Policy," p. 93.

31. Elliott, *United States Foreign Policy*, p. 95.

32. Corwin, *The Constitution*, pp. 11, 14, 15.

33. Dean Acheson, *Present at the Creation—My Years in the State Department* (New York: W.W. Norton, 1969), p. 594; Schlesinger, "Making of Foreign Policy," p. 96; U.S. Department of Justice, *Memorandum Reviewing Inquiries by the Legislative Branch During the Period 1948-1950 Concerning the Decision Making Process and Documents of the Executive Branch* (Washington, D.C.: U.S. Government Printing Office, 1959), p. 104.

34. Stennis and Fulbright, *Role of Congress*, pp. 27, 29; Acheson, *Present at the Creation*, p. 634.

35. Rossiter, *American Presidency*, pp. 417-40.

36. Edward S. Corwin, "The President's Powers," *New Republic*, January 29, 1951, pp. 15-16.

37. Dwight D. Eisenhower, *The White House Years: Waging Peace 1956-1961* (Garden City, N.Y.: Doubleday, 1965); Emmet John Hughes, *The Ordeal of Power* (New York: Atheneum, 1963).

38. Republican National Committee, *Official Report of the Proceedings of the Twenty-fifth Republican National Convention* (Washington, D.C.: the committee, 1952), p. 309.

39. This view was supported by Eisenhower's chief adviser on congressional affairs, Bryce Harlow, in an interview on January 14, 1972. Also see Arthur Krock, "The Purpose of the Message and Its Form," New York Times, January 25, 1955, p. L-24.

40. Schlesinger, "Making of Foreign Policy," p. 98.

41. Krock, "Purpose of the Message." Also see his "When Coordinate Powers Enter the Twilight Zone," New York Times, January 27, 1955, p. L-22.

42. John F. Kennedy, speech delivered January 14, 1960, as quoted in Hirschfield, *Power of the Presidency*, p. 131.

43. Arthur M. Schlesinger, Jr., *A Thousand Days: John F. Kennedy in the White House* (London; Mayflower Books, 1967), p. 535. Hereinafter referred to as *Thousand Days*.

44. John F. Kennedy, "News Conference on Foreign and Domestic Matters," New York Times, November 15, 1963, p. 1.

45. Lyndon Baines Johnson, *The Vantage Point: Perspectives of the Presidency, 1963-1969* (New York: Holt, Rinehart and Winston, 1971); George Reedy, *The Twilight of the Presidency* (New York: World Publishing Company, 1970).

46. Senator J. W. Fulbright, as quoted by Hugh Gallagher, *Advise and Obstruct* (New York: Delacorte, 1969), p. 318.

47. U.S. Congress, Senate, Committee on Foreign Relations, *U.S. Commitments to Foreign Powers*, testimony of the Hon. Nicholas deB. Katzenbach, Undersecretary of State (Washington, D.C.: U.S. Government Printing Office, 1967), p. 71.

48. Senator J. W. Fulbright, "American Foreign Policy in the Twentieth Century Under an Eighteenth Century Constitution," *Cornell Law Quarterly* 47 (Fall 1961): 1-13.

49. Schlesinger, "Making of Foreign Policy," pp. 99-100.

50. Samuel P. Huntington, *The Common Defense* (New York: Columbia University Press, 1961), p. 135.

51. Stennis and Fulbright, *Role of Congress*, pp. 29-30.

52. Schlesinger, "Making of Foreign Policy," p. 100.

53. Rossiter, *American Presidency*, p. 15.

54. Korematsu v. United States, 323 U.S. 214 (1944).

55. Youngstown Sheet and Tube Co. v. Sawyer, 343 U.S. 579 (1952).

56. Little v. Barreme, 2 Cr. 170, 177 (1804); Corwin, "The President's Powers," pp. 15-16.

57. Commager, "Does the President Have too Much Power?," pp.23-24.

58. The Prize Cases, 2 Black 635 (1863); Hirschfield, *Power of the Presidency*, p. 166.

59. Rossiter, *American Presidency*, pp. 14-15.

60. U.S. v. Curtiss-Wright Export Corporation, 299 U.S. 304 (1936). See discussion of this case in Corwin, *The Constitution*, pp. 4, 41, 108; Hirschfield, *Power of the Presidency*, p. 166; Rossiter, *American Presidency*, p. 14.

61. U.S. v. Belmont, 301 U.S. 324 (1937).

62. Youngstown Sheet and Tube Co. v. Sawyer, 343 U.S. 579 (1952).

63. Orlando v. Laird, 317 F. Suppl. 1013 (1970).

64. Hirschfield, *Power of the Presidency*, p. 112.

65. Bagehot, *English Constitution*, p. 217.

66. James A. Robinson, *Congress and Foreign Policy: A Study in Legislative Influence and Initiative*, rev. ed. (Homewood, Ill.: Dorsey Press, 1969).

67. U.S. Congress, Senate, Committee on Foreign Relations, *War Powers Legislation*, testimony of Professor Alexander M. Bickel, 92nd Cong. (Washington, D.C.: U.S. Government Printing Office, 1972), p. 549.

68. Raoul Berger, *Executive Privilege: A Constitutional Myth* (Cambridge, Mass.: Harvard University Press, 1974), pp. 1, 140.

69. Woodrow Wilson, *Constitutional Government in the United States* (New York: Columbia University Press, 1900), p. 74.

70. Rossiter, *American Presidency*, p. 15; Rossiter, cited in Edward S. Corwin, *The President, Office and Powers 1787-1957* (New York: New York University Press, 1957), p. 66.

71. James MacGregor Burns, *Presidential Government: The Crucible of Leadership* (Boston: Houghton Mifflin, 1965), p. 330.

## CHECKS AND BALANCES:
## THE FUNCTION
## AND DYSFUNCTION
## OF OVERLAPPING POWERS

As was shown in Chapter 1, analysis of the Constitution and its drafting sheds light but dimly on the sharing of legislative and executive powers in foreign affairs.

That the republic possessed the full attributes to national sovereignty was assumed; but upon the distribution of the powers within the federal government, necessarily concomitant to that external sovereignty, a consensus among the drafters was never achieved. As the Supreme Court later affirmed, had they never been mentioned in the Constitution, these powers to deal with other sovereigns through war, diplomacy, trade, and travel would nevertheless have inhered in the federal government.[1]

In the allocation of these powers among the branches of the government, in fact, the Constitution embodies not one but two incompatible concepts of executive power, reflecting the unreconciled differences among the drafters. One assumes that the Executive exists solely to serve the Congress, wherein resides the will of the people.[2] The other assumes that it ought, within generous limits, to be autonomous and self-directory.[3] This dualism has led to a permanent struggle for power between the two branches.* All that the Constitution really does is to confer upon the President, in Article II, certain powers capable of affecting our foreign relations and, in Articles I and II, certain other powers

---

*"In short, the Constitution itself reflects not one but two conceptions of executive power....Its consequence has been a constantly renewed struggle for power between the political branches." Edward S. Corwin, "Some Aspects of the Presidency," *Annals of the American Academy of Political and Social Science*, November 1941, p. 122.

of the same general nature upon the Senate, and still other such powers upon Congress as a whole.[4]

The war and treaty powers, for example, have been unending sources of struggle between the branches. No constitutional solution will ever end this struggle, because each branch has indisputable rights that overlap—or, as Hamilton described it, "Joint Possession." Article II grants the President the executive power to take care that "the laws be faithfully executed," and Article I grants Congress all legislative powers "to make all laws which shall be necessary and proper for carrying into Execution...all Powers vested by this Constitution in the Government of the United States or in any department or office thereof" (Article I, section 8). The President is endowed with the sole power of "Commander in Chief." Congress is directed "to raise and support armies," to provide for "disciplining the militia, and for governing such part of them as may be employed in the service of the United States." No further guidance is given as to the content of these powers.

Well, what do those words then mean? Does "the legislative power" include the right to exercise a surveillance or superintendence of the Executive, including the deployment and direction of military forces in the field? Does control of the purse strings include the right to refuse to raise armies or navies at all or to hamstring and inhibit the President in directing military operations undertaken as Commander in Chief? Does advice and consent to treaties include the right to abrogate, "so far as the people and authorities of the United States are concerned," any treaty to which the United States is a party, or to abrogate or refuse to implement executive agreements?

Is "the executive power" of that passive variety defined by Locke, or is it the power to act "according to discretion for the public good, without the prescription of the laws, and sometimes even against it," as exercised by Lincoln, Theodore and Franklin Roosevelt, and others in time of crisis? Do the "laws" that he must faithfully execute include treaties? Executive agreements? International law? Who should control the federal budget? What is the constitutional meaning of the word "war"?

There can be no disputing that a final and precise solution to the sharing of constitutional powers in foreign affairs is impossible. The framers have given us a system that a critic might justly characterize as contradictory, overlapping, and rife with unanswered questions. One more favorably disposed could, however, with equal justice characterize it as a system of ingenious flexibility. Justice Louis Brandeis perhaps discerned the central virtue of this inefficiency in his dissenting opinion in *Myers* v. *U.S.*, in which he said:

> The doctrine of the separation of powers was adopted by the Convention of 1787 not to promote efficiency but to preclude the exercise of arbitrary power. The purpose was not to avoid friction but by means of the inevitable friction incident to the distribution of

governmental powers among three departments, to save the people from autocracy.[5]

The arbitrary power that Brandeis feared could occur as well in Congress as in the Executive.

The other side of that coin, however, was noted by Walter Bagehot, who observed that the great weakness of this built-in friction was not simply that it encouraged deadlocks between the President and Congress, but that it yielded no solution and no formula for finding one.[6] Some scholars, in culling nearly two centuries of constitutional interpretation, tradition, practice, and custom, have found this dysfunction realized through the building into the structure and procedures of both branches an "unconscionable quantity of checks and balances" that result in great difficulties for efficient policy making.[7]

Other observers, however, have found in the historical evidence a validation of the "ingenious flexibility" provided by the overlapping powers. They see the growth of a system that adapted readily to unforeseen military and diplomatic contingencies. They point to the amendment procedure as the evidence that the overlapping powers have provided each generation with the opportunity—indeed, the obligation—to adapt the document and its system to historical experience and contemporary problems.[8]

Bagehot, however, provides the best answers to his own strong objection. The Constitution, he said, would long ago have been brought to a bad end by the overlapping distribution of its powers were it not for the American genius for politics, moderation in action, and regard for law. "Sensible shareholders, I have heard a shrewd attorney say, can work *any* deed of settlement; and so the men of Massachusetts could, I believe, work *any* Constitution."[9]


## THE POLITICAL NATURE OF THE PROBLEM


As was seen in Chapter 1, the predominance of one or other of the branches in the exercise of the foreign-policy powers has ebbed and flowed in response to two determining factors: epic events and strong personalities. So much have dramatic periods shaped the roles of each branch that one distinguished constitutional scholar has suggested that there are indeed two Constitutions: one for peaceful periods and another for crises.[10] But one need only mention Jackson, John C. Calhoun, Lincoln, Henry Cabot Lodge, Roosevelt, Arthur Vandenberg, and Lyndon Johnson to grasp the unique direction given by the *dramatis personae*.

The periods of executive dominance, or at times preemption, in the exercise of the foreign-policy powers took place during the terms of decisive men responding to unusual circumstances: Washington in the vulnerable early days of the republic; Jefferson and the Barbary Pirates; Polk and the Mexican War; Lincoln and the Civil War; Theodore Roosevelt and the Panama Canal; Wilson and World War I; Franklin Roosevelt and World War II; Truman, Eisenhower, Kennedy, Johnson, and Nixon in the long Cold War. During these periods of crises, Congress proved unable to check wide expansions of executive powers— approving, acquiescing, or retroactively authorizing the deployment of forces overseas, initiation of hostilities, suspension of elements of the Bill of Rights, and even the spending of unappropriated money.

Clearly the sharing and separation of foreign-affairs powers did not exist during some of the periods mentioned above. Were those executive actions constitutional? The Presidents involved believed so: Congress, while protesting some, approved others and repudiated none. The Supreme Court, in the few instances addressed by it, upheld their constitutionality.[11]

The history of the periods mentioned above, and their aftermaths, indicates that in large measure powers exercised in emergency do not rub off on the office itself. Instead, these periods have in each case provoked a reaction toward a restricted Executive and an expanded Congressional role. Congress has at times expressed its pent-up criticism in devastating incursions upon executive powers.[12] Jackson, for example, was followed by a series of shackled Presidents, culminating in Buchanan (punctuated only by the brief interlude of Polk). Lincoln was followed by a succession of Presidents who were utterly powerless against Congress in foreign affairs. Roosevelt and Wilson brought on the rejection of the League of Nations, the Neutrality Acts, and the triumph of isolationism imposed by Congress. Franklin Roosevelt gave Truman an office that was promptly forced to swallow a rapid succession of ever more noxious doses of disarming and disrupting legislation until Stalin came to the rescue.

Thus the peaks of Presidential domination of the foreign-policy powers have been likened to high-water marks on the banks of a river; they mark past floods, but they add little to the volume of the stream.[13] Braking and supplanting the initiative of the Executive is still the general pattern of Congressional action in foreign affairs during "normal times."

One must note, however, that the years of peace since 1945 do not qualify as "normal times." The unease and danger of the Cold War, with its lurking nuclear threat, seriatim crises, and limited conflicts, reinforced the position of the Executive and prolonged its broadened powers. This position was sustained and buoyed by American public opinion that vastly preferred a firm leadership centralized in facing "international Communism" and by an intellectual community enamored of the presidency.

Congress itself in the words of Ruhl Bartlett, "acquiesced in or ignored, or approved and encouraged this development," largely because it, no less than the Executive, did not question the axioms of the Cold War threat.

It would, of course, be going too far to say that a President welcomes a

Berlin blockade, a Cuban missile crisis, or a Middle East war;[14] but there is no denying that executive power waxes directly.

The postwar period of Cold War and crises has been unique in the larger rhythm described above. Because it diverged from the balance of normal times and has lasted so long, it has caused some thoughtful observers to conclude that finally circumstances have combined to lodge a monopoly of the foreign affairs powers permanently in the Executive, to the point that separated powers checked and balanced between the branches no longer exist.[15]

Some responsible critics have even gone so far as to characterize the current balance as a Presidential dictatorship in foreign policy.* Yet with the development of détente and the ending of the United States role in Vietnam, the dialectic once again asserted itself. The resurgence of Congressional dominance was speedily sealed by the events of Watergate.

Orthodox intellectual opinion has swung 180 degrees against the Executive and finds heretofore undiscovered merits in Congress;[16] public opinion lags considerably but has certainly lost its unquestioning allegiance to the presidency.

Executive foreign and defense policies received their first serious challenge in three decades during the Ninety-first Congress. The Ninety-second Congress waxed even stronger, significantly modifying executive policy and overriding executive rejections of war powers and Indochina restrictions. Where, in the last three decades, it was fashionable to ridicule Congress for its parochial inefficiency, there are now hoots at the presidency described by one observer as "like catcalls in a vaudeville house," while irreverence for Congress is severely frowned upon. Such evidence suggests we are well along toward a return to "normal times."

There is of course an entirely different dimension to the growth and scope of all executive powers. The vastly expanded role of the federal government necessitated by the industrial, technological, communications, and social revolutions of the last 50 years has fallen almost entirely upon the executive branch. Congress, in terms of its responsibilities, remains basically as it was in the earliest years of the Republic; yet it has systematically expanded, delegated, and created ever increasing responsibilities for regulation, social services, and administration within the Executive. This aggrandizement cannot have failed to have an impact upon the foreign-policy powers.

---

*"It may not be too much to say that, as far as foreign policy is concerned, our governmental system is no longer one of separated powers but rather one of elected, executive dictatorship." Senator J. William Fulbright, in Stennis and Fulbright, *Role of Congress*, p. 49; U.S. Congress, Senate, 92nd Cong., 1st sess., February 5, 1971, *Congressional Record*, p. S887.

A not unrelated corollary is the recent burgeoning of our intercourse and dealings with the rest of the world and the greatly expanded responsibilities thereby laid upon the Executive. Measured even in terms of the short history of our republic, this is a new state of affairs to which naturally our political institutions have had little time to adjust. The reality is less than 50 years old, and a widespread public concern, less than 25. This dimension, however, is beyond the scope of our study.[17]

## THE INFLUENCE OF PERSPECTIVE

We have seen that constitutional legitimacy has embraced a startling breadth of executive actions and legislative undertakings over time. The Supreme Court has fixed neither the outer boundaries nor the inner divisions of the foreign-affairs powers.[18] In such landmark cases as *Martin* v. *Matt*, The *Prize Cases*, *Ex parte Milligan*, *U.S.* v. *Curtiss-Wright*, *U.S.* v. *Pink*, *Youngstown Steel*, *Korematsu*, and *Orlando* v. *Laird*, in which these issues were before a Court that was constitutionally and practically in a position to delineate those powers, it refused to do so in any but the most guarded terms. The Court has been respectful of the other two branches, complimentary, and on occasion even awed; but it has always refrained from the expansive flights of dicta applied so often to other great constitutional questions.[19]

As noted earlier, in this relative absence of adjudication, tests of foreign-affairs powers must depend on the imperative of events and contemporary circumstances rather than on abstract theories of law.[20] It is only by reference to what administrations and Congresses have actually done (and gotten away with) that the broad grants of the Constitution take form.[21]

The grave rhetoric of constitutional crisis that inevitably attends this perennial struggle must, therefore, be taken with a grain of salt. To borrow a quip from Clinton Rossiter, the Constitution has always been the last refuge of the out-argued politician. Refusals of Congressional demands for documents, for example, are justified by the Executive, not on the grounds that they are politically embarrassing or administratively unwise but that they are "unconstitutional." Executive powers similarly come under vigorous attack as "unconstitutional," chiefly from those who object to the direction and substance of a specific policy more than the powers being exercised in pursuit of it. The shriller the policy debate becomes, the more likely that it will end in warnings of constitutional usurpation.

Richard Nixon perceived such usurpation in 1951 of powers involving troop commitments, executive agreements, and executive privilege. In 1971 he also saw constitutional crises on these same issues—but of a quite different sort.

In 1961, J.W. Fulbright, fearing the "localism and parochialism" of Congress, argued for the ceding of more powers in the conduct of foreign affairs by Congress to the Executive. In 1971, he argued for the ceding of those same powers, but in a rather different direction.[22]

The Korean War, the dispute over the Formosa Straits, the Bay of Pigs, and (most virulently) the Indochina War gave vigor and wide currency to fears of constitutional usurpation by the Executive. The rejection of the Treaty of Versailles, the Neutrality Acts, the Army-McCarthy hearings, the Connally Reservation, the Tonkin Gulf Resolution, and the Rhodesian Chrome Amendment called forth grave commentaries of legislative interference in executive powers.

Partisanship, it must finally be noted, is another very important contributor to "constitutional crises." Its converse, bipartisanship in foreign policy, is not an American tradition. It came into being in World War II and was revivified by the early Cold War and the attendant efforts of Democratic leaders, intellectuals, and sympathetic journalists to enlist Republican support for the postwar interventionism of the Truman administration. The assiduous cultivation of the GOP foreign-policy spokesmen by Secretaries of State Edward Stettinius, James Byrnes, and George Marshall became an institution in itself.[23] As a word, "bipartisanship" has a kind of beneficial power of its own; but the reality extends just as far as both parties have the same perception of a problem, and often not that far. The methods of reaching such perceptions are traditionally different in each party.

The Republican Party traditionally accepted a strong Hamiltonian conception of the executive role in foreign affairs. Wilson and Franklin Roosevelt were quite outside the Jeffersonian-Whig tradition of the Democratic Party's faith in Congress. The dialectic of opposition thus created strange patterns of constitutional allegiance, and even stranger constitutional arguments. The Executive operated by Democrats was suddenly revealed to the Republican opposition as inherently liberal-internationalist and even imperialistic, and the President himself as a high-handed trampler of Congressional powers. The word "dictatorship" was prominently and gravely heard in Republican circles during the Wilson, Franklin Roosevelt, Truman, Kennedy, and Johnson administrations. During those same years the political, intellectual, and media leaders of Democratic persuasion spoke somberly of the reactionary nature of Congress, seeing in it an almost exclusively negative and obstructive institution.[24]

During Eisenhower's and Nixon's administrations, however, an amazing transformation occurred. The Robert Tafts, Everett Dirksens, and David Lawrences found undiscovered charms and legitimacy in executive powers, while the Adlai Stevensons, J.W. Fulbrights, Henry Commagers, and Arthur Schlesingers awoke to unsuspected constitutional dangers and executive usurpations.[25] And so it goes—the elected party leadership will support a President of the same party. And as the trend in Congress has been to strengthen the party leadership at the expense of committee chairmen, the support of the Executive by its party leadership, whether majority or minority, has grown stronger.[26] As noted above, the temptation to clothe one's partisan or policy arguments and attacks in the pin-striped suit of constitutional discourse is usually overwhelming. The serious student of these matters may approach such debates with considerable skepticism.

## ATTRIBUTES OF THE EXECUTIVE

While it is not necessary to agree with Jefferson that the transaction of business with foreign nations is altogether executive, it must be admitted that the nature of diplomacy, commerce, war, and defense favors the Executive. Negotiation, conflict, crisis, and the simple practice of other nations do not readily adapt themselves to the peculiarities of parliamentary control.[27] The executive branch, by its organic nature, has attributes and capabilities that determine its powers and behavior. The organic nature of Congress is, of course, wholly different but no less determinant of the substance of both its powers and its behavior. These inherent factors are modified by certain outside circumstances.

It is a fact of history that the expanded role of the federal government has been lodged almost entirely in the executive branch. In foreign affairs this has been greatly accelerated in response to the military and strategic imperatives since the end of World War II.[28] The vast machinery of foreign and defense affairs is lodged in the executive branch. By contrast, since the founding of the Senate Committee on Foreign Relations in 1816, Congress can point only to the Congressional Research Service, General Accounting Office, Office of Technological Assessment, the Congressional Budget Office, and some expansion of staff.

The quality and vastness of the personnel resources of the executive branch are unmatched by any organization in the world. These legions of military, foreign, and civil service personnel are of course employees of the three branches of the federal government; but in the context of the struggle between the branches, they are on the executive rolls. In terms of numbers, the resources of Congress are infinitesimally smaller.

In terms of expertise, the disparity is even greater. In the executive departments, the richness and sophistication in scientific, technological, military, diplomatic, statistical, medical, educational, geological, fiscal, legal, and sociological skills, including their most arcane branches, are truly awesome.

The continuity and stability of career services, with men of tens of years' experience in particular problems, and the skill bred only of long years in appraising situations, provide an invaluable institutional wisdom totally absent in the notoriously transient staffs of Congress. The volume and complexity of international transactions and the durability and complication of substantive issues make this expertise increasingly necessary just to stay in the game.[29] There is a temptation in Congress to oversimplify—to be drawn, in Dean Acheson's words, "to courses high in debating appeal whose impracticalities are revealed only through considerable factual knowledge."[30]

The corollary attribute to executive expertise is intelligence acquisition, the established channels of which are an executive monopoly. The diplomatic, consular, military, electronic, photographic, and covert production of information on conditions in foreign countries flows to the Executive; and only the Executive has the capability to digest these daily volumes of raw data into rational and usable assessment. Congress possesses none of that, save what it acquires secondhand from the Executive or haphazardly from random direct sources. A significant portion of such intelligence requires protection from premature disclosure or protection of sources from any disclosure. The Executive itself has never fully achieved such protection, but an open democratic assembly is far less able to provide it.

The greatest organic strength in the executive branch lies in administrative unity: functional organization, hierarchical administration, unity of command, and internal discipline. These are the necessary attributes of problem solving, decision making, and policy execution. The orchestration and coordination of the many complex and controlled military, diplomatic, and domestic moves in, say, a Cuban missile crisis would be impossible without a single determining energy.

The spontaneity and unpredictability of international affairs quite often require prompt and even immediate response. The attributes of administrative unity enable the Executive to plan and execute appropriate responses with dispatch.*

One hundred Senators and 435 Representatives, as individuals, independent committees, policy caucuses, or legislative houses, possess none of the attributes of administrative unity. The slow and open deliberations of a democratic legislature are attuned to the process of continuing compromise rather than to the taking of decisive action. In Congress, controversy means delay and missed opportunities. †

---

*"The interlaced character of human affairs requires a single determining energy; a distinct force for each artificial compartment will make but a motley patchwork, if it live long enough to make anything." Bagehot, *The English Constitution*, p. 221.

†"It is highly unlikely that we can successfully execute a long-range program for the taming, or containing, of today's agressive and revolutionary forces by continuing to leave vast and vital decision-making powers in the hands of a decentralized, independent minded

Another essential requirement for successful conduct of foreign affairs is the ability to take a long-range view of situations, fashioning policy in light of long- and middle-range goals and effects. Success is the business of seeing problems before they happen, and devising and executing preventive policies. The Executive is attuned to such a perspective; Congress cannot afford it. Public opinion, to which Congress must be directly responsive, tends to lag behind the facts of an international problem with which the Executive must cope.[31] In the extreme, Congress has even been guilty of dealing with the future by legislating against the errors of the past.[32] (See, for instance, the repeal of the Tonkin Gulf Resolution described in Chapter 3.)

One does not have to agree with Richard Neustadt that the presidency is the "sole crown-like symbol of the Union"[33] to accept that the executive branch has a national constituency and is responsible to "the whole people," in Woodrow Wilson's phrase. It is thus in a unique position to stand for the national interest, as against the local and regional interests of Congressional constituents or the special interests of the organized lobbies.[34] This fact is of special importance in foreign affairs.

It is a fact of life that there is virtually no political profit for a Congressman in the serious pursuit of foreign affairs. The role of critic after the fact, or of dramatic accuser, however, can produce useful publicity. And a latent American exasperation with "foreigners" has often exerted an obvious influence on Congressional action, especially when coupled with the political requirements of domestic and constituent concerns.[35] Every member must stay close to the latter concerns. Only in the absence of opposition, interest, or consensus back home can a legislator be free to judge an issue by the larger national interest— and only then if he is free of the party whip, the pressure of a vital lobby, or of committee loyalties. Most regrettable of all, Congress is particularly vulnerable to the powerful narrow-interest lobbies: not merely the sordid black bag of the industry and labor lobbies, but zealous forces of Common Cause, the Liberty Lobby, Reserve Officers Association, Greek-Americans, and the Sierra Club, each stampeding vulnerable members to their own narrow view of the national interest.[36]

---

and largely parochial body of legislators." Fulbright, "American Foreign Policy," p. 7. See also Alastair Buchan, "Partners and Allies," *Foreign Affairs*, July 1963, p. 627.

"In Congress controversy can lead to delay, to inaction, to unworkable compromise; to missed opportunities. Minorities can obstruct; special interests can sometimes manipulate policy more easily on the Hill than in the executive branch. The accident of committee leadership and membership can skew policy away from the national interest to more parochial concerns. No one should be sanguine about these risks. The danger of getting hopelessly bogged down in a congressional quagmire is clear and present." Katzenbach, "Foreign Policy, Public Opinion and Secrecy," p. 19.

Because, along with the Vice-President, he is the sole nationally elected government official, with the unique stature that entails, the President brings to the Executive a mighty psychological power, the force of symbolic personalized leadership. Whether the man's style is charismatic or not, the office provides an outlet for the universal human desire to personalize trust. The more abstruse, exotic, or dangerous the problem, the stronger the tendency to place trust in one man. Lincoln and Roosevelt, for example, could never have acted with such independence of Congress had they lacked solid public support and personalized trust. Without this trust the executive branch is vastly weakened, as the administrations of Andrew Johnson, Herbert Hoover, Lyndon Johnson, and Nixon have demonstrated.

While Woodrow Wilson may have exaggerated in saying that "inside the United States, the Senate is mostly despised,"* it is nevertheless true that the normal tedium of debate, incomprehensibility of procedure, and confusing array of elderly spokesmen vying for attention carry little danger of captivating the millions into emotional allegiance to Congress. And it is indeed true that confronting a popular President and attempting to impose restraints can be politically dangerous to a member. His constituency can easily confuse such opposition with obstruction of Presidential efforts in the national interest.[37] The force of this personalization of trust is perhaps best understood in a period of its absence, as in the second Nixon administration.

This trust, and hence executive power, is greatly intensified by a general perception of national danger. "The circumstances that endanger the safety of nations are infinite," said Hamilton in "Federalist No. 23," "and for this reason no constitutional shackles can wisely be imposed on the power to which the care of it is committed."[38] While there have usually been voices of dissent during war and crisis, and even committees on conduct of the war, Congress has never been disposed during such periods to seriously challenge executive actions of arguable constitutionality.[39] Neutrality acts and war powers acts are a Congressional luxury of postwar periods only.

Indeed, the force of Congress during conflict and crisis has weighed as often on the side of bellicosity and more forceful executive action as on the side of restraint and executive restrictions.† The reasons are obvious enough:

---

*"Outside of the United States the Senate does not amount to a damn. And inside the United States, the Senate is mostly despised. They haven't had a thought down there in fifty years." Woodrow Wilson, quoted by John F. Kennedy in Hirschfield, *Power of the Presidency*, p. 131.

†"One need go back no further than the Cuban missile crisis to recall, as Robert Kennedy has told us, that the Congressional leaders including Senators Russell and Fulbright, 'felt that the President should take more responsible action, a military attack or invasion and that the blockade was far too weak a response.'" Schlesinger, "Making of Foreign Policy,"p. 107.

popular opinion is always with the Executive in crisis, and woe unto the Congressman who lays himself open to the charges of "stiffening the resolve of the enemy," "pulling the rug from under the President," or "abandoning our soldiers in the battle." Congressmen well know that in moments of crisis, the Executive will always have the drop on them, by having the President appeal over the head of Congress to the people.[40] Television and the press conference have made possible the strengthening of the President's bond with the public in a way that has no parallel for the 535 members of Congress. As far back as 1933 it was said that Roosevelt "has only to look toward a radio to bring Congress to terms."[41]

"Let him once win the admiration and confidence of the country," wrote Woodrow Wilson, "and no other single force can withstand him, no combination of forces will easily overpower him. His position takes the imagination of the country. He is the representative of no constituency but of the whole people."[42] This, one hardly need add, would not accurately describe the office in the period since Watergate.

## ATTRIBUTES OF CONGRESS

The attributes and circumstances shaping Congressional powers in foreign policy are less sharply identifiable and more difficult to catalog than those of the Executive. The very deficiencies noted above—multipolarity, diffuse authorities, paucity of machinery, thinness of expertise and personnel, lack of intelligence sources, plodding, and workaday character, freedom from secrecy, lack of continuity, and above all localism and parochialism—are also the bases of its strength and promise.

The sanction of elections ties members inescapably to the will and mood of the people. Every member must be responsive to the constituency he represents. In the Executive, only the President is elected. The vastly powerful Secretaries of State and Defense, the Service Chiefs, and the Director of Central Intelligence and their many subordinates respond to no constituency but the President. While elected by the "whole people," the President himself serves three competing constituencies: his bureaucratic government constituency, his partisan constituency, and his foreign constituency of allies and adversaries.[43]

Congress is in a sense the political matrix from which foreign policy must be drawn. It alone is the institution capable of setting the boundaries of acceptable policy. In contrast with the initiative and execution functions requiring those virtues found in the Executive, Congress alone is organically suited to shaping the broad flow of foreign affairs in terms of direction, goals, and philosophy—and, in so doing, molding popular understanding to accept and support the wisdom of good policy.

Congress monitors, reviews, questions, criticizes, challenges, defines, modifies, approves, vetoes, and provides or withholds the appropriations for executive action. It stimulates executive action through both informal and legislative means, and occasionally—and usually with less happy results—mandates and initiates policies and operations against strong executive opposition.[44] Despite much rhetoric to the contrary, the activity and influence of Congress in foreign affairs are immense—indeed, probably greater than those of any legislature in the world.[45]

Each of the virtues of the Executive noted above has a reciprocal and checking counterpart among Congressional attributes. Congressional freedom from the inertial moment of the vast machinery of government allows a detachment from entrenched institutional viewpoints, spontaneity of perception, and the opportunity to view forests rather than trees.

The lack of armies of experts enables the common-sense view of the layman to temper the often-narrow specialist proposals of the Executive. The arcane insights of specialists have usually been accorded an attention and importance in foreign affairs far beyond their worth. The most important issues of foreign policy are not the proper preserve of the natural, technical, and political scientist, but are amenable to the widely shared insights and common wisdom found among Congressmen.

Congress, moreover, has a kind of expert talent not often found in the Executive: virtuoso politicians long in the tooth. And there is, of course, the "Congressional leadership." Presidents come and go, but the powerful chairmen, whips, speakers, and majority/minority leaders are immortal. Not only do individuals physically hold the posts for as long as a quarter of a century or more; but when they pass from the scene, their understudies of equal devotion to Congress take their chairs without missing a stroke. They vary widely in education and even wisdom, but are invariably the same in political cunning and the dark arts of maneuvering against the boys "downtown." There is no such thing as a "weakened" Congress in the way the term can be used accurately to describe a presidency. Because of seniority and the leadership, Congress is always strong.

The corollary to the executive cult of the expert, as J.W. Fulbright has often reminded us, is the tyranny of secret information. The chaos of the classification system in the Executive is legendary. While Executive Order 11652, issued March 8, 1972, has begun the process of rationalization, it will take many more years to reach that point.[46] But virtually all "secrets" that are really relevant to the responsibilities of Congress reach the interested members (and the press) with minimal delay. Because of the very openness of Congress, moreover, the public is usually guaranteed access to the really important intelligence and developments not otherwise available from the Executive. The revelations attending the proceedings of the committees chaired by Frank Church and Otis Pike in the Ninety-fourth Congress are cases in point.

The "high prerogative" men of the Executive are always quick to remind that Congress is incapable of acting with unity and dispatch, as required by the pace of international events. But "in the legislature," as Hamilton wrote:

> ...promptitude of decision is oftener an evil than a benefit. The differences of opinion, and the jarrings of parties in that department of the government, though they may sometimes obstruct salutary plans, yet often promote deliberation and circumspection, and serve to check excesses in the majority.[47]

It is such deliberation and circumspection that can restrain unwise initiatives from a unified Executive about to act with dispatch—say, in rescuing the French at Dien Bien Phu. The deliberate skill and circumspect judgment of a Senator Richard Russell in piloting a bitterly polarized and explosive issue through the investigative or legislative process, to arrive at a national consensus of gloriously broad generalities to which the wise and just then repair, is a democratic function of incalculable value.[48]

While it is unquestionably true that in foreign policy, the Executive proposes in all important matters, it remains equally true that Congress disposes in the same proportion. The activism of Congress in scrutinizing and substantially modifying executive initiative has kept pace with the increase in the latter. This Congressional role has received much less scholarly and media attention because its methods, as Madison described them, "being at once more extensive and less susceptible of precise limits, it can, with the greater facility, mask, under complicated and indirect measures, the encroachments which it makes on the co-ordinate departments."[49] The Executive gets all the headlines for initiating an Alliance for Progress or a Guam Doctrine or East-West trade; but it is Congress that gives them substance, and usually of a far different texture than intended by the Executive. A more recent observer has likened the process to the boss who pays his employees and then gets them into a crap game in which he takes back all their money.[50]

After proposing its grand policy schemes, the executive attention to them is delegated from the chief to his subordinates. Their ability to protect and defend them from major Congressional surgery is quite limited.

The isolationist legislation of the 1920s and 1930s, the violence annually wreaked on foreign aid, the long opposition to recognition of Mainland China, and the long-held restriction on the use of East-West trade as an executive tool are well-known examples of the negative impact of Congress on executive initiatives. But less widely understood are the actual initiatives and positive modification of foreign policy by Congress in the role of prodder and goad to the Executive. People tend to forget that Congress forced distasteful policies upon Madison in the War of 1812, on McKinley in the Spanish-American War, on

Truman regarding aid to Taiwan, on Kennedy in Vietnam, and on Nixon over Rhodesian chrome. Congressional influence has also been predominant in the area of structure, organization, and process in foreign affairs. The National Security Act of 1947 and the reorganization of the military and intelligence establishments, the United Nations Charter, and the Atlantic Pact were largely the result of Congressional initiative or equal participation, as was the evolution of the National Security Council system.[51]

A closely related aspect of this Congressional policy activism is the increasing disposition noted by scholars, and especially marked since the mid-1950s, to oversee administrative detail and to superintend both the execution of policy and the performance and selection of personnel in the executive branch.[52] This movement has included serious efforts even to "prescribe the mission of our troops in the field, in accordance with a foreign...policy of the United States which it is for Congress to set when it chooses to do so."[53]

A primary source of Congressional strength in such efforts is the deeply entrenched bonds tying the executive bureaucracy to Congress. Every Congressman of seniority has cultivated numbers of career civil servants, military, foreign service, or intelligence officers throughout those agencies dealing in his areas of committee or constituent interest. The pattern of such symbiotic relationships typically stretches over three or more administrations. For the bureaucrat, the relationship yields benefits (or protection) to his agency or bureau office, or perhaps to his job. It can assist in promotion and even such things as service academy appointments to favored sons. The Congressman of course gains access to information and an influence on the day-to-day application of policy. Nearly all of the chief political and permanent career officers of the Executive are also under a constant temptation to do what the senior Congressmen of their jurisdiction want them to do. They consult formally, informally, and often covertly; and their decisions on both policy and personnel are heavily influenced by those consultations.

The scrutiny, modification, and even initiative in policy by Congress provides another invaluable service. In subjecting executive proposals to the counsel and analysis of advisers owing no allegiance to the White House, an antidote is provided to the regal isolation of the presidency, wherein all circumstances conspire to exclude criticism from the Oval Office. No one, as George Reedy has pointed out succinctly, has ever invited a President in person to "go soak his head,"[54] but that inestimable function can be, and frequently has been, bravely performed on the floors of Congress, often with salutary effect.

## NOTES

1. U.S. v. Curtiss-Wright Export Corporation, 299 U.S. 304 (1936).

2. See, for instance, James Madison, "The First Letter of 'Helvidius'," cited by R.S. Hirschfield in *Power of the Presidency* (New York: Atherton, 1968), p. 57.

3. See, for instance, Alexander Hamilton, "The First Letter of 'Pacificus'," cited in Hirschfield, *Power of the Presidency*, p. 51. "The general doctrine of our constitution then is, that the *executive power* of the nation is vested in the President; subject only to the *exceptions* and *qualifications* which are expressed in the instrument."

4. John Stennis and J.W. Fulbright, *The Role of Congress in Foreign Policy* (Washington, D.C.: American Enterprise Institute for Public Policy Research, 1971), p. 23.

5. Myers v. United States, 272 U.S. 52 (1926).

6. Walter Bagehot, as cited in *Saturday Review*, February 14, 1970, p. 11.

7. William Elliott, *United States Foreign Policy* (New York: Columbia University Press, 1952), p. 63.

8. See, for instance, William Anderson, "Intention of the Framers: A Note on Constitutional Interpretation," *American Political Science Review*, June 1955, p. 340. Also see Arthur Schlesinger, Jr., "Congress and the Making of American Foreign Policy," *Foreign Affairs Quarterly* 517, no. 1 (1972).

9. Walter Bagehot, *The English Constitution* (London: Fontana Library, 1963), p. 220.

10. Clinton Rossiter, *The Supreme Court and the Commander in Chief* (Ithaca, N.Y.: Cornell University Press, 1951), p. 129.

11. Ibid.; Corwin, *The Constitution*, pp. 89-132.

12. See, for instance, Elliott, *United States Foreign Policy*, p. 45; Schlesinger, "Making of Foreign Policy," p. 89; Owen S. Stratton, "Presidential Power—Too Much or too Little?," New York *Times Magazine*, January 20, 1957, p. 11.

13. Stratton, "Presidential Power," p. 11.

14. Nicholas deB. Katzenbach, "Foreign Policy, Public Opinion and Secrecy," *Foreign Affairs*, October 1973, pp. 1-19.

15. Francis O. Wilcox, quoted in *Saturday Review*, February 14, 1970, p. 11.

16. See, for instance, James Burns, *Presidential Government* (Boston: Houghton Mifflin, 1965); Emmet Hughes, *The Living Presidency* (New York: Coward, McCann and Geoghegan, 1972); Arthur Schlesinger, Jr., *The Imperial Presidency* (Boston: Houghton Mifflin, 1973); Raoul Berger, *Executive Privilege* (Cambridge, Mass.: Harvard University Press, 1974); Louis Fisher, *President and Congress* (New York: Free Press, 1972).

17. See Katzenbach, "Foreign Policy, Public Opinion, and Secrecy."

18. Rossiter, *Supreme Court*, p. 5.

19. Ibid., pp. 3-4. Also see Martin v. Matt, 25 U.S. 19 (1827); Prize Cases, 67 U.S. 635 (1862); *Ex parte* Milligan, 4 Wall. 2 (1866); U.S. v. Curtiss-Wright Export Corporation, 299 U.S. 304 (1936); U.S. v. Pink, 315 U.S. 203 (1942); Youngstown Sheet and Tube Co. v. Sawyer, 343 U.S. 579 (1952); Korematsu v. U.S., 323 U.S. 214 (1944); Orlando v. Laird, 443 F. 2nd 1039 (2nd Cir. 1971).

20. See Schlesinger, "Making of Foreign Policy," p. 108; and Louis Henkin, *Foreign Affairs and the Constitution* (Mineola, N.Y.: Foundation Press, 1972), pp. 205-24.

21. Hirschfield, *Power of the Presidency*, p. 240; Louis Koenig, *The Presidency and the Crisis* (New York: Kings Crown Press, 1944), pp. 42-44.

22. Schlesinger, "Making of Foreign Policy," p. 107; also see J.W. Fulbright, "American Foreign Policy in the Twentieth Century Under an Eighteenth Century Constitution," *Cornell Law Quarterly* 47 (Fall 1961): 1-13.

23. See David S. Broder, "The Limits on Being Bipartisan," Washington *Post*, August 29, 1973, p. 16.

24. Burns, *Presidential Government*, p. 313; Burton Sapin, *The Making of United States Foreign Policy* (New York: Praeger, for the Brookings Institution, 1966), p. 54.

"Kennedy quoted with approval Woodrow Wilson's statement that 'the President is at liberty, both in law and conscience, to be as big a man as he can,' and said almost eagerly, that if the next President 'is the man the times demand,' he would discover 'that to be a big man in the White House inevitably brings cries of dictatorship.'" David S. Broder, "Kennedy's Presidential Style," Washington *Post*, November 21, 1973, p. 18.

25. Schlesinger, "Making of Foreign Policy," p. 105; Stennis and Fulbright, *Role of Congress*, pp. 52-53; Henry Steele Commager, "Presidential Power: The Issue Analyzed," New York *Times Magazine*, January 14, 1971, p. 11.

26. Burns, *Presidential Government*, p. 330

27. Clinton Rossiter, *The American Presidency* (New York: Mentor, 1956), pp. 15-16.

As Walter Lippmann wrote, "In the final acts of state the issues are war and peace, security and solvency, order and insurrection. In these final acts the executive power cannot be exercised by the representative assembly." Washington *Post*, June 25, 1970, p. 19.

28. E.A. Kolodziej, *The Uncommon Defense and Congress* (Columbus: Ohio State University Press, 1966), p. 439.

29. George Kennan, *American Diplomacy 1900-1950* (Chicago: University of Chicago Press, 1951), pp. 73-94. See also Richard E. Neustadt, "The Reality of Presidential Power" in Hirschfield, *Power of the Presidency*, p. 281.

30. Dean Acheson, *Present at the Creation* (New York: W.W. Norton, 1969), p. 600.

31. See Adolf Berle, Jr., cited in U.S. Congress, 82nd Cong., 2nd sess., July 1, 1952, *Congressional Record*, p. A4392.

32. Stennis and Fulbright, *Role of Congress*, p. 28.

33. Richard E. Neustadt, *Presidential Power: The Politics of Leadership* (New York: John Wiley, 1960), p. 270.

34. Owen S. Stratton, "The Weakness of the Presidency," in Hirschfield, *Power of the Presidency*, 303.

35. See Acheson, *Present at the Creation*, p. 560.

36. Stanley L. Falk and Theodore W. Bauer, *National Security Management: The National Security Structure* (Washington, D.C.: Industrial College of the Armed Forces, 1972), p. 94.

37. Hirschfield, *Power of the Presidency*, p. 249. See also Sidney Hyman, *The American President* (New York: Harper, 1954), pp. 293-308.

38. Hamilton, "Federalist No. 23," *The Federalist Papers* (New York: New American Library, 1961), p. 153.

39. Stennis and Fulbright, *Role of Congress*, p. 18.

40. Katzenbach, "Foreign Policy, Public Opinion and Secrecy"; Elliott, *United States Foreign Policy*, p. 65.

41. Hirschfield, *Power of the Presidency*, p. 223.

42. Cited in ibid., p. 243.

43. See Jacob Javits, "The Congressional Presence in Foreign Relations," *Foreign Affairs* 49 (January 1970): 231; see also Neustadt, *Presidential Power*, p. 270. For an opposing view, see Burns, *Presidential Government*, p. 263: "Increased authority and scope have not made the Presidency a tyrannical institution; on the contrary, the office has become the main governmental bastion for the protection of individual liberty and the expansion of civil rights. The office represents the electorate at least as effectively and democratically as Congress...."

44. See, for instance, James A. Robinson, *The Monroney Resolution: Congressional Initiative in Foreign Policy* (New York: Holt, 1959).

45. Holbert N. Carroll, "The Congress and National Security Policy," in David B. Truman, *The Congress and America's Future* (Englewood Cliffs, N.J.: Prentice-Hall, 1965), p. 152.

46. U.S. President, *Public Papers of the Presidents of the United States* (Washington, D.C.: Office of the *Federal Register*, National Archives and Records Service, 1973), Richard M. Nixon, 1972, p. 401.

47. Alexander Hamilton, "Federalist No. 70," *The Federalist Papers* (New York: New American Library, 1961), pp. 426-27.

48. For an example see Acheson, *Present at the Creation*, p. 526; and, for another, Lyndon Johnson, *Vantage Point* (New York: Holt, Rinehart and Winston, 1971), p. 451.

49. James Madison, "Federalist No. 48," *The Federalist Papers*, p. 310.

50. Stratton, "Weakness of the Presidency," p. 301.

51. Rossiter, *The American Presidency*, p. 15; Elliott, *United States Foreign Policy*, p. 53; Falk and Bauer, *National Security Management*; Samuel P. Huntington, "Strategic Planning and the Political Process," *Foreign Affairs*, January 1960, p. 287.

52. For a survey of this development see Kenneth N. Waltz, *Foreign Policy and Democratic Politics: The American and British Experience* (Boston: Little, Brown, 1967), pp. 100-01. Arthur Schlesinger writes: "In the years since the Second World War, Congress through its enlarged use of its powers of appropriation and investigation, had become increasingly involved in the details of executive administration, thereby systematically enhancing its own power and diminishing that of the President." *A Thousand Days* (London: Mayflower Books, 1967), p. 256.

53. Professor Alexander Bickel, cited in Schlesinger, "Making of Foreign Policy," p. 106.

54. George E. Reedy, *The Twilight of the Presidency* (New York: World Publishing, 1970), p. 14.

# 3

## THE WAR PROCESS:
## THE COOPER-CHURCH
## AMENDMENT

### BACKGROUND

War has been identified as that state in which a nation prosecutes its rights by force. Thus defined, war normally does not involve declaration or the legal formalism of customary international law. One study of conflict in Europe and America between 1700 and 1870 identified 107 cases of hostilities that began without declarations of war, and only ten preceded by such declarations.[1]

The Supreme Court, in a case arising out of the undeclared conflict with France in 1798, described the differences between formal declared war and the more common variety as being in the former case "solemn war," and the latter "imperfect war":

> If it be declared in form, it is called solemn, and is of the perfect kind; because one whole nation is at war with another whole nation....In such a war, all the members act under a general authority, and all the rights and consequences of war attach to their condition. But hostilities may subsist between two nations, more confined in its nature and extent; being limited as places, persons and things; and this is more properly termed imperfect war; because not solemn, and because those who are authorized to commit hostilities act under special authority and can go no further than to the extent of their commission.[2]

A scholarly study of the involvement of the United States in war identifies 149 cases of the use of force by the United States between the undeclared war with France in 1798 and Pearl Harbor. A more recent study done by the

Library of Congress identifies 165 cases of the use of U.S. armed forces abroad between 1798 and 1970. During this same period, however, the United States has actually declared war only five times, and four of those were made only after hostilities were already in progress.[3] It is to this broader phenomenon of war, and the interaction between Congress and the Executive in dealing with it, that the present chapter is addressed.

As was noted earlier, recourse to the intention of the framers provides no definitive guidance as to the sharing of the war powers.[4] It is generally accepted that the prevailing view was expressed by Madison: "...those who are to conduct a war cannot in the nature of things, be proper or sage judges, whether a war ought to be commenced, continued or concluded." The power formally to place the nation in a state of "solemn" war ab initio was undoubtedly intended for Congress alone.[5]

But as against this power it is equally clear that it was intended, in Hamilton's words, that "If, on the one hand, the legislature have a right to declare war, it is, on the other, the duty of the executive to preserve peace."[6] Also, the powers to do so "...ought to exist without limitation, because it is impossible to foresee or define the extent and variety of national exigencies, or the correspondent extent and variety of the means which may be necessary to satisfy them."[7] It is the President alone who is held constitutionally responsible for the nation's readiness to meet an enemy assault.[8]

Between these two principles, however, the answers to the really substantive war powers questions were left for events to decide. What is the meaning of "the power to repel sudden attacks"? What of hostilities such as the war with Tripoli, or limited punitive or protective police actions not directed against foreign states? What is Congress' power over the movement or deployment of the armed forces that it may provide, maintain and make rules for—in time of hostilities and in time of peace? These issues offer so many complexities, such infinite variety, such inconsistent precedent and practice, and so little agreement as to scope and exercise.

Proponents of executive dominance will cite scores of instances in which these questions were answered by unilateral executive action without either authorization or interference by Congress, in which authority was asserted and exercised to commit forces to armed conflict, to deploy forces throughout the world in protection of U.S. interests, and to assume complete conduct of hostilities once begun.

Opponents will cite scores of cases in which the Executive sought advance approval for action, or acquiesced in Congressional prohibition or initiative in force deployment.[9]

Practice has not legitimized a clear pattern. Congress has generally not interfered in time of major hostilities, nor has it generally objected to executive initiatives with armed forces abroad without prior consent—but there are important exceptions to both general rules, usually coinciding with the periods of

Congressional ascendancy described in Chapter 1. The 1801 action against
Tripoli, the Boxer Rebellion in 1900, the Panama action in 1903, the Mexican
expedition of 1915, the Russian expeditions of 1918-20, Nicaragua in 1926, the
occupation of Greenland and Iceland in 1941, Korea in 1950, the Bay of Pigs in
1961, the Dominican Republic in 1965, and Cambodia in 1970, as well as scores
of lesser measures, were actions of war undertaken by the Executive with no
formal and, usually no informal authorization or subsequent censure from
Congress. In nearly all, however, there were strong criticisms voiced and resolutions introduced by Congress; but all were finally acquiesced in or approved
ex post facto.[10]

Another perspective may be perceived, however, by recalling that in
addition to the five declared wars (which are really studies unto themselves of
Congress-Executive interaction), there were the following situations where the
Executive felt constrained to obtain prior authorization from Congress or,
failing, drew back from planned action: the war with France in 1800, actions
against the Barbary Pirates in 1802 and 1815, the Florida expeditions of 1812-
16, the attempted annexation of Texas in 1844, hostilities with Mexico in
1914-17, troop deployments to Europe in 1951, assistance to the French in Indochina in 1954, Formosa in 1955, Lebanon in 1958, Cuba in 1962, Vietnam in
1964, and Cambodian military assistance in 1971.[11]

## INDOCHINA

The subject of Congress' authorization of executive action in Indochina
has been the subject of much controversy. Opponents of the war resorted early
to constitutional arguments contending that there was no Congressional sanction
for the policies pursued by the Executive in Indochina. They dismissed the 20-
odd authorizations and appropriation statutes facilitating the actions, and the
nearly unanimous passage of the Tonkin Gulf Resolution as the same meaningless "approval" given to Theodore Roosevelt to bring back the White Fleet he
had already sent halfway round the world.[12]

A sounder view is found in the slightly overstated pronouncement of a
senior member of the Senate:

> ...the fact is, Congress is and has been involved up to its ears in the
> war in Southeast Asia. It has known what has been going on from
> the start and has given its approval in advance to almost every-
> thing that has occurred there. Far from being the innocent dupes of
> a conspiring executive, Congress has been wholly involved in the
> policy decisions concerning Vietnam during the entire span of
> American commitment there.[13]

Beginning with the appropriation of $75 million as an "emergency fund to be expended in the general area of China" in the Mutual Defense Assistance Act of 1949,[14] Congress began its fateful partnership with executive involvement in Southeast Asia. Congress increased its commitment each year until 1954, when specific appropriations of $400 million for military assistance to Indochinese forces were added by Congress to the economic assistance.[15] Senator Mike Mansfield, returning in 1953 from a fact-finding visit to Vietnam and neighboring states for the Senate Committee on Foreign Relations, declared in his report to the committee that continued military aid was "both justified and essential."[16] Appropriations were renewed yearly after much debate, until they were precipitously reduced in 1973, with historic consequences. To be sure there were dissenting voices in Congress, but that did not negate the action of the institution. This partnership was explicitly acknowledged by both branches; as President Eisenhower avowed, "there is going to be no involvement of America in war unless it is a result of the constitutional process that is placed upon Congress."[17] The now-famous April 1954 meeting between Dulles and Congressional leaders over using force to aid the French in Indochina demonstrates that President Eisenhower declined to move in the area without Congressional sanction.[18]

In February 1955 the Senate ratified the SEATO Treaty and Protocol, including South Vietnam by a vote of 82 to 1.[19] In 1959 the Senate Committee on Foreign Relations conducted an intensive investigation of the now massive assistance to Vietnam, and praised the program as successful in its final report.[20]

The year 1964 represents a major threshold. The U.S. presence in South Vietnam had swelled to 18,000 with Congress' full knowledge and continued appropriations.* In the summer of 1964 it had become evident that a quantum increase of U.S. effort would be needed in Vietnam to avoid a Communist takeover. Like Eisenhower in 1959, President Johnson believed he should have "the advance support of Congress for anything that might prove to be necessary," and accordingly, following the Tonkin Gulf incident, he met with Congressional leaders and "told them that I believed a congressional resolution of support for our entire position on Southeast Asia was necessary and would strengthen our hand. I said that we might be forced to further action, and that I did not 'want to go in unless Congress goes in with me.'"[21] Elsewhere, however, he expressed

---

*This was not, of course, unanimous; and the increasing commitment was viewed with growing misgivings by a sizable minority in Congress. In September 1963, 32 Senators, led by Frank Church of Idaho, cosponsored a resolution calling for a cutoff of aid to South Vietnam unless its government put reforms into effect. While the resolution itself did not pass, a milder version, leaving it up to the President's discretion, was included in the foreign aid bill. Wilcox, *Congress, the Executive and Foreign Policy*, p. 28.

the belief that "the resolution was not necessary to do what we did."[22] This view was shared by the resolution's subsequent floor manager, Senator Fulbright, who felt that it merely approved the use of existing Presidential powers, serving only as a show of unity.[23]

The resolution itself, drafted in the White House, provided in section 2 that the United States was prepared, as the President determined, to take all necessary steps, including the use of armed force, to assist any member or protocol state of the SEATO Treaty that requested assistance in the defense of its freedom.[24]

It has subsequently been suggested by some participants that Congress was somehow misled and did not contemplate authorizing the actual escalation of the war. This theory is not borne out by the record. It is useful to reproduce a relevant portion of the debate, in an exchange between Senators John Sherman Cooper and J. William Fulbright:

> *Cooper*: Does the Senator consider that in enacting this resolution we are satisfying the requirements of Article IV of the Southeast Asia Defense Treaty? In other words, are we now giving the President advance authority to take whatever action he may deem necessary respecting South Vietnam and its defense, or with respect to any other country included in the treaty?
>
> *Fulbright*: I think that is correct.
>
> *Cooper*: Then, looking ahead, if the President decided that it was necessary to use such force as could lead to war, we will give the authority by this resolution?
>
> *Fulbright*: That is the way I would interpret it. If a situation later developed in which we thought the approval should be withdrawn, it could be withdrawn by concurrent resolution. That is the reason for the third section.
>
> *Cooper*: I ask these questions....
>
> *Fulbright*: The Senator is properly asking these questions.
>
> *Cooper*: I ask these questions because it is well for the country and all of us to know what is being undertaken.[25]

The remarkably prophetic fears of the few critics such as Senators Ernest Gruening and Wayne Morse were given due hearing, but were overwhelmingly rejected as the resolution swept through the Senate 88 to 2 and the House 416 to 0.[26]

The assertion that Congress was a conscious partner in authorizing executive actions in Indochina seems validated by the record. It has further been upheld by the courts in several rulings. In a 1971 decision the First Circuit Court held that Congressional action made legitimate the course pursued by the Executive up to the point where Congress may assert a conflicting claim of authority.[27] Up to the spring of 1970 it had not done so. The Cooper-Church amendment became the first serious attempt by a faction in Congress to assert such a conflicting claim, and it is this attempt that we shall now examine in detail.

While Cooper-Church was the first serious attempt to curtail the Executive's policies in Indochina, criticism in Congress, as in the universities and media, began to build steadily following the substantial combat increase and launching of air attack against North Vietnam in early 1965. Nevertheless support as measured in actual authorizing and appropriating votes remained high through 1968.* By 1966, however, hearings by the Senate Foreign Relations Committee revealed a deeply negative attitude in the committee. In August 1967, an AP poll of Senators revealed that 40 had come to oppose the Executive's policy, and 44 still supported it.[28] The House, while containing some vigorously critical voices, maintained solid support throughout the period.

In July 1967, the first mildly negative legislation was introduced in the Senate by Senator Fulbright, finally passing on June 25, 1969, without executive opposition. It merely expressed the sense of the Senate that future foreign commitments require specific Congressional approval.

The first legislation that specifically attempted to limit executive policy was the Military Procurement Authorization Act, passed in November 1969. This included a ceiling of $2.5 billion on funds for "Vietnamese and other free world forces in Vietnam, Laos, and Thailand." This was a modest restriction, considering that the Executive had requested only $2.26 billion.[29] This measure was followed in December by passage of the Defense Appropriations Act, containing a Church amendment precluding the use of American ground combat troops in Laos or Thailand.[30] (This was the direct result of the Symington hearings on Laos, which will be examined in detail in Chapter 5.) It is important to note that both of the above restrictions were not opposed by the Executive.

---

*For instance, a supplemental request for Vietnam for more than $12 billion was passed on March 15, 1966, in a House vote of 389 to 3 and a Senate vote of 87 to 2. In March 1967, another supplemental request for Vietnam amounting to more than $12 billion was passed by a House vote of 385 to 11 and a Senate vote of 77 to 3. *Congressional Quarterly Almanac XXII* (Washington, D.C.: Congressional Quarterly, 1966), p. 153. *Congressional Quarterly Weekly Report* 25 (March 31, 1967): 493.

## THE CAMBODIA INCURSION

On January 6, 1970, Prince Sihanouk left Cambodia for his annual vacation of several months. Cheng Heng was acting chief of state, and the government went on as usual under Sihanouk's prime minister, Lon Nol, and deputy prime minister, Sirik Matak. In late February and early March, there were indications that the Cambodian military was becoming increasingly dissatisfied with the presence and activities of the North Vietnamese forces in Cambodia. The reasons for this dissatisfaction are complex. Khmer nationalism and traditional anti-Vietnamese hostility were undoubtedly major factors, but the fiduciary relations between the North Vietnamese and the Cambodian army remain to be explored. Prince Sihanouk has stated that the financial benefits resulting from his agreement with the North Vietnamese regarding the use of the harbor of Sihanoukville, and regarding arrangements to transport North Vietnamese supplies from the harbor to the Cambodian sanctuaries over Cambodian roads and in Cambodian trucks, went into the Cambodian army coffers.

In any case, dissatisfaction had become deep; and by early March there were riots in the eastern provinces of Cambodia and in Phnom Penh against the North Vietnamese presence and the government's lack of preventive action.

On March 13, Sihanouk left Paris for Moscow and Peking, apparently to seek their assistance in reducing the North Vietnamese presence in Cambodia. Five days later the Cambodian National Assembly, by unanimous vote, declared that Prince Sihanouk was removed as chief of state. Lon Nol and Sirik Matak were retained in charge of the government, with Cheng Heng remaining as acting chief of state. The reasons for Sihanouk's removal by the assembly included the growing economic and social problems, anti-royalist sentiment, and his capricious and high-handed style of dealing with his cabinet and the National Assembly, as well as the growing nationalist resentment against Vietnamese misuse of Cambodian territory.[31]

The North Vietnamese presence in Cambodia had existed for about five years before that time, during which period base areas, supply depots, hospitals, and logistics networks had been established along the South Vietnamese border for the purpose of supporting Viet Cong and North Vietnamese operations. These became known as the "sanctuaries."

Sihanouk's removal took the Nixon administration completely by surprise. While there were immediate charges of a CIA conspiracy, the President and his senior advisers in fact viewed the event with some dismay. Until then it had been their judgment that the military benefits of having Sihanouk take action against the Cambodian sanctuaries, or having U.S. or South Vietnamese forces move into the sanctuaries, was far outweighed by the disadvantages of abandoning Cambodian neutrality. Sihanouk had been able to exercise a moderating, though decreasing influence on the North Vietnamese presence; and though that influence had grown larger than he had wanted to tolerate, he had been able to prevent the sanctuaries from becoming fully operational combat bases. Moreover, Sihanouk had taken a position of benign neglect of U.S. air operations against those sanctuaries, making it clear that he was not entirely unhappy with such strikes, so long as they were in areas devoid of Cambodian population.[32]

On the same day as the ouster, a senior NSC official held a secret briefing for Congressional leaders in the Roosevelt Room at the White House to update them, primarily on Laos and secondarily on Cambodia. Participants in this meeting were left in no doubt that the official was not pleased by the development, and that he had no expectation that involving the Cambodian army against the North Vietnamese would bring any benefit to American policy. He expressed the intention of the administration to make no change in its policy toward Cambodian neutrality and to respect the status quo and hope that events would stabilize. The leaders present made it explicitly clear that they were concerned that events in both Laos and Cambodia might lead by inadvertent steps to de facto U.S. commitments.

The administration decided to pursue a policy of reestablishing the status quo diplomatically and militarily under the new regime in Cambodia. Three days after the NSC briefing, in response to a press conference question, the President announced that the United States had established relations on a temporary basis with the Lon Nol government, that United States interests were best served by the protection of Cambodian neutrality, and that he called on North Vietnam to take the same position.[33]

The North Vietnamese found themselves in an increasingly difficult position. They began to come under pressure from the Cambodian army, and they suddenly found their vital flow of supplies from Sihanoukville completely cut off. Going on the offensive by the beginning of April, the North Vietnamese had begun to launch strong attacks against Cambodian forces throughout eastern Cambodia. By mid-April they had extended these attacks into central Cambodia, attacking the towns of Saang, Takeo, Snoul, and Mimot, and numerous small government positions.

On April 20 the President addressed the nation to report on Vietnam. In that address he took note of the attacks by some 40,000 Communist troops in Cambodia and warned that if such activities had the effect of jeopardizing the U.S. forces remaining in Vietnam, he would not hesitate to take "strong and effective measures." He went on to announce his decision to withdraw 150,000 more troops from Vietnam in the coming year.[34]

The argument could be made that because of the precarious logistic situation and the pressure from the Cambodian army, the North Vietnamese had no real choice but to attempt to secure eastern Cambodia. In any case, the very day the President spoke, the North Vietnamese captured Saang. The North Vietnamese pressures into central Cambodia, and especially the interdiction of highways, increased dramatically through the remainder of April. By the twenty-sixth they had interdicted traffic on the Mekong and had cut all roads south and east of Phnom Penh. The conclusion was reached at the White House that the North Vietnamese had decided on a course of securing their sanctuaries in eastern Cambodia, and quite possibly were attempting to open a secure corridor to the Gulf of Siam in order to reestablish the supply by sea lost when Sihanoukville was closed.

During this period the President met quietly with key Congressional leaders to apprise them of developments and to seek their thoughts. He talked to others by telephone[35] By the afternoon of April 29 the decision to commit U.S. forces against North Vietnamese troops in the Cambodian sanctuaries had been made. There were numerous high-level meetings hastily arranged to deal with the problems of informing Congress, of handling the press, and of informing the American people—and, not least, to deal with problems of White House staff dissension.

The opening skirmish in Congress began on April 30, before it was known that the President would go on television that evening to make an announcement. Perhaps reacting to the obvious vibrations that something indeed was afoot, Congressman Ogden Reid of New York introduced an amendment to the Military Procurement Bill in the House that would extend the prohibition against ground forces being used in Laos and Thailand to cover Cambodia as well.[36] There were worried calls from the Republican leadership in the House to Bryce Harlow early that afternoon warning, that the Reid initiative could precipitate trouble.

On the Senate side of the Capitol, the administration opponents were up and sniffing the air nervously. Senator Charles Goodell hastily introduced an amendment completely banning any U.S. personnel in or over Cambodia for any purpose. Senators George McGovern and Mark Hatfield rushed in the amendment that they had been preparing for some time, which sought to cut off all funds for the conflict in Vietnam after December 31, 1970, unless Congress declared war.[37]

We see here the first evidence of a phenomenon that was to plague those members of Congress who wished to enact limiting legislation. Throughout the period under study, the opponents of the Executive's policies were never able really to coalesce on a single vehicle. Those who initiated measures—Goodell, Hatfield, or Frank Church—each seemed to take a proprietary pride in his particular measure; and as a result, the efforts were never really concentrated on one but were divided among several.

On the evening of April 30, President Nixon went on national television to inform the American people of his decision to launch a joint operation with the South Vietnamese to attack the major enemy sanctuaries on the Cambodian-Vietnam border. He recalled the warning he had issued in his April 20 report on Vietnam, stating that he had "concluded that the actions of the enemy in the last ten days clearly endanger the lives of Americans who are in Vietnam." He pointed out that the purpose of the operation was not to occupy the areas but to drive the enemy forces from the sanctuaries, to destroy the military supplies, and then to withdraw.[38]

Just prior to the President's address, a senior official of the National Security Council gave a background briefing for the White House press corps in which he clarified the intentions and the limited scope of the operation about to be announced. He addressed himself quite clearly to the concerns that had become evident in the preceding months of Congressional debate and the private discussions that he had had with leading members of Congress, concerns about the great danger of escalation of the conflict and of widening the American commitment into Cambodia. He stressed that it was limited to an area extending about 20 miles inside Cambodia, and that it was concentrated on disrupting the communications and command and control network and destroying the supply depots. He emphasized that American forces would be kept in Cambodia only as long as necessary to destroy the supplies in the area. He stated that he did not expect the length of the operation to be much more than six weeks to two months, but he specifically refused to be tied to a specific date. He did not exclude the possibility that the sanctuaries could be reestablished after such withdrawal, but the primary purpose was to gain the added months of delay for further progress in Vietnamization. He specifically stated that he was sure that Congressional concerns were taken into consideration before the decision was made.

On the question of the aid to the Cambodian government mentioned in the President's speech, the official emphasized the limited nature of the assistance in the types of small arms that would be provided. Weapons requiring foreign advisers or of great technical complexity would not be provided. In response to a question about why Secretary of State William Rogers, in his appearance before the Foreign Relations Committee three days earlier, had not informed them of the impending operation, the official cited military necessity as one of the factors.[39]

The issue of prior consultation with Congress was to become quite contentious in subsequent months. The President stated that during the period of April 20-30 he consulted with a great number of people, including members of the Senate and of the House. When asked point-blank why he did not go to the Senate or the House for approval for the operation, the President pointed out that it had not been an attempt to expand the war into Cambodia or to launch a war on Cambodia but, rather, to clean out enemy sanctuaries used to attack American forces in Vietnam. If it had been the former case, he said, he would have gone to the Senate. He emphasized that the element of surprise was important and that, in his judgment, the losses would have been 3,000-4,000 men, rather than the 330 actual casualties, had the element of surprise been absent. He recalled rather pointedly that President Kennedy had notified Congressional leaders only two and a quarter hours before he gave his orders instituting the Cuba blockade in 1962.[40]

The President's attitude was a polite representation of a very deep and bitter hostility that had developed during the first year and a quarter of the administration between the Congressional critics of executive policy, led by Senator Fulbright, and the Executive. It involved not only Indochina but also strategic arms, European policy, and nearly all foreign policy issues. In the atmosphere that had developed, it was utterly unthinkable, in the White House view, to provide the Congressional critics with advance warning of impending action, for it was assumed that recourse would be had immediately to the press in order to try to preempt such action.

## THE DEBATE BEGINS

Not by accident, perhaps, Congress was not in session the day following the address. Reaction in the Senate Foreign Relations Committee, however, was not long in coming. On the morning of May 1 the committee took the unusual step of requesting a conference with the President to discuss American military involvement. Against the advice of the Secretary of State, the President agreed with the position of his White House advisers not to grant such a meeting to the Fulbright committee. In what was not unintentionally taken as a calculated slight, the White House instead invited the committee to a joint meeting with the House Foreign Affairs Committee at 5 p.m. the following Tuesday. At the same time the President invited the Senate and House Armed Services Committees to meet with him earlier that same day. The initial committee response was predictable,[41] but they came to the meeting. The motive for recommending such handling of the Fulbright committee was not entirely spite. NSC and White House Congressional strategists had decided on a long-term policy of building up the role and importance of the House Foreign Affairs Committee as worthy of at least equal treatment with the Senate committee, and of both Armed Services Committees with the Foreign Affairs Committees.

While the White House expected vigorous dissent to follow the announcement, there is no question that the intensity and virulence of protest on the campuses and the bitterness of the reaction from some quarters of Congress completely shocked it. Following the shootings at Kent State and Jackson State, the staff around the President was in a state of crisis. On one side Henry Kissinger and his staff of seasoned policy analysts, along with Bryce Harlow and his staff of experienced politicians, were calmly counseling a policy of conciliatory rhetoric and open dialogue with the Hill but unswervingly firm adherence to the policy embarked upon. On the other side the young advertising men and lawyers of the Haldeman staff, all newcomers to Washington, were in headlong panic, urging a rethinking of the Cambodia action and perhaps limiting it immediately through the acceptance of legislation worked out with Congress. Members of Kissinger's staff, during the week following Kent State, were treated by their domestic colleagues rather as the crew of the Titanic may have been by its passengers. The effects of this near-panic by his domestic staff were soon apparent in the confidence of the President.

Participants in the President's meetings with the Armed Services and Foreign Affairs Committees on that day found his attitude surprising, and reported to the press that the President pledged to restrict the operation of U.S. forces to 30 kilometers inside Cambodia. The President's military advisers were aghast.[42] The following day the President's Press Secretary, Ronald Ziegler, backtracked, saying that the restriction was a general limit on scope, but confirmed that the President had said it and that he had promised to seek Congressional authorization before exceeding that limit. He announced, further, that the President had pledged to the Congressmen that both U.S. and South Vietnamese forces would be withdrawn in six to eight weeks, and that no U.S. units would be used in Laos. Ziegler confirmed that the President pledged that no commitment would be made to support or defend the Lon Nol government.

## THE BATTLE IS JOINED

On May 7 the Senate began its own offensive in earnest. The majority leaders, meeting in the Democratic Policy Committee and the Democratic Conference, drew up a strategy to enact restrictive legislation as soon as possible. Letters were sent to all legislative chairmen of the Senate, stating in part:

> In view of recent events concerning the introduction of U.S. forces into Cambodia, it is requested that your committee consider on the basis of highest priority, all measures dealing with that specific action, or connected with it.
>
> It is deemed in the highest national interest that all such proposals be reported to the Senate as soon as possible to afford their early complete and expeditious consideration by the full Senate.

Of the several restrictive amendments that had been hastily drafted, the Senate majority settled on the Cooper-Church amendment as the primary vehicle and agreed that the Fulbright Committee should report out the Foreign Military Sales Bill as soon as possible, to act as the vehicle for Cooper-Church. Nevertheless, Senators Hatfield and McGovern announced that they would proceed with their amendment to cut off all funds for Southeast Asia by December 31.

Because of the well-developed intelligence sources possessed by the White House legislative liaison personnel, the White House was aware of the leadership strategy and had drafts of the proposed amendments within minutes after their policy has been established. Position papers, question and answers, and recommendations were immediately requested by the White House from the State, Defense, and Justice Departments in order to prepare to oppose the legislative offensive and to deal with the constitutional and political arguments that would be raised in debate.

By the afternoon of May 8, the NSC and White House strategists had received the department recommendations and the position papers. The Justice Department, in a well-reasoned brief written by William Rehnquist (subsequently appointed to the Supreme Court), firmly recommended all-out opposition to the legislative proposals on constitutional grounds, arguing that as an attempt by Congress to make short-range, tactical decisions on the conduct of a military operation, the legislation was an unconstitutional invasion of Presidential power. The Defense Department strongly urged opposition to such legislation for constitutional and military reasons. The Department of State's acting legal adviser recommended against opposing the legislation because it would be likely to spark an acrimonious debate.

Concurrently the National Security Council staff, looking ahead, examined the effects on U.S. policy if the foreign military sales legislation should become completely bogged down in a Cambodia debate and not be enacted. The bill extended authority to grant concessionary credit terms to friendly nations in the developing world for purchase of military equipment that they could not afford on commercial terms. The State Department had always been lukewarm on this legislation, while the defense Department was its primary sponsor. It was the National Security Council, however, that had the greatest interest in seeing it enacted, since it had come to be seen as the primary implementing legislation for the Guam, or Nixon, Doctrine of helping nations to pick up the burden of their own defense rather than depending on U.S. intervention. Failure to obtain legislation, it was concluded, would severely affect Greece, Israel, Jordan, and Korea and cause problems for Argentina, Morocco, Lebanon, Brazil, Chile, and Venezuela. In retrospect, it is amusing to note that included in this program for nations unable to pay commercial terms were Iran and Saudi Arabia.

In the late afternoon of May 8 the acutely nervous counsels of some of the President's advisers continued to be felt. The NSC staff was asked to draft possible compromise language for restrictive legislation to replace Cooper-Church. And then, to the complete surprise of the NSC staff, the President announced at his evening press conference that American units would begin their withdrawal from Cambodia the following week, that "the great majority of all American units will be out by the second week of June, and all Americans of all kinds including advisers will be out of Cambodia by the end of June."[43]

There were very good military reasons for not informing the North Vietnamese of the schedule for U.S. withdrawals from Cambodia and certainly for not setting a date for complete withdrawal.[44] This the senior NSC official had specifically refused to do in his April 30 background session. On May 9 the State Department formally pledged to end the operation by July 1, and probably earlier, in a letter to Senate Fulbright.

Thus, in just over one week Congress had succeeded in imposing de facto restrictions of both scope and duration on the Executive's policy in Cambodia.

When Congress returned from the weekend on May 11, the Foreign Relations Committee reported out the final version of the Cooper-Church amendment with a total number of 30 cosponsors; it was scheduled to come to the floor on the following Wednesday.*

Meanwhile, the executive branch had begun a policy of compromise on the amendment, over the objections of the NSC. Although during the previous week the Justice and Defense Departments and NSC had strongly recommended opposing the amendment, the Department of State sent a formal letter to Senator Fulbright in which it placed the administration in the position of taking no objection to subparagraph 1 of the amendment, which prohibited ground forces in Cambodia, and suggested "clarifying subparagraphs 2 and 3." No objection was raised in the letter about subparagraph 4, precluding the use of United States air power in Cambodia.†

---

*The text of the Cooper-Church amendment to the Foreign Military Sales Bill, as contained in Senate Report No. 91-865, is as follows:

In order to avoid the involvement of the United States in a wider war in Indochina and to expedite the withdrawal of American forces from Vietnam, it is hereby provided that, unless specifically authorized by law hereafter enacted, no funds authorized or appropriated pursuant to this act or any other law may be expended for the purpose of: (1) retaining United States forces in Cambodia; (2) paying the compensation or allowances of, or otherwise supporting, directly or indirectly, any United States personnel in Cambodia who furnish military instruction to Cambodian forces or engage in any combat activity in support of Cambodian forces; (3) entering into or carrying out any contract or agreement to provide military instruction in Cambodia or to provide persons to engage in any combat activity in support of Cambodian forces; or (4) conducting any combat activity in support of Cambodian forces.

†The letter from the State Department to Fulbright read in part:

As a general principle we do not consider it desirable that actions of the Commander in Chief should be subject to statutory restrictions. In any case, no such amendment should restrict the fundamental powers of the President for protection of the armed forces of the United States. As it stands, however,

In order to head off what the NSC perceived as spreading panic and to attempt to devise a coherent strategy, a meeting was held on the evening of May 11 in the Situation Room. At this meeting, attended by NSC staff, Assistant Secretary of Defense Nutter, Assistant Secretary of State David Abshire, Secretary of Defense Melvin Laird's legislative assistant, Richard Capen, and the President's Congressional liaison assistants Kenneth BeLieu and William Timmons, a strategy was agreed upon in which the administration's public position would be one of overall opposition to the amendment while the departmental legislative liaison people would explore possibilities for compromise behind the scenes.

On May 13 Timmons met with the chairman of the House Foreign Affairs Committee, Thomas E. "Doc" Morgan, and the ranking Republican, Ross Adair. He was encouraged to hear from them that they were firmly committed not to accept Cooper-Church in any House-Senate conference if it were eventually passed by the Senate. They expressed confidence that it had no chance of passage in the House. That afternoon a task force was organized in the White House with personnel from the Justice, State, and Defense Departments to draft speeches and talking papers for Senate opponents of the Cooper-Church amendment. The next day William Rehnquist was given responsibility for overall coordination of the substantive constitutional positions to be used in the coming debate.

---

the amendment might be so interpreted, thus limiting the President's authority to take actions which he finds to be essential for the defense of United States forces. Subject to this reservation we have no objection to subparagraph 1. We believe however that subparagraphs 2 and 3 are subject to a great variety of interpretations which might adversely affect the President's policy on Vietnamization and steady replacement of American combat forces in Vietnam.

The NSC objected to all four of the subparagraphs for different reasons. Subparagraph 1 was objectionable because it would obviously require the termination of the sanctuary incursions that were believed to be essential to the continued success of Vietnamization. Moreover, there was a strong desire on the part of the NSC to maintain the option or the threat of going back into the sanctuaries at any time after the operation then under way had been terminated. Subparagraph 2 was objectionable because it was believed to be desirable to maintain the option to provide training, in compliance with the Nixon Doctrine, to prepare the Cambodian army to improve its capabilities, and that the use of Thai or other third-country personnel for such activities could be advantageous. There was also a possible option that Thailand might send combat units to Cambodia to fight alongside the Cambodian army against the North Vietnamese. Subparagraph 3 was objectionable for the same reasons. Subparagraph 4 was opposed because it was thought desirable to maintain the ability to provide direct air support to the Cambodian army at some time in the future if it were necessary. There was also concern with the ambiguity of what constituted "combat activity," since the term could be construed to prohibit normal reconnaissance or air supply missions.

On May 15, there was a very important strategy meeting held in Senator Hugh Scott's office just off the Senate floor. In addition to Scott, Senators Margaret Chase Smith and Milton Young were present and the Executive was represented by NSC staff, Abshire, Capen, BeLieu, and Timmons. Senator Scott began the meeting by attempting to convince the administration officials of the wisdom of supporting an amendment that he wanted to introduce. It would retain much of the rhetoric and thrust of Cooper-Church but remove its fund cutoff requirement, and even include the Presidential loophole "to protect the lives of American troops etc." The NSC staff responded that the NSC was becoming increasingly concerned about the impact of Cooper-Church and the Senate debate on nations overseas. Therefore, it was argued that the administration's position was becoming as important as the actual legislative effect of whatever might be passed. Administration endorsement of any amendment that had the effect of prohibiting assistance to Cambodia would in effect be a repudiation of the Nixon Doctrine. The Djakarta conference of Asian nations was about to begin, and the NSC held high hopes for positive results from this initiative in regional security and self-help. The NSC was also concerned that administration endorsement of any modification of Cooper-Church would provide the enemy with valuable foreknowledge, thus enabling them to deploy their forces and direct their efforts much more efficiently. In sum, the NSC, it was reported, believed that public endorsement of any modification, regardless of how watered-down, of a Cooper-Church amendment, would damage the chances of achieving a final negotiated settlement of the war.

Scott replied that this was an unrealistic position, because the sponsors of Cooper-Church had a clear margin of victory on an up-or-down vote. At this point Senator Smith strongly intervened in support of the NSC position, saying that she personally was absolutely adamant that there could be no compromise with a principle of this constitutional magnitude and there should be no amendment of any kind restricting the President in this way. It was then agreed that Scott should examine exactly how many votes his compromise could pick up on a final tally and that the group would reconvene later.

Meanwhile, on the House side there were some developments encouraging to the administration. After much publicity, a House Democratic caucus was held on the morning of May 14 at the initiative of Representative William F. Ryan and other opponents of administration policy in an attempt to get Democratic endorsement for a Cooper-Church amendment. Only 86 Democrats attended, less than a quorum of the 244 total Democratic House membership. House leaders concluded that a majority of the approximately 200 House Democrats who were in town refused to attend the caucus because of their opposition to Cooper-Church.[45]

During the remainder of that week and over the following weekend, White House political assistants attempted to mobilize outside interest groups on the implications of Cooper-Church, seeking to make the depth of "silent majority" support for the administration's policy known to Congress.

## THE TURNING POINT

The real turning point in this interaction between the two branches on Cooper-Church came about in a dramatic meeting on Tuesday, May 19. The occasion was the Republican leadership meeting, normally held alternate Tuesday mornings in the Cabinet Room, at which the President and the Republican members of Congress discuss legislation and administration policy. Everyone present assumed that the purpose of the meeting was to agree on a compromise amendment in order to end the increasingly bitter Senate debate. To everyone's amazement, the President began the meeting by stating that he strongly opposed any restriction whatsoever. He recalled that when he was Vice-President, President Eisenhower had told him that while Eisenhower would never under any circumstances have used nuclear weapons in Asia, he would never publicly admit this because of the great advantage to a potential adversary. So, too, any version of Cooper-Church would offer similar help to the enemy. He said that regardless of what happened to the amendment in the House, passage in the Senate would mean that the enemy at home and abroad would have a field day.

The President then stated that the Cambodian operation was a great success, and called on Secretary Laird for a review of the situation. Laird reported that the operation was proceeding well ahead of schedule, that 1,300 men had already been withdrawn, and that operations were already beginning to phase down and all deadlines would be met.

The President then called on Secretary Rogers, who reported that the Djakarta meeting of Asian nations had just been completed and had been a great step forward for Asian regional security, with no participation from the United States. Rogers then suggested that the principal portions of Cooper-Church were consistent with the President's policy, but it was desirable to get out by July 1, without giving the enemy the appearance of grave division in the U.S. government.

The President then called on Bryce Harlow, who pointed out that the latest vote count in the Senate showed the sponsors of Cooper-Church with about a ten-vote margin. He noted that roughly 20 Republicans and some Democrats had expressed a willingness to debate at length, and that many of them felt the people were with the President and time was on the administration's side. Mike Mansfield, he reported, had sensed that and was therefore determined to bring Cooper-Church to an early vote. Further, Senator John Sherman Cooper had indicated a willingness to compromise, and Secretaries Rogers and Laird had been considering possible language. But one of the problems with compromise was that it would alienate the President's hard-core supporters in the Senate, who were committed to no restrictions at all.

Commenting on the possibility of adopting a strategy of filibuster, the President said he believed that sentiment would improve in the Senate during such extended debate, but that the debate itself would give aid and comfort to the enemy, and that he would prefer to have it out of the way. On the other hand, he also pointed out that uncertainty was one of the best assets the United States had in Southeast Asia and that passage would remove a considerable amount of that uncertainty for the enemy's strategists.

Senator Smith took issue with the President, telling him that he was really in a much stronger position than he believed, and that timing was very bad for any such amendment. She said that she would vote for an even stronger amendment if the troops were not out by July 1; but under the present circumstances she could not vote for any amendment, no matter how watered-down.

Senator Scott reported that the present vote would be about 57-40 in favor of Cooper-Church, but that as many as 20 Senators supporting Cooper-Church would vote for a Scott-type amendment to it and that he had talked to Senator Cooper, who was receptive to such an amendment. Scott felt that unless the administration accepted a compromise, some of the votes would deteriorate and go over to the Hatfield-McGovern amendment. Senator Griffin said that he believed the President was gaining more support in the Senate for no restrictions at all, and that this was no time to compromise.

The President called on Congressman Ford, who had just returned from Michigan. Ford reported that support for the President's policy was growing among the people. He stated that time was on the President's side and that the strategy should be to delay; then the whole question would become academic by July 1.

Senator Allott reported that all the hawks were willing to go into a full filibuster until July 1. He pointed out that if Cooper-Church passed, every politician facing reelection the following autumn would be facing the charge that Congress saved the country from the Republicans' war. Senator Tower injected that he strongly supported Senators Allott and Smith in urging a filibuster.

Secretary Laird said that he would much rather see the question fought out in conference than go into a filibuster. The President replied that there probably was no real way to get acceptable language, and that it would be far better to be able to wait until the President had had an opportunity to make a final report to the nation on the operation.

Secretary Rogers took a strong position against a compromise, because it would look like capitulation; but if debate were extended, there would be a far better chance of ultimately getting an acceptable compromise.

The President said that the trouble with the compromise offered by Cooper was that the interpretation must inevitably be that it was the Senate that got us out of Cambodia.

Congressmen Arends and Morton both strongly supported extending debate, because they believed time to be on the side of the administration.

Secretary Laird reiterated the importance of the Foreign Military Sales Bill and argued that the place for confrontation was therefore in the conference rather than on the Senate floor. He agreed, however, that two or three weeks' further debate would do no harm.

The President ended the meeting with the conclusion that the best course would be to compromise only later, when "they" were ready to talk, and that he firmly intended to have an opportunity to report to the American people before the Senate spoke. The meeting adjourned with an agreement to avoid mentioning the word "filibuster" but, instead, to refer to the need for serious consideration of such a vital constitutional question.

The Republican leadership thus returned to the Hill to embark on a filibuster of unknown duration. Secretary Laird expressed great displeasure with the outcome of the meeting, but Secretary Rogers and the NSC were quite pleased.

On May 21 Senator Cooper proposed a new compromise that would soften the preamble to read "in concert with the declared objectives of the President of the United States to avoid the involvement of the United States in Cambodia after July 1, 1970...." The administration refused to endorse this, since the NSC remained adamant that subparagraphs 2, 3, and 4 must be deleted as well. The Cooper modification to the preamble was subsequently adopted on the twenty-sixth by vote of 82 to 11.[46]

By the end of the following week, the possibilities for any compromise had narrowed even further. The main focus of attention had been on the preamble and subparagraph 1, on Presidential powers and the fund cutoff; but the National Security Council staff felt equally strongly about sections 2 and 3, having the effect of explicitly repudiating the Nixon Doctrine, and section 4, as precluding the use of U.S. air power in Cambodia, an option they felt could prove to be essential for continued success of Vietnamization if the position of the Cambodian army deteriorated badly.

Another significant factor was that with the cooling of the domestic situation, and the increasing evidence of success in the Cambodian operation, the domestic advisers to the President began to regain their composure.

Another further important factor working to prolong the debate was that it began to take on a life of its own as senatorial participants warmed to the task. Ably assisted by platoons of nameless ghostwriters in the executive branch, on one side, and legions of academic and journalistic opponents of administration policy lending their ghostwriting talents, on the other, the senators seemed almost to relish the opportunity of taking to the floor on matters of high constitutional principle, to speak at great length and much frequency.

By June 1, debate had gone on for nearly three weeks and no compromise was in sight. Amendments had been offered by Senators Robert Byrd, Ted Stevens, Robert Dole, Cooper, Church, Mansfield, George Aiken, Jack Miller, John Williams, Albert Gore, Peter Dominick, and James Eastland.

By June 1, the administration's position had crystallized to the following language, circulated to administration spokesmen:

> The Cooper-Church amendment is unacceptable for two basic reasons: 1) It seeks to place severe restrictions upon the President's power to take such actions as he deems necessary to safeguard United States forces in Vietnam. Such restrictions would be an unconstitutional interference with the President's authority as Commander in Chief under Article II.2) It represents a repudiation of the Guam Doctrine of regional cooperation and self-help, by prohibiting the President from considering certain types of assistance to the Cambodian government. The Administration has not endorsed any amendment to Cooper-Church.

On June 2, the administration, at the initiative of Senator Robert Byrd of West Virginia, made its first attempt to work out an acceptable compromise. The next day the President made an interim report to the nation on the Cambodian operation over nationwide television. In it he gave the background to the decision to move into the sanctuaries and recounted in detail the nature of the operation and the accomplishments in weapons captured and base areas destroyed, noting that the success of those operations guaranteed that the June 30 deadline he had set for withdrawal of all American forces from Cambodia would be met. He carefully avoided the mention of the withdrawal of South Vietnamese forces and noted that U.S. air missions would continue to interdict the movement of enemy troops and matériel in Cambodia "where I find that is necessary to protect the lives and security of our men in South Vietnam." Other than the pledge to fulfill his promise to complete U.S. withdrawal by July 1, and a noting of the success of the Djakarta conference in relation to the Guam Doctrine, there was no mention of the debate on Cooper-Church.[47]

On June 4, negotiations were successfully concluded between BeLieu and Senator Byrd for administration support of his amendment to Cooper-Church.* A Presidential letter was drafted by the NSC staff and Bryce Harlow, signed by the President, and hand-carried to Senator Scott for his release. The letter

---

*Byrd Amendment No. 664 read as follows:

By adding the following words to paragraph 1: "Except that the foregoing provisions of this clause shall not preclude the President from taking such action as may be necessary to protect the lives of United States forces in South Vietnam, or to facilitate (rather than hasten) the withdrawal of United States forces from South Vietnam."

endorsed Senator Byrd's *effort* as going a long way toward eliminating the more serious objections to the Cooper-Church amendment. It avoided formal endorsement of the amendment as such, but was very close to it. It also expressed the hope that the Senate would pass an amendment to Cooper-Church in support of the Guam Doctrine.*

Because the Byrd amendment went only to the question of powers of the Commander in Chief, leaving sections 2, 3, and 4 untouched, this was an apparent softening of the administration's opposition. This was not the case, however, since the filibuster was intended to continue until those matters were settled.

On the afternoon of June 3, Senator Dole's amendment, which conditioned Cooper-Church upon the release of all POW's, was rejected by a vote of 54-36. This represented a fairly accurate gauge of strength on the final tally, and served as an impetus both to prolonging debate and to seeking an eventual compromise.[48]

In conjunction with the endorsement of the Byrd effort, a meeting was held in Senator Scott's office on June 4, attended by Senators Scott and Robert Griffin, Assistant Secretary Abshire, Timmons, and BeLieu from the White House, and Capen from Secretary Laird's office. In addition to giving the go-ahead for full floor support for Byrd, the intense NSC concern over subparagraphs 2 and 3 was the subject of discussion. It was agreed that Senator Scott would negotiate further with Senator Cooper on some alternative revisions drafted by the NSC.

The administration got considerable encouragement from the House of Representatives on June 6, when it rejected a Reid amendment (that itself had been considerably softened by a Findley substitute on protecting the lives of American troops) by a resounding vote of 321-32. Following that, other anti-administration amendments were offered by Congressmen Robert Leggett,

---

*The President's letter read in part:

As you know I am opposed to the language of the Cooper-Church provision in its present form. Nevertheless, I fully appreciate the concerns of many senators anxious that the Cambodian expedition not involve our nation in another Vietnam type conflict...The Byrd Amendment reaffirms the Constitutional duty of the Commander-in-Chief to take actions necessary to protect the lives of United States forces and is consistent with the responsibilities of my office. Herefore, it goes a long way toward eliminating my more serious objections to the Cooper-Church Amendment...I should hope that the Senate would also adopt an amendment supporting the Nixon Doctrine of American material and technical assistance towards self-help....

U.S. President, *Public Papers of the Presidents*, Richard M. Nixon, 1970, p. 486.

Jonathan Bingham, William Ryan, and Allard Lowenstein and were rejected by similar margins.[49]

By June 9 administration support of Senator Byrd had strengthened him to the point where his unofficial count was to win on a vote of 48-44. Fearing such a success, Cooper-Church supporters counterattacked, Senator Charles Percy attempted to get White House support for a weakening of the Byrd amendment that would insert the words "having United States forces in Cambodia except where the use of such force is necessary *pending Congressional approval* to respond to a clear and direct attack upon forces of the United States from Cambodia." The administration declined to support it.

On June 9, responding to the growing threat from the Byrd amendment, Senator Church launched a counterattack, calling it a second Gulf of Tonkin Resolution. To appeal to the sponsors of the Byrd amendment, he pledged that the Cooper-Church amendment should not be read to affect the power of the Commander in Chief to protect U.S. forces and that it could not, even if it intended to, by mere bill, add or take away from those constitutional powers. He ridiculed the Byrd amendment as having been worked out in consultation with and endorsed by the White House.[50]

This interpretation by one of the amendment's sponsors, which would serve to narrow the effect through legislative history, had a real impact on a few wavering Senators who had agreed to support Byrd but now felt that this modified legislative history would accomplish the same thing. The White House and NSC staff, in their command post in Senator Scott's office, saw the balance tip against the Byrd amendment and were deeply concerned. They knew that while legislative history was nice to have, the reality of Cooper-Church would be that, if enacted, the executive branch would break the law if it took any further actions in Cambodia. Senator Mansfield had made this very point in a speech later that evening.

Members of the National Security Countil staff worked long into the night developing rebuttals for administration supporters to counteract the Church speech in the following day's debate. On the morning of June 10 an administration official met with Senator Byrd and discussed possible ways of dealing with the Church agruments.

That afternoon Senator Byrd offered a modification of his amendment that called on the President to consult with Congressional leaders prior to using any U.S. forces in Cambodia if, as Commander in Chief, he determined that the use of such forces was necessary to protect the lives of U.S. forces in South Vietnam or to facilitate their withdrawal.

After further debate, in which Cooper-Church sponsors argued that the amendment would still gut Cooper-Church, Senator Byrd returned to the floor on June 11, offering a further modification to the effect that Cooper-Church "shall not preclude the President in the exercise of his constitutional authority, powers and duties as Commander in Chief, from taking only such temporary

action as is clearly necessary to protect the lives of United States forces...
etc."[51] He went on to deny that his amendment would gut paragraph 1 of
Cooper-Church, and pointed out that his amendment did not touch paragraphs
2, 3, or 4. In this belief, Byrd was joined with the administration, which by this
time had decided it could not accept Cooper-Church even if the Byrd amendment had passed, for the very reasons that Byrd had just pointed out. This
second softening modification of his amendment was undertaken against the
wishes of the administration. There was thus little disappointment when, later in
the day, a roll-call vote brought defeat to the Byrd amendment by a vote of
52-47.

A curious fillip was added in passage by an overwhelming vote of 91-0 of
the Mansfield-Dole amendment late on June 11. It read as follows: "Nothing
contained in this section shall be deemed to impugn the constitutional power of
the President as Commander in Chief."[52]

The Executive gained a bit more favorable legislative history during debate
on this amendment through colloquy between Senator Jack Miller and Senator
Church.

Senator Church, speaking for the proponents of Cooper-Church, stated
that they had no intention whatsoever, under that amendment, to criticize the
President for his action in the Cambodian sanctuary operation.

As debate ground on past the middle of June, the administration was quite
confident that the filibuster could be maintained until all U.S. forces were out,
and that was the primary objective of the strategy daily engineered in the command post in Senator Scott's office.

One following the debates in the *Congressional Record* would get the distinct feeling of déjà vu when Senator Byrd, along with Senators Griffin and
William Spong, introduced on June 17 almost the same amendment that had
previously been defeated. One observer likened the debate to two punch-drunk
boxers supporting each other in the ring. The new Byrd amendment added a
sentence to the Mansfield amendment that had been previously adopted so that
it now read:

> Nothing contained in this section shall be deemed to impugn the
> constitutional power of the President as Commander in Chief, *in-
> cluding the exercise of that constitutional power which may be
> necessary to protect the lives of United States armed forces wherever
> deployed.*

The outside observer may be pardoned for failing to see any substantive
difference between the defeated wording of the first Byrd amendment—"...this
clause shall not preclude the President from taking such action as may be
necessary..." and the language of the newest Byrd amendment. His bewilderment may also be forgiven in finding that this new Byrd amendment met with

only desultory opposition from the Cooper-Church proponents and passed overwhelmingly on June 22 by a roll-call vote of 79-5.[53]

While the Senate proceeded with no end in sight, the Executive arrived at an approved policy for doing without the Foreign Military Sales Bill through a series of legislative devices that could continue authority for spending in lieu of the bill. This was approved on June 19. With that, the last remaining incentive to see the Senate action concluded was removed from executive deliberations, and its legislative strategy was conducted accordingly.

As we have seen, the Executive was at least as concerned about sections 2 and 3 of Cooper-Church as it was about section 1, because 2 and 3 struck directly at the Nixon Doctrine. Yet this issue played little part in the seven weeks of debate. It was not until June 29 that Senator Griffin, in consultation with the NSC staff, offered an amendment to modify subsection 3 to endorse the Nixon Doctrine of encouraging regional cooperation by changing the text to read:

> No funds authorized or appropriated pursuant to this act or any other law may be expended after July 1, 1970 for the purpose of... (3) entering into or carrying out any contract or agreement to provide military instruction by United States personnel or to provide United States personnel to engage in any combat activity in support of Cambodian forces.[54]

The Cooper-Church advocates and the press came to call this the "mercenary" or "Hessian" issue, after the Symington Subcommittee on Commitments Abroad revealed, on July 7, that under a secret agreement the United States had been paying Thailand $50 million a year as a subsidy to support its combat division in South Vietnam. (See Chapter 5.)

Thai Prime Minister Thanom Kittikachorn did not help the administration's position by announcing on June 1 that his nation was prepared to send volunteers to help Cambodia if they would be armed and equipped by the United States.[55]

In the course of debate Senator Church had characterized the Nixon Doctrine as a policy of "Hessians unlimited. The Nixon Administration is interested in 'hired guns.'"[56] The administration, however, again gained a favorable legislative history when Church finally adopted the position that his amendment gave it "a good bit of leeway" to provide aid to allies.

> It does not prevent us from arming or equipping or supplying a Thai or Lao force sent into Cambodia, but it would prevent us from hiring them to fight...all the Thais would be required to do is to pay for forces.[57]

If our outside observer were to be utterly confounded in attempting to ascertain the will of the Senate in the four votes taken on the Griffin amendment on June 30, he may again be pardoned. In the first vote the Griffin amendment endorsing the Nixon Doctrine passed by a vote of 47-46. In a motion to table a motion to reconsider the Griffin amendment, Griffin lost in a reversed vote of 47-46.[58] A vote was then taken on the motion to reconsider, which was approved 49-46. The Griffin amendment was then reconsidered and finally lost in a vote of 45 yeas to 50 nays, with 4 not voting.[59]

## TONKIN GULF REPEAL

One of the most interesting and instructive developments during the course of the Cooper-Church debate was the amendment offered on June 22 by Senator Dole, to add to the Foreign Military Sales Bill an amendment repealing the Tonkin Gulf Resolution.

The story of this amendment really begins in the preceding January. During the first session of the Ninety-first Congress, Senator Charles Mathias of Maryland had introduced a Senate joint resolution that would repeal the Formosa Resolution of January 1955, the Middle East Resolution of March 1957, the Tonkin Gulf Resolution of August 1964, and the Cuban Resolution of October 1962. With the start of the second session in January 1970, the executive branch was requested to provide its position on S.J. Res. 166 in preparations for hearings that were to begin on February 3 in the Senate Committee on Foreign Relations.[60] Information reached the White House from sources within the Foreign Relations Committee that the chairman intended to use this vehicle, specifically focusing on the Tonkin Gulf repeal, as the major thrust of his attack on the administration's Southeast Asia policy in the second session, and that he planned a major floor debate for the spring and summer to culminate in a dramatic vote that, he believed, would repeal the Tonkin Gulf Resolution and thus force the administration to withdraw immediately from South Vietnam.

By January 15, the White House had received legal analyses from the Justice and State Departments, while the NSC had evaluated the policy impact of the passage of such a resolution. State found no legal effects whatsoever if all four resolutions were repealed, pointing out that the present administration's policy was not dependent on any grant of authority in Tonkin Gulf for its continued policy in Southeast Asia. Justice raised some cautions about the possible need of a substitute resolution if Tonkin Gulf were to be repealed. The NSC staff warned against the adverse impact abroad, especially in each of the areas affected if all four resolutions were repealed. Repeal of these resolutions could be interpreted as a repudiation of administration policy in all four areas, thus presenting the dilemma that if the administration opposed and lost, it would be seen to have been repudiated, while if it joined in the repeal, it would be seen to be joining in the repudiation.

On January 23, a meeting was held at the White House between Bryce Harlow, Undersecretary of State Elliot Richardson, and NSC staff to decide on a course of action, because the hearings were soon to begin and Richardson himself had been called to testify. It was tentatively decided that the Tonkin Gulf Resolution presented the greatest problem, that there were probably sufficient votes in the Senate to repeal Tonkin Gulf, and that the administration's posture toward it could be decided only by the President.

During the following week Harlow, Richardson, and NSC staff drafted a lengthy analysis of the implications of various courses of action, and a decision memorandum was sent to the President.

On February 3, the Foreign Relations Committee began its hearings on S.J. Res. 166 and, as expected, the media focused on the Tonkin Gulf repealer section, describing it, in Walter Cronkite's words, as a "Bi-partisan effort... aimed at reasserting the Senate's constitutional right of advise and consent in foreign policy."[61]

The final conclusions reached by the executive branch analysis were the following:

1. The Tonkin Gulf Resolution was a legitimate expression of Congressional authorization for the Executive to commit troops to the defense of South Vietnam.

2. An increased commitment of troops to Southeast Asia would probably require further authorization actions by Congress.

3. While such a resolution may have been necessary to make the original commitment ab initio, it has no real relevance to the President's powers as Commander in Chief over those troops legitimately in the field in South Vietnam.

4. Hence the repeal of Tonkin Gulf would have no effect on the legitimacy of the President's current policies, since no increased commitment was contemplated; rather, the withdrawals had already commenced.

5. Repeal of Tonkin Gulf would have a debilitating effect on the South Vietnamese, give a very damaging signal of encouragement to the North Vietnamese, and be seen abroad as a general repudiation of the administration's Indochina policy.

6. There were almost certainly enough votes in the Senate to repeal Tonkin Gulf unless the administration made an all-out fight.

7. If the administration had to fight, it was taking on all of the liabilities associated with Tonkin Gulf and the Johnson policy of slow escalation.

8. To engage in such a battle would be to accept Fulbright's grounds and provide him with the major debate that he was looking for.

On February 26, the President decided on the following administration position:

Executive testimony should reflect that these congressional resolutions were a matter of congressional business. Since the administration did not depend on any of the resolutions in question for authority for its current policies, it would take no position for or against the repeal of those resolutions.

Executive testimony should reflect that the President would not veto the resolution if it came to him for signature.

All testimony must be cleared in advance by the White House.

The State Department would be charged with preparing immediately measures to ameliorate the damage abroad in the event that the resolutions were repealed.

The President also approved a nine-page letter drafted by the NSC and Richardson, formally stating the administration's position for the Foreign Relations Committee.

In line with the President's decision, the letter stated: "The Department believes that repeal of the resolution specified in section 1 is a matter within the discretion of the Congress. We neither advocate nor oppose congressional action."

Each of the resolutions specified in section 1 was passed in response to a crisis situation in the affected area....In these moments of crisis, the use of these resolutions as a highly visible means of executive-legislative consultation was instrumental in demonstrating unified support for our policies to the world and the American public and in indicating congressional approval for the possible employment of U.S. military forces in support of these policies.

The crisis circumstances giving rise to these resolutions have long since past [sic]. As indicated by the specific analyses below, the administration is not depending on any of these resolutions as legal or constitutional authority for its present conduct of foreign relations, or its contingency plans.

Equally important, the administration does not consider the continued existence of these resolutions as evidence of congressional authorization for or acquiescence in any new military efforts or as a substitute for the policy of appropriate and timely congressional consultation to which the administration is firmly committed.

The letter then went on to analyze each of the resolutions in detail.

### The Tonkin Gulf Resolution

As noted above, this administration has not relied on or referred to the Tonkin Gulf Resolution of August 10, 1964, as support for its Vietnam policy.

Repeal at this time, however, may well create the wrong impression abroad about U.S. policy.

The President has made our policy in Vietnam clear on numerous occasions. We seek a negotiated settlement and are proceeding with efforts to bring the war to an end even if such negotiated settlement proves unattainable. The Congress could, of course, draft and adopt a new resolution to complement and support that policy.[62]

This letter was sent to the committee on March 12, and on March 16 Secretary Richardson testified in defense of that position, emphasizing that the administration did not rely on any of the resolutions, but pointing out that they did contain valid expressions of policy.[63]

The Foreign Relations Committee chairman, apparently without having read all nine pages of the letter, exclaimed that it was "the most enlightened and progressive and conciliatory and pleasant memorandum I've received in a long time."[64]

On April 10, the Foreign Relations Committee approved a modified resolution calling for repeal of the Tonkin Gulf Resolution by a unamious vote.[65] Richardson's prediction of adverse signals abroad was realized when, on April 15, both Radio Hanoi and Tass heralded its passage as a major setback for the administration's policy.[66]

The great debate on the floor was to have begun promptly after the publishing of the committee report on May 1, but the announcement of the Cambodia incursion on April 30 completely preempted it. In an interesting footnote, the committee staff, without authorization but presumably reflecting the pique of the chairman, hastily revised the report just before its release, inserting language that accused President Nixon of "conducting a constitutionally unauthorized, presidential war in Indochina," and assailed the President for sending U.S. troops into Cambodia "without the prior consent or even the prior knowledge of Congress or any of its committees." Committee chief of staff Carl Marcy submitted his resignation over the incident after Senator John Williams of Delaware protested, but the resignation was declined.[67]

The White House thereafter decided to have Senator Dole introduce and sponsor a repeal of the Tonkin Gulf Resolution at an appropriate moment during the Cooper-Church debates, in order to steal its thunder and to defuse the issue.

Thus, on June 22, Chairman Fulbright was found in the somewhat awkward position of testily opposing the repeal of the Tonkin Gulf Resolution, proposed in the administration's behalf by Senator Dole. Fulbright was joined in this effort by some of the President's staunchest supporters who failed to appreciate the subtlety of the administration's position and fought to maintain the Tonkin Gulf Resolution on the books. Thus Senator Sam Ervin of North Carolina argued that if it was repealed, the resolution "would be a repeal of the authority of the President to command our troops in combat in that area of the world...."[68] Senator John Stennis argued, "It would jerk the rug out from under the authority that has been exercised for all of these years."[69] Senator Ervin expressed the bewilderment felt by a number of administration supporters when he said:

> I cannot view it as anything but intellectual and constitutional schizophrenia that the Administration should stand here and fight the Church-Cooper amendment for all these weeks and then make through its spokesman the proposal on the floor of the Senate that the Senate repeal the only action taken by Congress which gives the President authority to use the armed forces of this country in combat in Southeast Asia.[70]

Chairman Fulbright was rebuffed in a vote to have the motion tabled by a vote of 67-15. He then found himself leading a minority against the repeal of the Tonkin Gulf Resolution as it was enacted by the Senate in a roll-call vote of 81-10.[71]

The whole episode was perhaps best described in an editorial written the following week:

> Now Senator Fulbright's team overshifts—far to the left—when playing against right-handed hitters. So, the skipper in the Administration dugout signaled for Senator Dole to hit to the opposite field. With a motion to repeal the Tonkin Gulf Resolution, Dole came through with a stinging drive over first base that rolled all the way to the bamboo fence—completely taking the scrambling fielders by surprise. They are now gathered around the pitcher's mound frantically planning how to play the next batter....
>
> One does not have to be a baseball fan to recognize that Senator Fulbright and his followers have been outmaneuvered on the Gulf of Tonkin Resolution. Fulbright is furious that his plans for lengthy, spectacular debate are now rather trifling.[72]

In a less publicized move that one member described as reminding him of Alice in Wonderland, the Senate repassed another repeal resolution in July by a vote of 57-5. This time Senator Fulbright voted for repeal, but the resolution was never enacted by the House and died. Senator Dole's repeal was signed into law on January 11, 1971, as part of the Foreign Military Sales Act.[73]

## FINAL PASSAGE

On the afternoon of June 29, the last American combat troops returned to Vietnam from the Cambodian sanctuaries. The determination by the executive branch to accomplish withdrawal before the Senate took action was achieved, and there was no further reason for delay. In the command post in Scott's office, the White House representatives suggested to administration supporters that they go ahead and vote for Cooper-Church in final passage and call it a victory. They were now confident that Cooper-Church would never survive a House-Senate conference. And they were generally satisfied with the results of the Senate debate, with the passage of the Byrd-Griffin amendment, and with the establishment of a legislative record that included concessions by the sponsors, Senator Church among them, of the principle that limited incursions back into Cambodia would be permitted under Cooper-Church and even an implied endorsement of the Nixon Doctrine of providing arms to Cambodia.[74]

At four o'clock on June 30, after more than seven weeks of consideration, a roll-call vote was taken on final passage of the Cooper-Church amendment. It passed by a vote of 75-20, with the administration's floor leaders, Scott, Griffin, and Dole, voting for final passage.[75]

The immediate preliminary response from Press Secretary Ziegler in San Clemente was to note that the results of the debate were somewhat confusing but that the Senate had clearly recognized the prerogatives and responsibilities of the President as Commander in Chief.[76]

On the evening of June 30, the President made a lengthy report to the American people on the Cambodian operation over nationwide television. In it he recapitulated the factors leading up to the decision to move against the sanctuaries, and detailed the military results of the operation. He pointed out that the Executive "scrupulously observed the 21-mile limit on penetration of our ground combat forces into Cambodia territory," and noted that while those self-imposed restrictions of time and geography might have cost some military advantages, they had served the purpose of underscoring the limited nature of the incursion for the American people. The President then announced the guidelines for further U.S. policy toward Cambodia: that there would be no U.S. ground personnel or advisers in Cambodia; that air interdiction missions against enemy resupply through Cambodia and against the base areas, to protect U.S. forces in Vietnam, would be conducted with the approval of the Cambodian government; and that military assistance to the Cambodian government would be provided. He explained the principles of the Nixon Doctrine as applied to Southeast Asia and reaffirmed the administration's commitment to them. He made no mention whatsoever of the Cooper-Church amendment or debate.[77]

In further explaining the administration's policy on the same day, a senior official of the National Security Council told newsmen that while no set of principles could cover every conceivable contingency, U.S. forces would not go back into Cambodia. He stated that U.S. air interdiction would not be assigned the task of close air support in Cambodia. He indicated that there would have been no point in staying beyond June 29, since by them the operation had completed its purposes. He said that he could foresee no circumstances in which United States forces would be reintroduced into Cambodia.[78]

On the morning of July 1 the White House-NSC team that had quarterbacked executive strategy for the seven weeks of debate cabled guidance for the President's use that evening, when he was to go on nationwide television once again for an hour-long interview with the anchormen of the television networks.

The first concern was the passage of Cooper-Church, and the team recommended that the President take a position based on the following points: that the language of Cooper-Church was, to say the least, ambiguous; that it would send a negative and confusing signal regarding U.S. intentions abroad; that the legislative history and the amendments sponsored by Senators Dole, Byrd, Griffin, Henry Jackson, and others clearly recognize the Congressional responsibilities of the Commander in Chief; and that the President was confident that the House of Representatives would modify the amendment's objectionable language.

The second most important concern in the minds of the NSC and the Justice Department was the controversial question of how the President could continue military operations in South Vietnam after the Tonkin Gulf Resolution was repealed. The guidance on this point was based on the following simple arguments: First, the Tonkin Gulf Resolution was a constitutional procedure in the exercise of shared war powers appropriate to a period of initial commitment to action under the SEATO Treaty and Article 51 of the UN charter—both treaties ratified by the Senate and currently in force; second, the administration was not pursuing or seeking a new commitment to action; rather, it was engaged in the liquidation of the initiative begun in earlier administrations; third, the Tonkin Gulf Resolution, appropriate as an instrument of initial commitment, had no continuing relevance to the deescalation of the conflict being conducted by the current administration. Other procedures of Congressional authorization under the Constitution were required and appropriate for such a period, including testimony, consultation, and the appropriations process.

That evening the President was interviewed by Howard K. Smith of ABC, Eric Severeid of CBS, and John Chancellor of NBC. As expected, one of the first questions was Smith's request for an explanation of what legal justification remained for continuing to fight in Vietnam once the Gulf of Tonkin Resolution was rescinded. To the acute distress of his advisers watching television in Washington, the President responded by justifying his actions on the extremely narrow basis of his right to protect the lives of American men. Smith reiterated his question: "But do you have a legal justification to follow that policy once the Tonkin Gulf Resolution is dead?"

The President reiterated his very narrow justification: "Yes sir Mr. Smith, the legal justification is the one I have given, and that is the right of the President of the United States under the Constitution to protect the lives of American men. That is the legal justification."[79]

Thus, in not using the legal position that the administration had approved and worked out, the President opened a Pandora's box of legal doubts about his power to continue administration policy in Vietnam. In fact, the better legal view was not the narrow one that the President suggested, but the position contained in the suggested substantive guidance sent to San Clemente. Limiting the justification to protection of U.S. forces in South Vietnam of course immediately begged the question of why this right would not also require the President to give these troops the greatest protection, that of immediate withdrawal from the hostile zone. The President had put a valuable weapon in the hands of his critics.

The President was much more effective in handling the questions on passage of Cooper-Church. His initial response noted, with tongue in cheek, "Fortunately, our founding fathers had great wisdom when they set up two houses of Congress." He then went on to say, with studied unconcern:

> I think the performance of the Senate over the past seven weeks, going up and down the Hill on Cooper-Church, has not particularly distinguished that august body, and the Cooper-Church that came out was not a particularly precise document and was somewhat ambiguous...now fortunately, it now goes to the House and the House will work its will on that amendment, and then it goes to conference...and I believe that the conference of the Senate and the House...will first be sure that the power of the President of the United States to protect American forces whenever they come into attack is in no way jeopardized...and second, that they will recognize that the Nixon Doctrine will be upheld...as far as the Senate is concerned that, while I will listen to them, I will pay attention to what they have said, I am going to wait until the House acts, until the conference acts, and I believe that the action, the joint action of the House and Senate, will be more responsible, I will say respectfully, than the action of the Senate was.[80]

On July 1, acting Secretary of State U. Alexis Johnson had called a meeting in the Department of State without White House representatives present, in which the department settled on a position recommending that the administration accept Cooper-Church in exchange for the Senate yielding on the sections 9 and 10, which severely restricted the military assistance program. The Department of Defense joined in this commendation. On July 3, word reached the White House that Senator Church was willing to trade sections 9 and 10 for the administration's acceptance of Cooper-Church.

The Speaker of the House and Minority Leader Ford were both unfavorably disposed toward Cooper-Church, and were most anxious to have a clear White House position before July 4, so that conferees might be appointed and instructed in the House. The matter was referred to the President, and on July 6, he decided that there should be no compromise on Cooper-Church. The NSC staff was accordingly instructed to take appropriate actions to adjust policy to do without the Foreign Military Sales Bill, and that afternoon the State and Defense representatives were summoned to the White House and instructed that all agencies should conform their actions to that position. The Speaker of the House, the Minority Leader, and the chairman of the House Foreign Affairs Committee were informed late that afternoon that the administration would rather not have a Foreign Military Sales Bill than have the current language of Cooper-Church become law.

On July 9, Congressman Donald Riegle offered a motion to instruct the conferees to accept Cooper-Church. The motion lost by a vote of 237-153, thus in effect rejecting Cooper-Church.[81] After the vote, Richard Cook, the White House liaison man, had a long meeting with the Speaker, during which it was concluded that there would be a long impasse in the conference, with the Foreign Military Sales Bill a probable casualty. Possibilities were explored for obtaining alternate authorities by different legislative methods. Chairman Thomas Morgan, who would lead the House conferees, believed, however, that the conference would have to accept some modified weaker version of Cooper-Church.[82]

## DEADLOCK

The House-Senate conference held its first meeting on July 15; and as it met, the White House delivered an unsigned memorandum giving the executive branch position. The memorandum took a very strong position against Cooper-Church, stating:

> The Administration opposes this amendment and urges that it be stricken. The restraints imposed by this section appear to affect the President's exercise of his lawful responsibilities as Commander in Chief of the armed forces.[83]

As expected, the positions were polarized from the very first meeting, with the House conferees taking an adamant stand for deletion of the amendment,

and the Senate conferees taking an equally firm position insisting upon retention.[84] On July 16, Senator Mansfield lamented, "It looks as though it will be a
drawn out impasse...we'll never have an arms bill at all."[85] The New York
*Times* and the Washington *Post* were quick to join several network commentators in chastising the executive branch for tying up this legislation by not ac-
cepting the will of the Senate in the Cooper-Church amendment.[86]

By July 22, the administration's supporters in the House were becoming
somewhat restive, since the supporters of Phantom jet sales to Israel were beginning to fear that the stalemate would prevent conclusion of another Phantom
deal.[87] On that day the House conferees queried whether the White House would
be satisfied if they were able to modify section 3 to meet the requirements of
the Nixon Doctrine. The administration's reply was that this was not sufficient,
that section 4 remained unacceptable and that sections 9 and 10 of the bill itself were also unacceptable, and that therefore the House conferees were requested to "hang tough."

On August 11, the President reviewed the impasse—still without sign of
breaking—and noted that if a Griffin-type amendment securing the Nixon Doctrine were to be included instead of subsection 3, he might consider a compromise.

On August 29, Secretary of Defense Laird on his own initiative sent a
letter to Chairman John Stennis of the Senate Armed Services Committee and to
Chairman "Doc" Morgan of the House Foreign Affairs Committee in which he
implied that the administration was ready to compromise. As was noted earlier,
Laird had always been unhappy with the administration's hard line against
Cooper-Church, and he was particularly unhappy that it was interfering with
his legislation in the Foreign Military Sales Bill. In the White House, however,
there was considerable consternation because Laird's letter had not been cleared;
and Chairman Morgan was promptly told that there was no change in the President's opposition to Cooper-Church.

Thus the impasse continued through September and October. On October
22, however, Secretary Laird once again broke ranks. In a speech calling for the
enactment of the legislation, he said:

> This foreign military sales authorization has been languishing
> in conference between the House and Senate for several months now
> in a dispute over an irrelevant provision. I hope that the Congress
> will no longer delay action on this vital legislation when it reassem-
> bles in November.

Once again the House conferees thought that the administration had changed
its mind and was ready to compromise, and once again the NSC-White House
position was reaffirmed to Chairman Morgan: no compromise was wanted, and
the administration would rather see the bill die.

By the end of October the House conferees had met only six times in four months, and no progress was in sight.[88] (A total of six meetings had been held on four days: July 15, 22, 29, and August 11, 1970.)

In November, all attention shifted away from the impasse over the Foreign Military Sales Bill and focused on the administration's ambitious Supplemental Assistance Bill, in which $500 million for Israel was combined with a new commitment of aid to Cambodia. The supporters of Cooper-Church immediately devoted their efforts to attaching a new Cooper-Church amendment to this piece of legislation while opposing the legislation itself—a difficult task.[89]

It was not until the Cambodia supplemental aid was finally resolved on December 22 that the way was cleared to resolve the Cooper-Church problem with the Foreign Military Sales Bill. On December 31 the conference met for the last time, the Senate conferees gave way, and Cooper-Church was deleted. The Foreign Military Sales Bill was signed by the President as Public Law 91-672 on January 12, 1971.

## CONCLUSION

The Cooper-Church amendment drew its strength from several sources. Some Senators simply feared the consequences of the Cambodia incursions and wished to bring them to an end, dreading the consequences of a widened war.[90] A major source of strength was those members who had become totally opposed to U.S. policy in Vietnam and saw Cambodia not merely as an issue of widening the war, but as an opportunity to mobilize a majority against the entire war policy. They were quickly joined by the various antiwar groups, such as Women's Strike for Peace, the Mobilization Committee, Common Cause, and others, to undertake what was described by one sympathizer as "the most extensive lobbying campaign ever undertaken for an anti-war measure."[91]

Still another source of strength was provided by those who saw it as an effort "to substitute congressional authority for Presidential authority in a theater of war."[92] Those who held this view—most of them members of the Foreign Relations Committee—saw it as the first step in curbing the "unconstitutional" growth of Presidential power.

While the initial perception of the State and Defense Department bureaucracies was characteristically to find some accommodation on the issue, the President and his National Security Council advisers, after some indecision, concluded that all-out opposition was required. The gravest threat seen by the White House was the encroachment of Congress upon the President's powers as Commander in Chief. They were fully in accord with Senator Stennis, who told a White House lobbyist, "...I know of no instance in recorded history when any Congress even seriously considered restricting the Presidential power to the extent that the Cooper-Church...amendments would have when American fighting men were actually engaged in battle."

On a more visceral level, the White House perceived this as the latest offensive of the antiwar coalition of some Senators, media collaborators, and of course demonstrators. By this time, that conflict was very emotional on both sides. While the President's National Security Council advisers prided themselves on their cool analytical detachment, it would be naive to think that there was not some emotional effect from narrowly evading physical harm while trying to sneak through demonstrations to get into work in the White House basement, or in being pelted with eggs at Harvard colloquia. In the spring of 1970 there was a siege atmosphere in the White House that was fed by a very deep frustration at what was seen as gross negative distortion in media coverage of the war. Cooper-Church was immediately seen as but the latest offensive of the besieging forces.

White House determination to fight the measure was also based on the military analysis of the Cambodia situation. it was the belief of the Pentagon, shared by the NSC staff, that destruction of the stockpiles and disruption of the logistics and communications in the sanctuary areas would effectively end the war in the southern half of South Vietnam for at least a year, a vital gain for their withdrawal strategy. The accuracy of this assessment was further confirmed in the weeks following the incursion, when the records from the port of Sihanoukville provided proof that, contrary to the assessments of the intelligence community, virtually the whole of the war in the Mekong Delta was being supplied through the sanctuaries by shipments offloaded at the Cambodian port. Cooper-Church was therefore seen as a direct threat to the success of the NSC strategy.

The response of the executive branch, then, was to fight Cooper-Church with every means at its disposal. Counsel was taken with supporters in Congress, and a filibuster organized and maintained until the military operation was completed. During the debate, pressure was maintained to modify the most objectionable part of Cooper-Church, which was finally done through the passage of the second Byrd modification. Cooper-Church was then passed by the Senate, with the executive branch asking its supporters to vote for passage. Because of remaining objections over sections 3 and 4, having to do with third-country assistance and U.S. air support, the administration through its supporters in the House, easily bottled up the measure indefinitely in a stalemated conference, until the matter was settled in the Cambodia supplemental aid, after which Cooper-Church was killed by the conferees.

The Cooper-Church effort did have a substantial impact, however. On the military level, the President twice restricted operations under pressure of Cooper-Church when he imposed a limit of penetration to 21 miles into Cambodia, and then pledged to withdraw all U.S. forces by June 30. By midsummer the President was giving assurances that there were no circumstances in which he

would send U.S. forces back into Cambodia. Many of the President's advisers, and all of the U.S. military commanders in South Vietnam, deplored these restrictions. They believed that U.S. forces could have achieved much more had they been permitted to operate 50 or more miles into the sanctuary areas, and to continue operations through the summer of 1970. They also strongly objected to providing North Vietnam with assurance that they would never again have to fear such a thrust into their sanctuaries.[93]

The impact on executive policies actually ran much deeper. It had a conditioning effect on all of the President's advisers and, in effect, narrowed the parameters of future options to be considered. Everyone was aware that ground had been yielded and that public tolerance had been further eroded. This was especially evident in dealing with the use of U.S. air support to Cambodian forces and in the possibility of Thai forces fighting in Cambodia. There was also the curious weakness in the logic of the executive position introduced by the President in his July interview.[94] By ignoring the carefully argued position worked out by the Justice Department and putting forward his right to take any military action to defend U.S. troops as the sole constitutional justification, he provided his Senate opponents with a damaging line of attack once all U.S. ground forces were out of action the following year.[95]

The Senate critics, however, had paid a price as well. First, they never did get Cooper-Church enacted. They failed to end the Cambodia incursion by legislation. Indeed, far from curbing Presidential power, passage of the second Byrd amendment can be interpreted as "...the most explicit reaffirmation of the inherent powers of the Commander in Chief ever to issue from a legislative body, in wartime or otherwise."[96] The critics, through inadvertence, also lost their potentially most damaging issue, the withdrawal of Congressional sanction from the war by repeal of the Tonkin Gulf Resolution. The administration, knowing there was a majority for repeal, carefully laid the groundwork in testifying that it no longer depended on Tonkin Gulf and then, through its floor manager, Senator Dole, moved and carried the repeal itself—thus completely defusing the issue and placing Senator Fulbright in the embarrassing position of voting against repeal.

The cause of Senate opposition was perhaps most set back by the tying into knots of Senate business for seven weeks of debate, ending in a conference stalemate and producing a legislative logjam that was not unraveled until the very eve of the new Congress the following year.

## NOTES

1. Arthur Schlesinger, Jr., "Congress and the Making of American Foreign Policy," *Foreign Affairs Quarterly*, 51, no. 1 (1972): 83.

2. The Eliza, No. 4 Dall. 37, pp. 40-41.

3. Edward S. Corwin, "Who Has the Power to Make War?" New York *Times Magazine*, July 31, 1949, pp. 11, 14, 15. For different lists based on wider criteria see U.S. Congress, House, *The Powers of the President as Commander in Chief of the Army and Navy of the United States* (Washington, D.C.: U.S. Government Printing Office, 1956); U.S. Congress, House, Committee on Foreign Affairs, *Background Information on the Use of United States Armed Forces in Foreign Countries* (Washington, D.C.: U.S. Government Printing Office, 1970).

4. Eugene V. Rostow, "Great Cases Make Bad Law: The War Powers Act," *Texas Law Review* 50 (1972): 833.

5. James Madison, "The First Letter of 'Helvidius,'" cited by R.S. Hirschfield, in *Power of the Presidency* (New York: Atherton, 1968), p. 57. Also see E.S. Corwin, *The Constitution and What It Means Today* (New York: Atheneum , 1967), p. 125; John Stennis and J.W. Fulbright, *The Role of Congress in Foreign Policy* (Washington, D.C.: American Enterprise Institute For Public Policy Research, 1971), pp. 39, 41, 42; and Schlesinger, "Making of Foreign Policy," p. 81.

6. Alexander Hamilton, "First Letter of 'Pacificus,'" cited by Hirschfield, in *Power of the Presidency*, p. 52.

7. Clinton Rossiter, *The Supreme Court and the Commander in Chief* (Ithaca, N.Y.: Cornell University Press, 1951), p. 8.

8. "He is never for one day allowed to forget that he will be held accountable by people, Congress and history for the nation's readiness to meet an enemy assault." Clinton Rossiter, *The American Presidency* (New York: Mentor, 1956), pp. 16-17.

9. "Both the historical and the judicial precedents tell each principal in the great debate exactly what he wants to know." Rossiter, *Constitution*, pp. 12, 13.

10. U.S. Congress, House, Committee on Foreign Affairs, *Background Information on the Use of United States Armed Forces in Foreign Countries*.

11. Schlesinger, "Making of Foreign Policy," pp. 95, 98, 99. Also see U.S. Congress, House, Committee on Foreign Affairs, *Background Information on the Use of United States Armed Forces in Foreign Countries*, and Chapter 6 of this book.

12. See, for instance, Senator Fulbright's remarks in U.S. Congress, Senate, 92nd Cong., 1st sess., February 5, 1971, *Congressional Record*, p. S888.

13. Senator Barry Goldwater, New York *Times*, August 25, 1971, p. 37.

14. *Congressional Quarterly Almanac* V (Washington, D.C.: Congressional Quarterly, 1949), p. 351. It is ironic that this Congressional initiative, largely engineered by the "China lobby" under the leadership of Senator William Knowland of California, was actually opposed by the Executive. Also see Francis Wilcox, *Congress, the Executive and Foreign Policy* (New York: Harper and Row, 1971), p. 25.

15. *Congressional Quarterly Almanac* IX (Washington, D.C.: Congressional Quarterly, 1953), p. 156.

16. New York *Times*, October 27, 1953, p. 5.

17. Ibid., March 11, 1954, p. 1.

18. Chalmers Roberts, "The Day We Didn't Go to War," *Reporter*, September 14, 1954, p. 31.

19. *Congressional Quarterly Almanac*, XI (Washington, D.C.: Congressional Quarterly, 1955), p. 281. "Senator Walter F. George, Chairman of the Foreign Relations Committee

at the time made absolutely clear that a purpose of the treaty was to warn aggressors of American intervention in order to protect Asian member and protocol states. The preservation of that freedom is a primary objective of the treaty." New York *Times*, August 25, 1971, p. 37.

20. New York *Times*, February 9, 1960, p. 3.

21. Lyndon Johnson as quoted in the Washington *Post*, October 20, 1971, p. 12.

22. Schlesinger, "Making of Foreign Policy," p. 101.

23. U.S. Congress, Senate, 88th Cong., 2nd sess., *Congressional Record* 110: S18409.

24. 78 Stat. 384 (August 10, 1964).

25. Washington *Post*, January 13, 1972, p. 18.

26. U.S. Congress, Senate, 88th Cong., 2nd sess., *Congressional Record* 110, S18133. Also see Stennis and Fulbright, *The Role of Congress*, p. 19.

27. Orlando v. Laird, Mitchell v. Laird, Berk v. Laird, and Massachusetts v. Laird, as cited in Arthur Schlesinger, Jr., *The Imperial Presidency* (Boston: Houghton Mifflin, 1973), pp. 288-94.

28. *Sunday Bulletin*, August 20, 1967, p. 1.

29. Military Procurement Authorization Act, PL 91-121, November 19, 1969.

30. Department of Defense Appropriations Act, PL 91-17, December 29, 1969. "(Section 643). In line with the expressed intention of the President of the United States, none of the funds appropriated by this act shall be used to finance the introduction of American ground combat troops into Laos or Thailand."

31. U.S. President, *The Cambodian Operation* (Washington, D.C., U.S. Government Printing Office, June 30, 1970), Richard M. Nixon. Background briefing given by a senior official of the National Security Council, July 1, 1970.

32. Press Conference by Prince Sihanouk, Phnom Penh, Cambodia, as reported in Foreign Broadcast Information Service Bulletin, May 13, 1969.

In the daily State Department press briefing of June 25, 1973, the Department spokesman reported that documents in the State Department included a memorandum of conversation between Chester Bowles and Prince Sihanouk on January 10, 1968, in which Sihanouk indicated to Bowles that he wanted the United States to retaliate against the North Vietnamese in the Cambodian sanctuaries with hot pursuit and with bombing. State Department files also contained a memorandum of conversation between Senator Mansfield and Prince Sihanouk on August 22, 1969, in which Prince Sihanouk pointed out to Mansfield that he would make no protest of U.S. bombing in the sanctuaries as long as it took place in areas without any Cambodian population.

33. U.S. President, *Public Papers of the Presidents of the United States* (Washington, D.C.: Office of the *Federal Register*, National Archives and Records Service, 1971), Richard M. Nixon, 1970, p. 288.

34. Ibid., p. 373.

35. Based on an interview with Bryce N. Harlow, April 1970.

36. U.S. Congress, House, 91st Cong., 2nd sess., April 30, 1970, *Congressional Record*, 116: 13774. This amendment finally came to a vote on June 6, losing 321 to 32.

37. Ibid., 13551.

38. U.S. President, *Public Papers of the Presidents*, Richard M. Nixon, 1970, p. 405.

39. Background briefing by senior official of the National Security Council, April 30, 1970.

40. U.S. President, *Public Papers of the Presidents*, Richard M. Nixon, 1970, p. 543.

41. New York *Times*, May 2, 1970, p. 1.

42. Based on interviews with staff members of the Joint Staff of the Joint Chiefs of Staff, conducted in November 1970.

43. U.S. President, *Public Papers of the Presidents*, Richard M. Nixon, 1970, p. 413.

44. Based on interviews conducted with senior U.S. military officials in Saigon, July 1970.

45. Based on interview with Richard Cook, Deputy Assistant to the President for Legislative Affairs, November 1970.

46. U.S. Congress, Senate, 91st Cong., 2nd sess., May 26, 1970, *Congressional Record* 116: 17083.

47. U.S. President, *Public Papers of the Presidents*, Richard M. Nixon, 1970, p. 476.

48. U.S. Congress, Senate, 91st Cong., 2nd sess., June 3, 1970, *Congressional Record* 116: 18015.

49. Ibid., June 5, 1970.

50. Ibid., June 9, 1970, p. 8630.

51. Ibid., June 11, 1970, p. S8801.

52. Ibid, p. S8817.

53. Ibid., June 22, 1970, p. S9444.

54. Ibid., June 29, 1970, p. S10156.

55. Washington *Post*, June 19, 1970, pp. 1-3.

56. Ibid.

57. U.S. Congress, Senate, 91st Cong., 2nd sess., June 29, 1970, *Congressional Record*, p. S10161.

58. Ibid., June 30, 1970, p. S10264.

59. Ibid., p. S10265.

60. U.S. Congress, Senate, Committee on Foreign Relations, *Legislative History of the Senate Committee on Foreign Relations, January 3, 1969 to January 2, 1971* (Washington, D.C.: U.S. Government Printing Office, 1972), p. 68. Hereinafter cited as *Legislative History*.

61. "CBS Evening News," February 6, 1970.

62. U.S. Congress, Senate, 91st Cong., 2nd sess., S. Rept. 91-834, May 1, 1970, pp. 32-36.

63. U.S. Congress, Senate, Committee on Foreign Relations, *Hearings on S.J. Res. 166* (Washington, D.C.: U.S. Government Printing Office, 1970).

64. Washington *Post*, March 14, 1970, p. 12.

65. U.S. Congress, Senate, Committee on Foreign Relations, *Legislative History*, p. 68.

66. *Foreign Broadcast Information Service*, April 16, 1970, p. K-5.

67. Washington *News*, May 6, 1970, p. 7.

68. U.S. Congress, Senate, *Congressional Record*, June 22, 1970, p. S9449.

69. Ibid.

70. Ibid., p. S9490.

71. Ibid., p. S9670.

72. Ibid., July 1, 1970, p. E6099.

73. Ibid., July 10, 1970, p. S11055.

74. Ibid., June 29, 1970, p. S21958; June 30, 1970, p. S22192.

75. Ibid., June 30, 1970, p. S10285.

76. Afternoon press briefing, Western White House, June 30, 1970.

77. U.S. President, *Public Papers of the Presidents*, Richard M. Nixon, 1970, pp. 545, 546, 552.

78. Background session by senior official of the National Security Countil, July 1, 1970.

79. U.S. President, *Public Papers of the Presidents*, Richard M. Nixon, 1970, p. 543.

80. Ibid.

81. U.S. Congress, House, 91st Cong., 2nd sess., July 9, 1970, *Congressional Record*, p. H6561.

82. Baltimore *Sun*, July 10, 1970, p. 1.

83. Unsigned memorandum circulated to members of the House-Senate conference.

84. New York *Times*, July 16, 1970, p. 1.

85. Washington *Post*, July 17, 1970, p. 6.

86. New York *Times*, July 18, 1970, p. 24; Washington *Post*, July 19, 1970, p. B-6.

87. U.S. Congress, House, 91st Cong., 2nd sess., July 22, 1970, *Congressional Record*, p. H7062.

88. U.S. Congress, Senate, Committee on Foreign Relations, *Legislative History*, p. 33.

89. Washington *Post*, November 22, 1970, p. 23. Also see Chapter 6 of this book.

90. See, for instance, Stennis and Fulbright, *Role of Congress*, p. 20.

91. John Rothchild, "Cooing Down the War: The Senate's Lame Doves," *Washington Monthly*, August 1971, p. 16.

92. *Newsweek*, July 27, 1970, p. 24.

93. Based, inter alia, on interviews conducted in Chu-Lai and Saigon, South Vietnam, July-August 1970, with senior U.S. army commanders.

94. U.S. President, *Public Papers of the Presidents*, Richard M. Nixon, 1970, p. 543.

95. See, for instance, Arthur M. Schlesinger, Jr., *The Imperial Presidency* (Boston: Houghton Mifflin, 1973), pp. 195-97.

96. Washington *Post*, July 4, 1970, p. 1.

# 4

## THE TREATY PROCESS:
## THE SPANISH BASE
## AGREEMENT

## BACKGROUND

The diversity of practice that marks the interaction between Congress and the Executive in the exercise of the treaty powers directly reflects the nature of international agreements themselves. Customary international law requires no precise rules nor settled patterns for the concluding of international agreements. These contractual arrangements between states come in almost an infinite variety and are given many names—multilateral conventions, treaties, pacts, accords, acts, declarations, protocols—none of which has an absolutely settled meaning. They are found in all degrees of solemnity and formality.[1]

As the analogue to the law of contracts, the only general requirement to conclude an international agreement seems to be the presence of both consent and capacity among all parties.

By custom there are normally two stages in the making of international agreements, its signature by "plenipotentiaries" of the contracting states and its subsequent ratification by the governments of those states. While these two stages are traditional for important treaties, they are not necessarily required in all cases.[2] Many agreements are effective upon signature and ordinarily contain a clause to the effect that, either expressly or by implication, they become binding on signature. If this clause is not present, there is a presumption that ratification is necessary, though this is not settled. Recent practice, especially in the area of multilateral conventions, has gotten away from formal ratification, using instead a clause providing that they shall become binding on "acceptance," which has the effect of allowing each party to choose the particular form in which it indicates its willingness to be bound. It is that latter element that is the essence of the agreement.[3]

The method by which an agreement is ratified by a party is of course a matter exclusively of domestic constitutional law. In modern democratic states, reference is normally had to the legislature before ratification of important treaties. Under some constitutions, such as that of the United States, this is a legal requirement, while under most parliamentary forms it is a tradition rather than a strict obligation.

Under the American Constitution it is usual to regard the process of negotiation and signature as belonging exclusively to the President, while the process of ratification belongs exclusively to the Senate. In fact the Constitution makes no such distinction. Article II, section 2, clause 2 provides that the President "...shall have power, by and with the advice and consent of the Senate to *make* treaties, provided two-thirds of the senators present concur." Thus the Senate is associated throughout the entire process of the making of treaties.[4]

This of course was consonant with the early view of the Senate as a small body of counselors available to the President. Hamilton wrote that the intention of the framers in the treaty power "was understood by all" as giving "the most ample latitude" to make every "species of convention usual among nations." But, being quite well acquainted with customary international law, the founding fathers knew well that international agreements were a source of domestic law, and thus not the exclusive domain of the Executive. In Hamilton's words, "A treaty is not an execution of laws: it does not presuppose the existence of laws. It is, on the contrary, to have itself the force of a law, and to be carried into execution, like all other laws by the executive magistrate."

The division of these functions came about almost immediately, however, with the President as negotiator and the Senate as ratifier. In fact, the joint "making" of treaties was attempted only once in the nearly 200 years of practice under the Constitution, when President Washington, in the first year of his administration, attempted to take counsel with the Senate regarding the negotiation of a treaty, with unfortunate results.[5]

It was from this disunion that the Senate Committee on Foreign Relations was born. It was created as a standing committee in 1816 for the express purpose of carrying out the advice and consent and approval clause of Article II.

Today the actual negotiation and signing of treaties is, by the vast weight of practice and opinion, the President's alone, though that fact does not mean that repeated challenges are not raised to that function from the Senate and from Congress. Moreover, according to E.S. Corwin, ratification belongs also to the President alone, although the vast weight of both practice and opinion has decreed that he may not ratify a formal treaty unless the Senate, by two-thirds' vote of the members present, approves or, in the case of an executive agreement, at least acquiesces.[6]

In granting consent, the Senate has made liberal use of its right to do so conditionally, stating its conditions in the form of amendments to the treaty itself or in the form of reservations attached to the act of ratification. The difference is that the former, if accepted by the President and the other party, change the nature of the obligations for all parties, whereas reservations merely limit the obligations of the United States under the proposed convention. The latter form has been the norm for multilateral conventions.[7] In effect, these reservations and amendments often are practical renegotiations of the agreement itself, and on occasion have resulted in the rejection of the entire agreement by either the President or the other state party. Between 1789 and 1929 about 900 treaties were negotiated by the President and ratified by the Senate. Another 200 were either rejected outright by the Senate or so amended or reserved by it that either the President or the other party rejected them.[8]

The general statement that negotiation has come to be accepted as the domain of the Executive alone should not be taken too literally. It is true that the sanction of the Supreme Court has been put upon the notion that "the President alone has the power to speak or listen as a representative of the nation. He *makes* treaties with the advice and consent of the Senate; but he alone negotiates. Into the field of negotiation the Senate cannot intrude; and Congress itself is powerless to invade it.[9] The Court notwithstanding, Congress has had a very direct influence during negotiations in many instances.

Between the end of World War I and 1965, the Senate was represented by observers, advisers, or delegates at 21 major international conferences. Since June 1965, Senators and, on a number of occasions, Senate staff members have been accredited as representatives, advisers, and observers to at least 68 international conferences, and Senators have served at 25 of the 27 sessions (to date) of the United Nations General Assembly. Senators participated in the United Nations Conference on International Organization in 1945, the Paris Peace Conference in 1946, the conference on the peace treaty with Japan in 1951, the Mutual Defense Treaty with the Philippines in 1951, the ANZUS Treaty, and the SEATO Treaty. For the last four of these treaties the Senators were delegates and actually signed the treaties.

Senators have participated with several different titles. The title of delegate or representative connotes the greatest degree of participation, although delegates and representatives are normally bound, to some degree, to follow administration instructions. Advisers and observers have a rather different status; and though they are normally privy to all of the deliberations of the delegation, they are not involved in the formal procedures as participants.[10]

Direct participation is not, of course, the only, or necessarily the most effective, method of involvement in negotiations. While there have been persistent requests by Congress to have members put on the SALT delegation, for instance, the influence of Congress has been strong and continuous throughout SALT-I and SALT-II through the extensive consultations and briefings that are held between the sessions in Geneva with the subcommittees of oversight.

The truism of British politics noted by Sir Ivor Jennings—"Negotiations with foreign powers are difficult to conduct when lynx-eyed opposition sits suspiciously on the watch"—applies equally well to the American system.[11]

If the Senate has managed to infiltrate the executive domain of negotiation, its incursion is nothing compared with executive circumvention of the Senate's ratification responsibilities. The method used has of course been the device of executive agreements, resorted to with ever-increasing frequency by the Executive since the middle of the nineteenth century. In the years immediately following the Civil War, the Senate, during an era of Congressional dominance, had exercised its ratification powers with a vengeance, amending and rejecting treaty after treaty negotiated by Presidents. In fact, it ratified no important treaty between 1871 and 1898. In 1868 the Senate further expanded its ability to rewrite treaties by revising its rules to permit the amending of treaties by a simple majority.

By 1885 an exasperated Professor Wilson (later to become President) lamented that in regard to ratifying treaties, the President was made to approach the Senate "as a servant conferring with a master...it is almost as distinctly dealing with a foreign power as were the negotiations preceding the proposed treaty." He noted wryly that the treaty-making power had become "the treaty-marring power."[12]

Some years later McKinley's Secretary of State, John Hay, who had considerable experience as Lincoln's private secretary, seriously doubted that "another important treaty would ever pass the Senate." He viewed advice and consent to treaties by the Senate as the Constitution's "irreparable" mistake, that "the attitude of the Senate toward public affairs makes all serious negotiations impossible."[13]

It was not surprising then that the Executive sought ways around this veto by any coalition of one-third of the Senate. One device early resorted to by Presidents was the agreement entered into on his own authority as Commander in Chief and Chief Executive, requiring no ratification. One of the traditional fathers of international law, Emerich de Vattel, attempted to postulate what required a formal treaty and what could be a less-than-formal agreement as follows: the former was required when "the acts called for must continue as long as the treaty exists," and the latter when obligations were "fulfilled by a single act."[14] The distinction, however, has never become settled either in customary international law or in domestic constitutional law.[15]

The device was resorted to as early as 1817, when the demilitarization of the Great Lakes was formally agreed to by a simple exchange of notes between British minister Charles Bagot and Secretary of State Richard Rush. Similarly, the Protocol of 1898 between the United States and Spain, in which her territories in the Caribbean were ceded to the United States, was a simple executive agreement with no reference to Congress. Such agreements became increasingly numerous after that, and included the famous "open-door" agreements, the Northwestern Fisheries Agreements, the agreement for ending the Boxer Rebellion in 1901, the Armistice ending World War I, the Litvinov Accords of the 1930s, the Yalta and Potsdam Agreements, and of course the subject of the present chapter, the Spanish Base Agreements.[16] During the first 50 years after independence, of 87 international agreements, 60, including most of the important ones, were full treaties. In the next 50 years there were 215 treaties and 238 executive agreements.[17]

In 1905, when the Senate declined to ratify a treaty with Santo Domingo, President Roosevelt simply put the agreement into effect for two years until the Senate capitulated. And he did not even bother to tell the Senate of a secret agreement he made with Japan regarding the Japanese protectorate in Korea.[18]

A recent review of the calendar of the Senate Foreign Relations Committee provides an interesting insight: in 1951, the year when the United States released Italy from military restrictions under the Italian peace treaty by simple executive agreement, the Truman administration submitted a protocol on the regulation of sugar. In 1953, the year in which the Eisenhower administration by executive agreement gave up its rights over the Amami Islands, the Executive submitted a convention modifying and supplementing an earlier convention with Belgium on double taxation. In 1954, the year in which the free territory of Trieste was divided between Italy and Yugoslavia by executive agreement, the Executive submitted as treaties a protocol on slavery and a double taxation agreement regarding the Netherlands Antilles. In 1968, the year in which the Bonin Islands were given back to Japan by executive agreement, the Johnson administration submitted as a treaty an agreement with Mexico regarding radio broadcasting and another on the safety of life at sea.[19]

Another variation of this device, resorted to in the more important matters in which Congressional support was deemed necessary but Senate veto feared, has been the presentation of an executive agreement to both houses of Congress for approval by joint or concurrent resolution. This device was first attempted successfully when Texas was annexed in 1845 by joint resolution. This was followed more blatantly a half-century later when Hawaii was annexed by a similar joint resolution, after a treaty had been rejected. Thereafter the war with the Central Powers was brought to a close in 1921 by joint resolution and the United States accepted membership in the I.L.O. by joint resolution in 1934. The most recent example of this device was the acceptance of the executive agreement on offensive weapons approved by joint resolution in 1972.

The relatively unchallenged success of these two devices, approved repeatedly by the Supreme Court, led Corwin to conclude that it is difficult to establish any limit to the power of the President and a Congressional majority to implement effectively any foreign policy upon which they agree, regardless of how the Senate may feel about the matter.[20]

This is not to say that serious attempts have not been made in the Senate to curtail this executive latitudinarianism. The perceived abuses of executive agreements by Presidents Roosevelt and Truman set off a conservative movement to bridle this power in the successive attempts and variations of the Bricker Amendment. It went through quite a few versions, but the common theme was that both treaties and executive agreements should become effective as internal law only through enabling legislation, as in the British system. In its last incarnation it failed to obtain the two-thirds majority necessary for a constitutional amendment by one vote.

After that failure, its supporters narrowed the attempt to a bill requiring all agreements to be transmitted to the Senate within 60 days of their execution. It passed the Senate in 1956; but since it excluded the House, that body never acted. The same measure, however, sweetened for the House by including its role in receiving such agreements, was passed over Nixon administration objections in 1972.[21]

By 1969 the major concern about the abuse of executive agreements centered on the issue of defense commitments to other countries. This of course was a reaction to the gradual involvement of the United States in Vietnam. Executive agreements regarding the sending of troops, the stationing of troops, and the establishment of bases around the world were pointed out as a method of making de facto national commitments without the participation of Congress.

The proponents of this view overlooked the fact that 97 percent of the agreements regarding the basing of U.S. personnel abroad were made pursuant to treaties approved by the Senate or statutes passed by Congress as a whole. Further, the vast majority of U.S. bases abroad had resulted from the eight security treaties made with 43 countries in the period following World War II that were still in force. Major bases existed in only four countries without treaty sanction—Cuba, Morocco, Ethiopia, and Spain.[22]

It is this basing arrangement with Spain that provided a major interchange between the branches on the respective treaty powers in 1969 and 1970. That interaction will now be examined in detail.

## THE SPANISH BASE AGREEMENTS

The agreement between the United States and Spain concerning the use of certain bases was signed on September 26, 1953. It authorized the United States to build and operate bases and facilities in Spain, and provided that the United States would support "Spanish defense efforts for agreed purposes by providing military end item assistance to Spain during a period of several years." Under Article V of the agreement, it was to run for ten years and thereafter could be automatically renewed for two five-year extensions. At the end of the ten-year term, however, or at the end of an extension, either government could give notice of intent to cancel. That would begin a six-month consultation period, at the end of which the United States would have one year to withdraw from Spain if no agreement was reached.[23]

The primary objective in obtaining the base rights was to provide advanced and alternative basing for the American B-47 nuclear bombers. Four major bases and numerous small communications and logistics facilities were established under the agreement. The three major Air Force bases were located at Torréjon near Madrid, Morón near Seville and Zaragoza in northeastern Spain. A very small naval facility was constructed at Rota near Cádiz that was later expanded into a nuclear submarine home port and naval air station. Although built by the United States, the bases have been legally Spanish and occupied jointly with elements of the Spanish armed forces.

The original cost to the United States of building these facilities was $395,600,000 (1953 dollars). The replacement cost at 1967 prices was put by the Department of Defense at $1,088,000,000.[24]

It is ironic that an executive agreement was apparently chosen for the 1953 arrangement with Spain at the recommendation of the Congressional leadership. In his book *Spain: The Gentle Anarchy*, Benjamin Welles wrote: "To coat the bill for Congress and liberal U.S. sentiment the Washington-Madrid link was designated as 'executive agreement' rather than a military alliance since it did not specify the mutual obligation of the two governments in case of war."[25] In a letter dated July 23, 1953, to the Senate majority leader, William Knowland, Secretary of State John Foster Dulles described a meeting that he had with Congressional leaders (Senators Knowland, Styles Bridges, Eugene Millikin, Alexander Wiley, Leverett Saltonstall, Lyndon Johnson, and Richard Russell; Representative Joseph Martin, Speaker of the House, Charles Halleck, Robert Chiperfield, and John McCormack) on July 9, 1953, in his office. Dulles expressed his desire to consult with these leaders to determine the most suitable way of handling the proposed Spanish agreement. The consensus, without dissent, was that since such agreements would be subject to Congressional appropriations in any case, the agreement should be concluded by the President without further authority.

The letter went on to recall that the majority leader had recommended that the administration proceed with an executive agreement, and informed Senator Knowland that on July 15 the President had approved that course of action.[26]

The first five-year extension of the Defense Agreement became effective on September 26, 1963. At that time a "joint declaration" (an executive agreement) was issued, providing that "a threat to either country, and to the joint facilities that each provides for the common defense would be a matter of common concern to both countries, and each country would take such action as it may consider appropriate within the framework of its constitutional processes."[27] The Welles book describes this language as coming from the Spanish Ambassador to the United States, who settled it to establish a defense commitment after reading the language of other U.S. defense treaties.[28]

The Spanish also obtained a commitment of grant military assistance over the five-year period amounting to about one-fifth the original assistance for the first ten years.

On September 26, 1968, the first of the five-year extension periods was to expire. On March 15, 1968, the Spanish formally requested the initiation of negotiations for the second five-year extension. This set in motion an inter-departmental review of the strategic situation in the Mediterranean and the relative value of the joint-use bases in Spain. That analysis concluded that the bases remained important to U.S. security and that the agreement should be extended.[29]

In June 1968, a Spanish military mission led by General Diez-Alegría, came to Washington and presented the United States with a "shopping list" of military equipment with a price tag, reportedly over $1 billion. They specifically requested all of this material as a direct quid pro quo for the extension of the agreement. Between June and September, a counter offer was developed by the State and Defense Departments and, after Congressional consultations, was approved by the President. It became clear during this period that the Spanish also had in mind the possible expansion of the agreement into a mutual security pact. On September 16, a Spanish delegation led by Foreign Minister Fernando Castiella resumed negotiations with Secretary of State Dean Rusk and other U.S. officials. During these negotiations the U.S. offer was ultimately increased to approximately $140 million, but the gap between that and the Spanish figure was still too wide to be bridged.[30] On September 25, Castiella informed Rusk that the U.S. offer was unacceptable and that he was invoking Article V of the defense agreement, thus initiating the consultation period of six months, and if the U.S. could not come to terms by March 26, 1969, complete U.S. withdrawal would be required.

## THE BURCHINAL MINUTE

On October 17, Castiella made a farewell call on Rusk, and at this meeting an agreement was reached on three points to try to get the negotiations back on track: First, as a matter of general policy, both Spain and the United States wanted the agreement to continue. Second, a high-level military meeting should be established to work out common strategic concepts as a basis for continued cooperation, and then to draw up a program of military assistance derived from those common strategic concepts. Third, there should be ultimate political negotiations to clear up remaining bilateral military and political matters.[31]

On November 16, following the NATO ministerial meeting in Brussels, Secretary Rusk visited Madrid and met both with Foreign Minister Castiella and with Franco. At the same time General Earl Wheeler, chairman of the Joint Chiefs of Staff, began discussions in Madrid with General Diez-Algería from which issued an "agreed minute" under which both countries would jointly study the threat to Spain's security and agree on general outlines of the requirements for meeting such threats. General David A. Burchinal, Deputy U.S. Commander, Europe was designated to conduct these discussions, beginning on December 4. After interagency discussions, formal guidelines for the talks were agreed to between the State and Defense Departments and were sent to General Burchinal for his use in the talks.[32]

The discussions began in Madrid on December 4, and resulted in an "agreed minute" defining the common threats that was signed by General Burchinal and General Diez-Algeria on December 6.

Rusk's purpose in taking this approach was of course to examine the subject in terms of needs rather than desires, so that Madrid could be backed off from its exorbitant demands for military assistance, at the time reported to have been reduced to a minimum of $700 million.

The Burchinal minute was received in the Pentagon on December 9 and circulated to the Department of State, causing an immediate furor. While he had been in Madrid in November, General Wheeler had made a speech in which he alluded to "the potential problem of political instability in North Africa";[33] and the Burchinal minute included a discussion of the threat of limited war in North Africa mentioning such possibilities as Algerian aggression and a proxy war in North Africa. Secretary of Defense Clark Clifford's Deputy Assistant Secretary for Latin American and African Affairs, William Lang, and the Assistant Secretary of State for Africa, Joseph Palmer, were particularly upset that some of the language could be interpreted as a U.S. security commitment to defend Spanish interests in North Africa, even though an agreed minute does not have the status of an intergovernmental agreement.

After considerable discussion, it was finally agreed that the minute would remain as written, since it had already been signed, but that a disclaimer would have to be included in the next paper, making it clear that these minutes did not imply intergovernmental understandings but were merely procedural.[34] The text of a "prefatory note" was then sent to Burchinal to be inserted in the next joint minute on "tasks and missions." The note was accompanied by an interdepartmentally agreed draft minute to be negotiated at the next round. On January 7, 1969, the negotiations were resumed and continued at Stuttgart and Madrid into February 1969.[35]

This was of course a particularly delicate time for policy negotiations, with an entirely new administration about to take office. It provides an excellent example of the difficulties facing a new administration in attempting to embark on a new foreign policy. The new administration was only vaguely aware of the process for which they would soon have responsibility regarding the Spanish bases.

Immediately following Dr. Kissinger's appointment in December, 1968, his full attention was taken up with the selection of his NSC staff and the designing of the new National Security Council machinery, along with the commencement of a major reexamination of Vietnam policy. One of the first global priorities of the new administration was to conduct an exhaustive study of U.S. strategic policy around the world, a study that later became known as "NSSM 3."

In the waning days of the Johnson administration, a major survey and analysis of U.S. bases around the world had been completed under the direction of General Robert Wood and Ambassador Robert McClintock. The study was the first effort in some ten years to review all of the U.S. overseas installations and facilities, examining overseas base requirements on the basis of alternative strategies and options. It was an excellent encyclopedic reference for the new administration, and was turned over to the Kissinger staff in December 1968. The intention was to await the completion of NSSM 3 and then to derive actual base requirements from the strategic options chosen by the President, using the Wood-McClintock study as a primary source. Such questions as the need for the Spanish bases were put off until such a comprehensive policy analysis could be undertaken. The NSC staff realized soon after their first meeting on January 21, 1969, however, that the negotiations with the Spanish could not await such a study. Supervision of the ongoing negotiations therefore became an immediate operational problem; and, as with so many things at the time, policy decisions were made on an ad hoc basis.[36]

On February 6, General Burchinal forwarded the proposed agreed minute on tasks and missions for approval by the State and Defense Departments. The Burchinal minute again created a furor. The "threat from North Africa" was still included, as was a statement to the effect that the United States was obligated to defend Western Europe, "of which Spain is an integral part." State pointed out that this would in effect extend NATO guarantees to include Spain.[37]

Under the new National Security Council system, responsibility for the negotiations had been charged to the undersecretary's committee. That subgroup of the NSC is given responsibility for matters not deemed to be of Presidential importance and also is charged with implementing decisions taken. The undersecretary's committee simply assumed the criteria of the previous administration that the bases were strategically necessary and that the problem with which they had to deal was reaching an acceptable compromise with the Spanish on the price that was to be paid. There were, however, a number of influential people in the bureaucracy who wished to see the responsibility taken out of the operational system and sent back up to the NSC for reexamination because they believed that the bases were not at all vital, and that commitments to Spain could be had only at the expense of our good relations with the Africans and the developing world. Assistant Secretaries Leddy and Palmer in the State Department were thought to hold that view, and the Bureau of the Budget and the Office of Assistant Secretary of Defense, International Security Affairs (ISA) were also sympathetic. A meeting of the undersecretary's committee was held on February 20 to resolve the problem of the Burchinal minute and what the next step should be. A strong representation was made on behalf of Palmer against General Burchinal, who was present. The issue was again his acknowledgment that Spain faced a threat from North Africa. The African Bureau of the State Department foresaw grave repercussions on our good relations with African states. The ire of both Leddy and Palmer over the Joint Chiefs of Staff handling of the matter, and particularly over Burchinal's role, was quite evident.

Contingency planning was begun for possible withdrawal from the bases, and instructions were given to Burchinal for the next round of negotiations on a military assistance package. In addition, it was concluded that a security treaty as a part of the base package was out of the question.

On February 25, a bomb was dropped. Flora Lewis, in a syndicated column carried in the Washington *Post*, laid out the entire negotiating struggle, quoting liberally from the sensitive classified documents involved.[38] Since the article followed very closely the line that the State Department had taken in interdepartmental meetings, and since very few people had access to the documents quoted, many observers in Washington assumed that Lewis had been given background information by an Assistant Secretary of State. Others suspected that the State Department had given the documents to the Senate Foreign Relations Committee, and that Lewis got her information there.

Predictably, the Spanish exploded at the article, assuming that it was a calculated move by the U.S. government and taking the position that it gravely affected the status of negotiations. They were outraged that discussions of so sensitive a nature between the two governments could not be protected on a basis of mutual confidence, and indicated that all communications with the United States would have to be viewed in that light in the future.[39]

In a move that led some to suspect that there had been collusion, Senators J. William Fulbright, Stuart Symington, and Mike Mansfield announced on February 25, the day the article appeared, that they intended to hold hearings to investigate the matter.[40]

Up to this point the Executive had high hopes of concluding the final political phase of negotiations before the withdrawal deadline of February 26. The Lewis article soundly dashed those hopes. Spanish Ambassador Merry del Val formally protested to Undersecretary U. Alexis Johnson what he saw as a deliberate attempt to sabotage the talks. While the Spanish suspected that the source of the leak was a Johnson administration holdover trying to sabotage the Nixon administration, they could not be sure—and were not reassured by Johnson's cavalier attitude. Naively, the Spanish welcomed the announcement of a Senate investigation, believing that the inquiry would clarify the issues in their favor.[41]

At a press conference on March 4, President Nixon was asked about General Burchinal's activities. He replied that he believed that no new commitments should be made unless U.S. interests were vitally involved; that no commitment should be made in Spain; and that he had checked into the report about Burchinal and that no commitment had been made.[42] By this time the

White House had become convinced that there were several high officials in the State Department left over from the previous administration who were determined to sabotage the policy. This was the first of many such instances.

On that same day Robert Wagner made his farewell call on Franco as he left his post as ambassador. Franco expressed distress at the newspaper leaks but indicated his interest in seeing the negotiations reach a successful conclusion.

## NEGOTIATIONS FALTER

On March 5, the New York *Times* weighed in with the first of many editorials against renewal of the bases.[43] By the second week in March, it had become obvious that the deadline of March 26 had no chance of being met. The Spaniards by this time welcomed the announcements by Senator Symington and Representative Leonard Farbstein of investigations, as an excuse to grant an extension of time.

The judgment in Washington was that the United States should not feel under any pressure, that the Spanish government very much wanted to conclude the base agreement and eventually would come to terms on U.S. conditions. The American negotiating position was further buttressed by a continuing assault on the base agreements by the New York *Times*.[44]

It is somewhat ironic, in light of the constitutional issue then being debated in the United States regarding the executive agreement status of the relationship, that the Spanish officials were maintaining that any extension beyond the March 26 deadline would require ratification by the Cortes, their parliament.[45]

During the third week of March, President Nixon decided to offer a new package involving slightly increased assistance, rejecting the idea of any security treaty, offering the establishment of a joint consultative committee, and authorizing an optional extension of the termination clause beyond the March 26 deadline. This position was conveyed to the Spanish on March 21, and the suggestion was made to begin negotiations at the political level. On March 24, Foreign Minister Castiella and his negotiating team arrived in Washington to begin negotiations the next day.

Once again Congressional intervention was not unhelpful to the American position. On the day that Castiella arrived, Senator Symington issued a major blast against renewal of the base agreements; and on the following day, opponents in the House of Representatives launched an attack on the floor.[46] This Congressional criticism had a marked effect on the Spanish negotiators and was reflected the next day in a spate of pessimistic press comment in Madrid.[47]

The negotiations were conducted at the State Department on March 25 and 26, following which, on the evening of the latter day, a joint communiqué was issued in which Castiella and Secretary of State William Rogers announced "agreement in principle."[48] This was of course a euphemism to cover the fact that agreement had not been reached. "Sources" at the State Department indicated to the press that the Spanish had insisted on a package of $300 million (down from $1.2 billion) and that the United States had countered with a maximum package of $240 million.[49]

On March 26, President Nixon received Castiella, whom he had known previously, for a meeting lasting more than an hour; and in that meeting he informed the Foreign Minister that he intended to visit Spain at a later date.

Press reaction in Madrid, reflecting the Spanish government's position on the extension, emphasized that there had been no agreement and that Spain could still decide to invoke complete withdrawal by March 26, 1970.[50]

On April 3, President Nixon nominated an old friend and experienced political associate, Robert Hill to be the new Ambassador to Spain. In his meeting with Hill, the President told him that he was picked for the job for the express purpose of delivering the base agreements on the proper terms and maintaining and improving the U.S. relationship with Spain.[51] Hill, a wealthy businessman from New Hampshire, had extensive diplomatic experience as a Foreign Service officer and as Ambassador to Costa Rica and to Mexico. He was selected also, in some measure, because of his extensive knowledge of Congress, where he had served on a Senate committee staff and as Assistant Secretary of State for Congressional Relations. He had a good personal relationship with key Senators and Congressmen interested in the base negotiations.

On April 5, the Washington *Post* added a new note of shrillness to its opposition to the agreements, printing two editorials calling upon the Senate to see that the agreements would be "tossed into the ash can."[52]

An interesting side effect of the increased attacks in the Senate and in the press was that members of the NSC staff and others in the administration who had serious doubts about the strategic necessity of the bases began to see more merits in the agreement by virtue of the kinds of people who were so vigorously attacking it.

On April 18, a curious fillip was added to the Burchinal incident of February, when Senator Symington deplored press treatment of the issue as having done "what may be irreparable damage to General Burchinal, a fine officer and a man who, as far as I know, has acted in the best tradition."[53]

On April 17, the Senate Foreign Relations Committee issued its committee report, S. Res. 85, the "National Commitments Resolution." The impact in Washington was minor, but in Spain it created a furor. One paper's headlines read: "Senate Committee Criticizes Government for Manner of Negotiating with Spain: Opinion of Some Senators Annoying to Madrid Which Has Not Tried to Secure Agreements Behind Congress' Back." It reported that the Spanish base problem had escalated because Senator Fulbright had claimed that renewal of the accords would be tantamount to usurping the Senate's constitutional power.[54]

## DEADLOCK

On April 21, Ambassador-designate Hill was heard before the Senate Foreign Relations Committee. Stories emanating from the committee along the lines already noted further frayed spanish nerves. The Madrid daily *Ya* which reflects exactly the government's position, declared: "We must not accept a 'diktat' ....Those agreements...have become too burdensome for us...an alliance on equal grounds may be appetizing but not the posture of an acolyte. We will not become a satellite country." And then the editorial struck a note that would later mark a curious change of Spanish attitude that was to plague future negotiations: "Without adequate countermeasures against the dangers involved [meaning a signed treaty] we believe that Spain should not revew the agreements with the United States."[55]

Thus we see that the Senate attacks on the idea that there was a de facto security commitment to Spain finally had the effect of convincing the Spanish that indeed there was one—and that there should be a fully formal treaty.

By the last week in April, a new Spanish approach had been formed. They began to take the position that a deliberate, and even leisurely, reevaluation of the situation should be made; but there was also no reason to start U.S. withdrawal. In addition, they came to be fascinated by the prospect of going for a full treaty in the Senate. The Spanish pointed out that they were particularly incensed by the spate of leaks in the U.S. press and by the paraphrasing of the sensitive passages of classified documents contained in the Senate Foreign Relations Committee report on commitments. They also made clear their resentment at the complete lack of response from the executive branch in defending the agreements against Congressional criticism. On the Spanish side there were increasing indications that the desire for a security guarantee and a treaty were becoming paramount. In light of the Congressional situation, this gave further cause for pessimism.

Moreover, in response to the vigorous campaign against the agreements being waged by the Washington *Post* and the New York *Times*, the Spanish government, through its controlled press, began a counterattack on the negotiations and on overall U.S.-Spanish relations.[56]

The stalemate seemed to have become a simple difference of goals, with the United States merely wanting to make a simple rental renewal agreement and the Spanish resenting being put in the position of a landlord, strongly desiring treatment as a full ally through a security agreement.

A further complication was added during this period when a report written by the General Accounting Office for Senator Symington began to circulate. Symington had sent a team of GAO investigators to explore the files in Madrid, and their report contained considerable criticism of Spanish policy and use of military assistance previously provided. This was seen in the executive branch as one more piece of evidence that the Foreign Relations Committee would use whatever means available to undermine the administration's policy.

## RESPITE

On May 14, Nuño Aguirre de Cárcer, head of the American Bureau of the Spanish Foreign Office, met with Undersecretary of State Johnson and for the first time raised the possibility of an extension of a year or so as a means of getting around the present impasse.

By the end of the month the executive branch had decided that the idea of an extension of from one to three years provided the best way out of the dilemma. It offered the considerable advantage of providing the opportunity for the systematic evaluation of what our future policy toward Spain should be, as well as time to make a reasoned valuation of the requirements for the bases in light of the larger strategic review being undertaken by the NSC. In a press briefing at the State Department on March 26, the administration acknowledged the outlines of the discussions under way.

On May 28, a leak (generally attributed to the Spanish delegation) to Benjamin Welles in the New York *Times* provided the outlines of the overall Spanish counterproposal, in which the relationship was to be put on a new basis of cooperation in such fields as space, peaceful nuclear development, education, culture, civil aviation, and investment; the base facilities would appear as but one among many elements. In response to Congressional criticism, the Spanish proposal called for gradual deemphasis of military ties and an acceptance of the U.S. offer of $175 million in military assistance. To enable the details of this more comprehensive agreement to be worked out—and, not incidentally, to allow time for Congressional opposition to cool—both sides agreed on a one-to-three-year extension of the current agreements.[57]

By June 1, the impasse seemed to have been broken. There were indications that the Spanish had accepted a compromise for a two-year extension of the old agreement. The Madrid press took a suitable 180-degress shift in its attitude toward the base agreements.[58]

On June 5, Undersecretary Johnson briefed the Foreign Relations Committee in closed session on the outlines of the agreement that had been reached, involving the two-year extension in return for $50 million in military assistance. In what was to become a habit increasingly vexing to the executive branch, Fulbright announced to the press the outlines of what Johnson had told them immediately following the closed-door session. Fulbright was reported to have told Johnson that he would oppose the agreement because it could be construed as a commitment to defend Franco's regime from internal and foreign foes. Johnson, however, was reported to have insisted that no such commitment existed, and he was said to have repudiated the memorandum by General Wheeler in which Wheeler was supposed to have told the Spanish that the presence of U.S. forces in Spain amounted to a more significant security guarantee than a written agreement.[59]

At the State Department press briefing on June 9, the administration spokesman indicated that there were certain things remaining to be negotiated, but that "we are closing the gap."

At this delicate juncture the executive branch suffered what it viewed as another act of guerrilla warfare from the Foreign Relations Committee. The staff investigators that Symington had sent to Spain the previous month had been fully briefed on all aspects of the bases, and of U.S. military activities in Spain, including a number of joint exercises that had periodically been conducted with U.S. and Spanish forces. On June 14, the Washington *Post* carried two articles revealing classified details of two exercises that the staff investigators reportedly believed to be further evidence of hidden U.S. military commitments to Spain. The exercises in question, "Pathfinder Express" I and II, were joint exercises in countering insurgent warfare. The *Post* opined hopefully that these newly revealed findings of the Symington staff would be "likely to cause a stir in Congress."[60]

The normally well-coordinated timing of such leaks was in this case several hours too late to have its expected effect on the Spanish. That very day in Madrid, the final details were agreed to and signature authorized. UPI reported that the *Post* story was leaked by the Senate Foreign Relations subcommittee in anticipation of the possible future signing of the agreement and also in advance of the expected vote on S. Res. 85, the National Commitments Resolution, the following week in the Senate.[61]

The Spanish government was greatly disturbed by the articles, and it was reported that some of the highest levels were advocating immediate denunciation of the agreements. Spanish chagrin was somewhat understandable, since they had participated in the exercise at the request of the United States and the executive branch had been conspicuous in its lack of defense back in Washington. The White House had been unaware that before the stories appeared, the State Department had presented the completed agreements to Senator Fulbright and the Foreign Relations Committee.

Predictably, the New York *Times* attacked the still unsigned agreement extensions, calling them "an unconscionable perversion of United States principles and policy."[62]

On June 18, there was an amusing exchange in the daily State Department press briefing. The day before, there had been considerable criticism from some members of Congress about a statement that Ambassador Hill had made in Madrid stating U.S. support for Spain's entry into NATO. The department spokesman pointed out that the latest guidance from Congress on the matter was a resolution from the Eighty-fifth Congress that declared, "It is the sense of the Congress of the United States that the Department of State should continue to use its good offices toward the end of achieving participation by Spain in the North Altantic Treaty and as a member of the North Atlantic Treaty Organization."[63]

On that same day, Spanish Foreign Minister Castiella left Madrid for Washington. On June 20, the Department of State released the following joint statement:

> Spanish Foreign Minister Castiella and Secretary of State Rogers today exchanged diplomatic notes extending the defense agreement of September 26, 1953, until September 26, 1970. Under the terms of the extension the two governments will use this period to determine the new relationship of cooperation between the two countries that would follow the present agreement. Secretary Rogers has invited Spanish Foreign Minister Castiella to return to Washington about July 15, to continue the negotiation which opened today.
>
> In conjunction with this extension, the United States government as authorized by the Congress, will provide grant military assistance and credit facilities to Spain for the purchase of military equipment.

## THE SECOND ROUND

On July 15, Foreign Minister Castiella resumed negotiations in Washington for a new agreement. It was evident, as the negotiations began, that the Spanish government feared the impact of the Senate critics on prospects for a long-term agreement, and resented the lack of executive branch willingness to defend the agreements.

At the initiative of the NSC, an extensive study of U.S. interests in Spain and the future of U.S.-Spanish relations was conducted through the late summer and autumn of 1969. A consensus emerged that the military value of the bases was extremely high in a potential general-war situation for the security of the Mediterranean. In nongeneral war situations the bases were much less essential. The communications facilities and Torrejón air base were useful links in U.S. worldwide lines of communication, but alternatives could be found. The Rota submarine base provided obvious advantages, but that too could be relocated. Although there were strongly held views to the contrary in some areas of the Department of State, the consensus was that political and cultural relations with Spain were to be encouraged as in the long-term interests of the United States.

As a result of this process, the executive branch had a much clearer and more settled view of the interests and value involved for the negotiation of a new agreement than had been the case in the just-completed negotiations for the extension of the old.

The coup in Libya that occurred in September 1969 provided a new peacetime military importance to the Spanish bases. The base at Zaragoza was blessed with one of the best bombing and training ranges for tactical aircraft in Europe. With the loss of Wheelus air base in Libya, training alternatives had to be found for U.S. aircraft based in Europe, and Zaragoza offered the best facilities.

Through the winter of 1969-70 there was no progress in the negotiations because of the policy evaluation going on in the executive branch and a change of regime at the Foreign Office in Spain, with Gregorio López Bravo, a young Opus Dei technocrat replacing Castiella. There of course had been informal exchanges of views between the Department of State and the new Foreign Minister during a visit to Washington in mid-March. The American government found the new Foreign Minister much more positive in his attitude than was Castiella, who all along was suspected of being basically anti-American. López Bravo was much more interested in the accomplishment of a new agreement of friendship and cooperation than with the details of the bases or the quid pro quo. The atmosphere of the discussions was considerably improved.

During this period Congress was kept informed through informal discussions between Undersecretary Johnson and Foreign Relations Committee members, and between Assistant Secretary David Abshire and a larger number of members.64 There was, however, a shift in thinking at the working level in the Department of State that caused concern in the White House. A movement gained strength to work for an agreement that would involve withdrawal from the bases, leaving only the educational and cultural aspects. This State Department idea, not unnaturally, soon emerged on the Hill as an alternative to proceeding with the current position.

After the initial discussions between López Bravo and Secretary of State Rogers in April, negotiations continued through the spring and early summer in Washington. They were conducted by Undersecretary Johnson for the United States and the new Spanish Ambassador to the United States, Jaime Arguelles. Military advisers who participated were part of both negotiating teams, but there were no military-to-military meetings like those during the previous round of negotiations.

By mid-June most of the details had been worked out; but the Spanish once again raised their desire to elevate the agreement to a treaty status, especially since there was to be no security clause similar to that in the 1963 agreement. The response from the State Department was considerably less negative to a treaty than had been the case the previous year. The constant pressure of the Foreign Relations Committee had brought most of the working level in the State

Department round to their point of view. On June 18, Secretary of Defense Melvin Laird met with foreign Minister López Bravo in Madrid for a discussion of the final details of the military quid pro quo package.

On July 24, Deputy Secretary David Packard and Undersecretary Johnson met in executive session with the full Foreign Relations Committee and briefed it on the details of the agreement and the military assistance package. As expected, the committee vigorously urged the submission of the agreement as a full treaty, but had no substantive criticism of the agreement itself. The chairman indicated that he had drafted, and intended to introduce, a Senate resolution requiring that the agreement, and any other agreement under which U.S. forces would be stationed abroad, be submitted as a treaty for ratification by the Senate.

At this point all was in readiness for signature of the agreement. Following the July 24 hearing, however, the Secretary of State had become convinced that the agreement should be submitted as a treaty. The White House was equally convinced that to submit the agreement as a treaty would be to guarantee, at the very minimum, a long delay that could not fail to sabotage the agreements with the Spanish. In any case, prospects for getting two-thirds of the Senate to ratify the agreements were at best doubtful. Following the July 24 hearing, the Department of State deliberately delayed the arranging of a signing, because it intended to proceed along the treaty route. The White House, however, was not aware of this delay and remained fully committed to accomplish the signing at the earliest opportunity—before Senator Fulbright had time to act.

On July 25, the White House became extremely concerned. The legislative liaison staff reported that the Foreign Relations Committee was circulating a resolution for cosponsorship, as Fulbright had promised. It read in part:

> ...it is the sense of the Senate that any agreement with a foreign country, including the prospective agreement with Spain, relating to the stationing of forces or other military uses by the United States of major defense bases or facilities on the territory of the country concerned should be in the form of a treaty subject to the advice and consent of the Senate for ratification.

On that date the White House also became aware of the State Department's instructions to the field to suspend arrangements for signing the agreements.

After telephone conversations with the American Embassy in Madrid, the NSC staff became convinced that Spanish patience was running out, and that if the State Department were allowed to continue its delay, in cooperation with the Foreign Relations Committee, that the entire agreement would probably come unstuck.

Meanwhile, the Foreign Relations Committee in addition to its moving the resolution as fast as possible, also intended to have open hearings, and requested that the State Department take no action until those hearings were set.

The NSC staff, recalling the State Department proposals to withdraw from the bases in any case, and realizing that if the agreement were not signed by September 26, the Spanish reaction would probably unravel the entire agreement, decided that action must be taken at once. The entire matter was therefore referred to the President; and on July 27, Secretary Rogers was instructed by the President to sign the agreements by the following Friday, July 31, if at all possible. Rogers maintained that this was impossible, and that such a move did not give due consideration to Senate views on the matter. Accordingly, he requested a reexamination of the question, and on July 30 he flew to San Clemente to discuss the matter with the President.

Meanwhile, having been informally assured by the Department of State that the matter was being reexamined, the Foreign Relations Committee had relaxed its schedule and was moving at a leisurely pace with its resolution. Senator Fulbright had scheduled a meeting with Secretary Rogers for Monday, August 3, and apparently intended no action until that time. On July 31, the New York *Times* carried an article datelined Madrid, reporting that the agreements had been submitted to the Foreign Relations Commission of the Spanish Cortes.

On that same day Senator Fulbright, on the floor of the Senate, again urged the State Department to submit the agreements in the form of a treaty. He specifically declined, however, to commit himself not to delay such a treaty so submitted.[65] As a bit of rather transparent sugar-coating, he assured the administration:

> I have no serious misgivings about Mr. Franco. When we look at all the countries we are doing business with, to me Spain is a more civilized and liberal dictatorship than the one in South Vietnam, if we want to make comparison...as a matter of fact, I think the Spanish people have made great progress....It is a dictatorship, but it is a relatively progressive one and has brought substantial benefits to the Spanish people."[66]

In an interview two days later on "CBS Evening News", however, Senator Fulbright took a contrary view as to the wisdom of our continuing the relationship with Spain.[67]

The conflict between the NSC and State Department, meanwhile, grew more intense. The draft statement that was to provide the administration position on the agreements was drafted in State and obtained by the NSC on August 1. The draft contained only the most lukewarm defense of the agreements, and was rewritten by the NSC to include a more detailed rationale for the retention of both the military and nonmilitary relations in the agreement, as well as an explanation of why a treaty was inappropriate.

At San Clemente on July 31, the decision to proceed as soon as possible with an executive agreement was reaffirmed, and Secretary Rogers so instructed. A further note of urgency was added by a phone call from the American Embassy in Madrid, advising that time was running out.

By Monday, August 3, Senator Fulbright had become aware of the intention of the administration to beat him to the punch. He took the floor that afternoon with a vigorous attack on the agreements. He served notice of his intention to proceed at once to amend the military appropriations bill to forbid the spending of any money for U.S. forces in Spain unless that agreement were approved by treaty or legislative convention. In another instance of unilateral declassification, Senator Fulbright cited Undersecretary Johnson's testimony in the executive session hearings of July 24. He quoted Johnson as saying:

> During our discussions with the Spanish in their efforts to get language which I would interpret as a commitment, they pushed very, very strongly for getting this language that was in the Joint (U.S.-Spanish) Declaration of 1963. I have said that we could not do that without entering into a mutual defense treaty, and this was a road that we did not want to go.

Fulbright then quoted verbatim from the secret memorandum of 1968 that had been given to the Foreign Relations Committee, in which General Wheeler was quoted as saying:

> By the presence of United States forces in Spain the United States gives Spain a far more visible and credible security guarantee than any document.

Fulbright went on to urge the Senate to act on his amendment "within the next two weeks," at which time he expected the agreement to be signed.[68]

The White House wasted no time in responding. On August 4, Foreign Minister López Bravo was invited to sign the agreement in Washington on August 6.

Even the State Department was stung by the Fulbright attack, and on August 4, at the daily briefing, the department spokesman accused Fulbright of leaking classified information given in good faith to the committee in executive hearings. Fulbright defended himself on the Senate floor that afternoon by saying that the State Department leaks as well: "They leak whatever they think helps their own interests."[69]

On August 4, Secretary Rogers visited Senator Fulbright for more than an hour and informed him that the administration had decided against submitting the agreement as a treaty. Meanwhile, unknown to Fulbright, Foreign Minister López Bravo was on his way to Washington, arriving late on August 5.

On August 5, a State Department spokesman, Robert McCloskey, somewhat sourly acknowledged that the agreement would be signed the following day by Foreign Minister López Bravo and Secretary Rogers. He pointedly disclaimed the department's responsibility in this maneuver, saying, "This is the decision of the administration." That afternoon Fulbright berated State for what he saw as a double cross: "Events of the past two weeks raise serious question as to the accuracy of representations" made by the State Department to the Foreign Relations Committee. He charged the administration with a deliberate attempt to short-circuit his plan to require open hearings on the agreement.[70]

In late afternoon of August 6, the following joint statement was issued by the Department of State:

> The Spanish Foreign Minister, Gregorio López Bravo, and Secretary of State William P. Rogers today signed an agreement of friendship and cooperation. This agreement which replaces the defense agreement of 1953 and extensions thereof, initiates a new era in partnership between the U.S. and Spain.
>
> The new accord comprehends various fields of existing cooperation between the two countries. Among them are education, agriculture, environment, space, science and technology, as well as defense. Such an agreement reflects the manner in which cooperation between the two countries has come to include new dimensions since the early 1950's. At that time, it was a matter of urgency to establish the joint use bases in Spain to strengthen the defensive capability of the West. Under the new agreement, the United States will be permitted to use certain Spanish military facilities, which are still of great importance in Western defense. The United States will undertake to assist Spain in strengthening its own defense system.
>
> In addition, the new agreement also takes into account the many non-military fields in which both countries now have close mutual interest. An example of such an area is space; Spanish tracking stations, manned by personnel from both countries have played an important role in the Apollo flights. The field of educational exchanges, having already become a fruitful area of cooperation, promises to assume an even greater importance with the adoption of an extensive educational reform program by the government of Spain.
>
> Both governments intend this agreement, the text of which is being made public, to promote the well-being and progress of our peoples and, moreover, to make a positive contribution to world peace in accordance with the purposes and principles of the charter of the United Nations.

At the same time the full text of the agreements, having no secret minutes, was released.[71]

Concurrently with the release of these two documents, the position paper that had been substantially revised by the NSC staff was issued as well, presenting the basic rationale for the administration's signing of the accords. In that rationale a brief recap of the history of the agreements was given, pointing out, and perhaps even slightly exaggerating, the extensive Congressional consultations at every step. It stated that after careful interdepartmental evaluation, the President had decided to continue to maintain the facilities in Spain. It summarized their importance in

> a. maintaining our general deterrent posture in the Mediterranean area,
> b. providing the infrastructure to support our forces deployed in Europe and the Mediterranean,
> c. Contributing to our worldwide strategic and tactical mobility. The facilities in Spain contribute to our deterrent strength, particularly by providing maximum coverage for our Polaris-equipped submarines. Thus all of our facilities in Spain are defensive and deterrent in nature and will contribute to the maintenance of peace and avoidance of conflict. Our overall Mediterranean security posture would be considerably degraded were these bases not available.

In attempting to draw attention away from the base rental elements of the agreements, the statement pointedly drew attention to the fact that

> ...both Spain and the United States government realize that times have changed significantly since 1953, and that true friendship and international peace must rest on the foundation of cooperation which goes far beyond strictly military base agreements. Therefore the agreement which has been negotiated covers a number of areas of cooperation, including education, science, cultural exchange and many others, in addition to military cooperation.

In dealing with the sensitive question of why it was not submitted as a treaty, the statement agreed

> ...that were the proposed agreement of friendship and cooperation to contain such a commitment as, for example, is contained in the North Atlantic Treaty,... [then] the agreement should be submitted to the Senate for its advice and consent to ratification. However... the proposed agreement contains no such commitment. [72]

The Senate critics of the agreements had pointed to two specific sections of the agreement. Chapter VIII and Article 30 read, in part:

> The governments of the United States and Spain are in agreement in considering that the threat to peace is the greatest problem faced by the modern world and that it requires that both governments remain vigilant and continue to develop their ability to defend themselves against such a threat. Consequently, both governments, within the framework of their constitutional processes, and to the extent feasible and appropriate, will make compatible their respective defense policies in areas of mutual interest and will grant each other reciprocal defense support as follows:
>
> Article 30. Each government will support the defense system of the other and make such contributions as are deemed necessary and appropriate to achieve the greatest possible effectiveness of those systems to meet possible contingencies.[73]

It was these sections that the critics contended constituted a security commitment in the agreement. In dealing with this charge, the statement argued that

> The agreement thus contains no language such as is found in our bilateral and multilateral mutual defense treaties. It is not provided that an armed attack against one party shall be considered an attack against the other, such as the North Atlantic Treaty and the Rio Pact provide, or that such an attack would be dangerous to the "peace and safety" of the United States or that the United States "would act to meet the common danger in accordance with its constitutional processes" as provided in our other mutual defense treaties.

Significantly the statement also included the paragraph: "In recognition of the concern expressed by some members of the Foreign Relations Committee the 1963 joint declaration language has been dropped. The joint declaration itself lapses upon the entry into force of the new agreement." The statement then summed up the position by saying, "The conclusion of this agreement as an executive agreement rather than as a treaty makes it even clearer that no commitment is involved."[74]

Although too late to have any effect, the Foreign Relations Committee finally was able to schedule open hearings on the agreements on August 26. Undersecretary Johnson and Deputy Secretary Packard added little new to the record; but they did manage to provoke a testy exchange between the agreement's critics and another committee member, Senator Gale McGee of Wyoming. Senator McGee told his committee colleagues that they had "strained the daylights" out of the Spanish bases issue and had learned nothing more in the public session than they knew from two earlier executive sessions. He criticized "perpetual fishing expeditions in Spanish waters" by the committee.[75]

It had become obvious by this time that there was no possibility of Fulbright's amendment to cut off funds obtaining anything near a majority in the Senate. As a result, an alternative resolution was offered by Senator Frank Church on September 22 (S. Res. 469) that said quite simply, "Resolved, that it is the sense of the Senate that nothing in the said agreement shall be construed as a national commitment by the United States to the defense of Spain." The administration saw little problem with this resolution, and on October 5 Assistant Secretary Abshire sent the official administration position in a letter to Senator Fulbright, which read in part:

> We would of course not object to the adoption of a resolution which merely reiterates the testimony previously set forth by administration officials. However, in light of the administration's public statements on this point we do not consider the resolution to be necessary.

The resolution passed the Senate on December 11, with extensive discussion but no real debate, since the administration did not oppose its passage. The Spanish government, not unexpectedly, felt its pride somewhat wounded by the passage of the resolution; but the administration simply smiled and told the Spanish not to worry. The issue of the Spanish base agreements was closed for another five years.

## CONCLUSIONS

The Spanish base agreements were of course far less controversial than Cooper-Church. At issue was the Senate's and Congress' role in establishing international commitments—in short, the treaty power. Unlike the war issue, which was high in everyone's consciousness, the issue of the Spanish agreements was largely theoretical; and concern outside the Senate Foreign Relations Committee was quite limited.

Support for the committee's effort to have the agreement submitted as a treaty drew on several sources. The overuse of executive agreements instead of treaties had been a source of Senate concern since World War II. There was almost certainly a majority in the Ninety-first Senate who would have favored the submission of the agreement as a treaty in the abstract. The majority never materialized, however, because of suspicion among many Senators concerned over the constitutional question—that the issue was being pursued by Senator

Fulbright and others in order to end the agreements altogether, rather than gaining Senate participation through a treaty. It was indeed true that several Senators had strong objections to having any relations with Franco Spain, and a larger number were opposed in principle to the maintenance of U.S. bases on foreign soil in peacetime. Yet others had concern that there was a de facto commitment to defend Spain involved in the relationship, and that it provided another example of the overextension of the United States as "world policeman."

Once again, according to its lights, the State Department wished to accommodate the Senate critics, not only because compromise is the job of diplomacy but also because, in this case, it had little sympathy for an agreement that essentially originated in, and served the interests of, the Pentagon.

The NSC, however, concluded that the Spanish bases were valuable in the Mediterranean and NATO power balance, and that the relationship with Spain was politically useful. The executive branch position therefore was to renew the agreements. At first there were no strong feelings one way or the other at the White House on the issue of making the renewal agreement a treaty. After analysis of the Senate situation, however, the NSC staff came to the firm conclusion that Chairman Fulbright could bottle up any treaty in his committee, or at best amend and reserve it to such an extent that it would be unacceptable to the Spanish. Moreover, it was judged probable that in the event of a real conflict, Fulbright could muster the 34 votes necessary to kill the treaty in a floor vote. The NSC judgment was that that was exactly Fulbright's intention.

In the end the Executive succeeded in renewing the agreement without submitting it as a treaty for two reasons. First, the opponents made it too obvious that they meant to kill the agreement, not merely change it to a treaty. With the vigorous assistance of White House lobbyists, this fact was sufficient to detach a significant number of Senators who agreed that constitutionally it should have been a treaty, but who also believed in the military need for the agreements. Second, the critics believed they had convinced the State Department to submit it as a treaty in the summer of 1971, as indeed they had, and therefore became complaisant. They apparently did not realize that such decisions were no longer being made by the State Department, and thus were caught completely unaware when the White House summoned the Spanish Foreign Minister and signed the agreement in the space of 72 hours.

Once again, however, there were far-reaching results from the interaction. The attacks from the Senate in the spring of 1969, with the accompanying leaks and adverse press comment, greatly unsettled the Spanish and came near to preventing renewal. While the Spanish valued the agreements politically, and profited financially, there were domestic benefits to be had by standing up to Uncle Sam. Spanish honor, easily bruised, was then brought prominently to the fore with the spate of derogatory speeches and articles that flowed.

As a result, agreement became impossible and the two year extension was arranged. During the negotiations that followed, however, the inveighing of the

Foreign Relations Committee and its media supporters became a very useful weapon in the skilled hands of U.S. negotiators, U. Alexis Johnson and Robert C. Hill.[76]

When the final agreement was reached the following summer, it contained substantially better terms than had been foreseen when the original negotiations began. Gone was the implied security commitment contained in the Joint Declaration of 1963.[77] Instead of the quid pro quo of more than $1 billion originally asked, the final assistance package totaled only $175 million over five years. In place of a purely military arrangement, the new agreement was based on mutual cooperation and cultural and educational exchange, of which U.S. use of Spanish bases was to constitute only a subsidiary part. In sum, the agreement was on a far sounder basis at much lower cost, thanks largely to the Foreign Relations Committee, although it did not rejoice.

As in Cooper-Church, the executive branch had lost ground on the constitutional issue during the debate. Congress shortly thereafter passed an amendment requiring all executive agreements to be transmitted promptly to Congress. When the Executive signed base agreements in 1971 with Portugal and Bahrain, the Senate promptly voted 50-6 that they must be submitted as treaties. The Executive rejected the request, arguing that making them treaties would imply important and permanent commitments. Several committees then began consideration of bills that would give Congress the right to veto any executive agreement. (At this writing these measures are under active consideration in Congress.)

A further price was paid in 1972, when the Executive signed an interim agreement on offensive weapons with the Soviet Union. The Executive wanted to avoid submitting this to Congress in part because of its interim term, but primarily because it feared tampering by Congressional skeptics who were unhappy with its terms. Because of the atmosphere created by the Spanish base agreement, it proved impossible to avoid submitting it for a joint resolution of approval. The executive fears of tampering were realized when Senator Henry Jackson of Washington succeeded in attaching a reservation to the resolution calling for equal numbers in a permanent agreement. The Soviets considered this a reservation to the agreement itself, when it was adopted by the House and signed by the President.[78]

While the Senate critics failed to block the Spanish base agreement or to have it submitted as a treaty, they did have a significant impact upon executive action and upon the agreement itself. If the Executive maintained its right to conclude executive agreements, it found that its scope for exercising it had been significantly reduced.

## NOTES

1. J.L. Brierly, *The Law of Nations*, Sir Humphrey Waldock, ed. (Oxford: Oxford University Press, 1963), p. 317.

2. Ibid., p. 320.

3. Ibid., pp. 321-33.

4. E.S. Corwin, *The Constitution and What It Means Today* (New York: Atheneum, 1967), p. 107.

5. E.S. Corwin, *The President: Office and Powers, 1787-1957* (New York: New York University Press, 1957), pp. 56-57. For a highly dubious attempt to refute Corwin, see Raoul Berger, *Executive Privilege* (Cambridge, Mass.: Harvard University Press, 1974), pp. 121-33.

6. Corwin, *The Constitution*, p. 108. Also see John Stennis and J.W. Fulbright, *The Role of Congress in Foreign Policy* (Washington, D.C.: American Enterprise Institute for Public Policy Research, 1971), pp. 4-5; and Myres McDougal and Asher Lans, "Treaties and Congressional-Executive or Presidential Agreements: Interchangeable Instruments of National Policy, " *Yale Law Journal* 54 (1945): 255.

7. Corwin, *The Constitution*, p. 109; Stennis and Fulbright, *Role of Congress*, p. 5.

8. Corwin, *The Constitution*, p. 108.

9. U.S. v. Curtiss-Wright Export Corporation, 299 U.S. 304 (1936). In delivering his opinion for the court Justice Sutherland (formerly chairman of the Senate Foreign Relations Committee) based his view in part on John Marshall's famous statement that "the President is the sole organ of the nation in its external relations."

10. Cited in U.S. Congress, Senate, Committee on Foreign Relations, Staff Study, February 6, 1973.

11. Sir Ivor Jennings, *The British Constitution* (London: University of London Press, 1959), p. 82.

12. Cited in Arthur Schlesinger, Jr., *The Imperial Presidency* (Boston: Houghton Mifflin, 1973), pp. 79-80.

13. Ibid., pp. 80-81.

14. Emerich de Vattel, *Le droit des gens*, as cited in Schlesinger, *Imperial Presidency*, pp. 80-81, and Brierly, *The Law of Nations*, p. 37.

15. Corwin, *The Constitution*, pp. 112-16.

16. Ibid., pp. 114-15.

17. Louis Fischer, *President and Congress* (New York: Free Press, 1972), p. 45.

18. Schlesinger, *The Imperial Presidency*, pp. 85-86.

19. Stennis and Fulbright, *Role of Congress*, p. 60-61.

20. Corwin, *The Constitution*, p. 114, fn. 51, and p. 116.

21. Schlesinger, *Imperial Presidency*, p. 312.

22. Ibid., pp. 312-13.

23. U.S. Congress, Senate, Committee on Foreign Relations, *United States Security Agreements and Commitments Abroad*, report by Subcommittee on U.S. Security Agreements and Commitments Abroad of Committee on Foreign Relations (Washington, D.C.: U.S. Government Printing Office, 1971), II, 2364, 2400, 2425.

24. U.S. Congress, Senate, Committee on Foreign Relations, *Spanish Base Agreement* (Washington, D.C.: U.S. Government Printing Office, 1970), p. 57.

25. Ibid., p. 56.

26. U.S. Congress, Senate, Committee on Foreign Relations, *Commitments*, II, p. 2344.

27. U.S. Congress, Senate, Committee on Foreign Relations, *Spanish Base Agreement*, p. 56.

28. U.S. Congress, Senate, Committee on Foreign Relations, *Commitments*, II, p. 2391.

29. Ibid., p. 2350.

30. Ibid.

31. Ibid., p. 2351.

32. Based on interview conducted with General David A. Burchinal in Madrid, April 1969.

33. Washington *Post*, February 25, 1969, p. 17.

34. U.S. Congress, Senate, Committee on Foreign Relations, *Commitments*, II, p. 2352.

35. Ibid.

36. Based on interviews with senior officials at NSC, January 1969.

37. U.S. Congress, Senate, Committee on Foreign Relations, *Commitments*, II, p. 2352.

38. Washington *Post*, February 25, 1969, p. 16.

39. Based on interviews conducted at U.S. Embassy, Madrid, April 1969.

40. New York *Times*, February 26, 1969, p. 1.

41. Ibid., March 1, 1969, p. 8.

42. U.S. President, *Public Papers of the Presidents of the United States* (Washington, D.C.: Office of the *Federal Register*, National Archives and Records Service, 1970), Richard M. Nixon, 1969, p. 193.

43. New York *Times*, March 5, 1969, p. 46.

44. New York *Times*, March 12, 1969, p. 46; New York *Times*, March 23, 1969, p. 3-E; also see Washington *Post*, March 17, 1969, p. 22; Washington *Daily News*, March 22, 1969; St. Louis *Post-Dispatch*, March 19, 1969. This adverse publicity buttressed the U.S. position by reducing the Spanish perception of the strength of the U.S. desire to maintain the bases in Spain and, hence, the price that the U.S. might be willing to pay.

45. New York *Times*, March 16, 1969, p. 5.

46. U.S. Congress, House, 91st Cong., 1st sess., March 25, 1969, *Congressional Record*, p. H2035; Washington *Post*, March 25, 1969, p. 1.

47. *Nuevo diario*, *ABC*, and *Ya*, March 20, 1969, p. 1.

48. Washington *Post*, March 27, 1969, p. 2.

49. Baltimore *Sun*, March 27, 1969, p. 1.

50. *Ya*, *Arriba*, and *ABC*, March 28, 1969, p. 1.

51. Based on interview with Ambassador Robert C. Hill, September 1969.

52. Washington *Post*, April 5, 1969, p. 15.

53. U.S. Congress, Senate, 91st Cong., 1st sess., April 18, 1969, *Congressional Record*, p. S3827.

54. *ABC*, April 19, 1969, p. 1.

55. Washington *Post*, March 23, 1969, p. A-6.

56. *ABC*, May 7, 14, 25, 26, 29; *La vanguardia española*, May 22, 1969; May 29, 1969; *Arriba*, May 29, 1969; *Ya*, May 29, 1969.

57. New York *Times*, May 29, 1969, p. 13.

58. *ABC*, June 3, 1969, p. 1.

59. Washington *Post*, June 6, 1969, p. 1.

60. Washington *Post*, June 14, 1969, pp. 1, 25.

61. *Stars and Stripes*, June 16, 1969, p. 1.

62. New York *Times*, June 18, 1969, p. 46.

63. U.S. Congress, House, 85th Congress, 1st Sess., March 20, 1957, *Congressional Record*, 103, pH4035.

64. Based on an interview with Assistant Secretary David Abshire, June 1970.

65. U.S. Congress, Senate, 91st Cong., 2nd Sess., July 31, 1970, *Congressional Record*, p. S12500.

66. Ibid., p. S12501.

67. "CBS Evening News," August 2, 1970.

68. U.S. Congress, Senate, 91st Cong., 2nd sess., August 3, 1970, *Congressional Record*, p. S12650.

69. Washington *Post*, August 4, 1970, p. 3.

70. U.S. Congress, Senate, 91st Congress., 2nd sess., August 6, 1970, *Congressional Record*, p. S12905.

71. U.S. Congress, Senate, Committee on Foreign Relations, *Spanish Base Agreement*, p. 1.

72. Ibid., pp. 10, 11, 12.

73. Ibid., pp. 2-6.

74. Ibid., p. 10.

75. Washington *Star*, August 27, 1970, p. 28.

76. Based on interviews with Undersecretary Johnson and Ambassador Hill, August 1970.

77. U.S. Congress, Senate, Committee on Foreign Relations, *Spanish Base Agreement*, p. 10.

78. For text and extensive debate see U.S. Congress, 92nd Cong., 2nd sess., September 14, 1972, *Congressional Record*.

# 5

## THE INVESTIGATION PROCESS:
## THE SYMINGTON SUBCOMMITTEE

### BACKGROUND

The power of Congress to investigate is nowhere to be found in the Constitution. Like so many other powers, it is a derived power flowing from the principle that each branch of the government has those powers not explicitly prohibited it that are necessary to carry out the duties and functions explicitly granted in the Constitution.

Almost certainly the founding fathers contemplated an inherent investigative power in the new Congress. The House of Commons had exercised investigative power since the sixteenth century, and the experience of most of the drafters in their colonial legislatures and the Continental Congress, where the parliamentary practice of investigation was prevalent, disposed them to accept this as a necessary concomitant of the legislative function.[1]

Many serious students of American government have been placing more importance upon the investigating and informing function of Congress than upon even its legislative function. As Woodrow Wilson put it:

Unless Congress have and use every means of acquainting itself with the acts and the disposition of the administrative agents of the government, the country must be helpless to learn how it is being served; and unless Congress both scrutinize these things and sift them by every form of discussion, the country must remain in embarrassing, crippling ignorance of the very affairs which it is most important that it should understand and direct.[2]

The first use of this implied power was not long in coming. In 1792, the House of Representatives decided to look into the defeat of General Arthur St. Clair's disastrous expedition against the Indians of the Northwest Territory. President Washington's cooperation with this committee helped to provide this important Congressional power with its present unquestioned legitimacy. From this case Congress established the precedent that the investigative power would be exercised through committees. A special or select committee was established for the purpose of the St. Clair investigation, and a majority of all investigations from then until the Reorganization Act of 1946 were carried out by such ad hoc committees, which expired with the conclusion of the particular investigation.[3] Another enduring precedent set by this investigation was the heavy role of party politics in the creation of the committee and in the suppressing of its final report.[4]

In 1828, the investigative power was further broadened by the granting of subpoena power for the first time to a standing committee—the House Committee on Manufactures. Heretofore the limiting of the investigative power to ad hoc committees acting in a judicial capacity had kept the scope of the investigative power quite narrow.[5]

At first the House of Representatives dominated Congressional investigations. It conducted 27 of the 30 investigations between 1789 and 1814. As time passed, however, the Senate took over the dominant position; and between 1900 and 1925 it conducted 40 of the 60 Congressional investigations.[6]

Since that first investigation in 1792, the exercise of this power has made many important contributions. In the words of Nelson McGeary, "They have illuminated many a dark problem, lighted scores of shadowy corners, and sometimes disclosed carefully hidden skeletons."[7] A proclivity established from this very first investigation was the Congressional fondness for the investigation of military operations. It is in this field also that most observers agree that the investigative power has made its least admirable contributions. Every conflict in which the United States has been involved, except the Spanish-American War, has been the subject of Congressional investigation. Undoubtedly the most infamous of such inquiries was that conducted by the Joint Committee on the Conduct of the Civil War, authorized in December 1861. It was mandated to investigate "past, present, and future defeats, the orders of executive departments, the actions of generals in the field, and the questions of war policies."[8] It had been set up in the aftermath of the defeat at First Bull Run, and immediately became a political vehicle for the Radical Republicans opposed to Lincoln.

As some later committees have attempted to do, it took over a partial control of military operations, investigating strategy, interrogating subordinate officers to gain evidence against particular generals, and demanding particular resignations or reassignments by President Lincoln. Setting yet another hallowed precedent, the proceedings of their sessions, while supposed to be highly secret, were usually leaked to the press without delay.[9]

As a result of its activities, the Confederate commander in chief, Robert E. Lee, observed that this committee was worth about two divisions of Confederate troops.[10]

President Lincoln, in exasperation to be echoed almost exactly by some of his twentieth-century successors, cried, "This improvised vigilant committee to watch my movements and to keep me straight...is a marplot, and its greatest purpose seems to be to hamper my action and obstruct military operations."[11]

Another exercise of the investigative powers that serves to discredit this Congressional role was the notorious Senate Special Committee Investigating the Munitions Industry, established in 1934. Despite Democratic control of the Senate, a progressive Republican, Gerald P. Nye of North Dakota, was appointed chairman; and he set out to use the committee as a vehicle to ride to the Vice-Presidential nomination in 1936 as the leader of an increasingly popular isolationism. Nye believed that the public was convinced that it was the "merchants of death" who had dragged the country repeatedly into war, and he set out to prove this case. The committee ran off in many different directions; and while it was able to disclose instances of bribery and corruption in the arms business, its overall impact was to fan the flames of isolationism in the pre-World War II period.[12]

Performances such as these led some observers to denounce the "senatorial debauch of investigations—poking into political intrigue...the level of professional searchers of municipal dunghills." [13]

The reputation of the Congressional investigative powers was somewhat refurbished by the very real contributions made by the Truman committee during World War II. Created in March 1941, nine months before the attack on Pearl Harbor, it sought to uncover and halt wasteful practices in war preparations. When the war broke out, it greatly expanded its authority "to make a full and complete study and investigation of the operation of the program for the procurement and construction of supplies, materials, vessels, plants, camps and other articles and facilities in connection with the national defense."[14]

Although many executive branch officials were less sanguine in their assessment of the committee, most observers believed in retrospect that the Truman committee was very effective in bringing about needed improvements in the administration, and in rationalizing the enormous expenditures for industrial production during the war.[15]

The investigative power was greatly strengthened immediately following World War II. Passage of the Legislative Reorganization Act (Public Law 79-601) in 1946 cut the number of standing committees in the House from 48 to 19, and in the Senate from 33 to 15. It authorized standing committees of both chambers to "exercise continuous watchfulness of the execution by the administrative agencies concerned of any laws, the subject matters of which is within the jurisdiction" of the respective committees. It also provided a permanent budget for investigating and the hiring of professional staff members for all standing committees.16 The effect of this act, in conuunction with the vast expansion of the federal bureaucracy during the 1930s and 1940s, resulted in a tremendous growth in the number of investigations in the postwar years. Compared with approximately 500 investigations from 1792 until 1946, the Ninetieth Congress alone authorized 496 investigations.17

## EXECUTIVE SECRECY

There is, needless to say, a fundamental conflict inherent between the Congressional powers of investigation and the executive need for secrecy. Like the Congressional power to investigate, the Executive's right to secrecy is nowhere mentioned in the Constitution, but derives from the executive powers granted under Article II. That the founding fathers assumed this to be the case is indisputable. The Constitutional Convention was closed by a bond of secrecy. Benjamin Franklin admonished his colleagues to maintain that secrecy after the Convention when, noting some of the doubts he had expressed about the Constitution during the Convention, he said, "Within these halls they were born and here they shall die."18

While nowhere explicitly granted to the Executive, paragraph 3, section 5, of Article I in the Constitution provides: "Each house shall keep a journal of its proceedings, and from time to time publish the same, excepting such parts as may *in their judgment require secrecy*."

*The Federalist* explicitly discussed the need for secrecy in the Executive in the area of diplomacy, where "Perfect secrecy and immediate dispatch are sometimes requisite," and in the area of intelligence, where "The most useful intelligence may be obtained if the persons possessing it can be relieved of the apprehensions of discovery."19

Over the years the kinds of information that the executive branch has, with limited success, attempted to keep secret, have fallen into five categories.

The first category, the protection of diplomatic negotiations, was perhaps most succinctly defended by, of all sources, the Senate Foreign Relations Committee in 1816, which stated: "The nature of transactions with foreign nations, moreover, requires caution and unity of design, and their success frequently depends upon *secrecy* and dispatch."20

Justice Potter Stewart most recently gave the court's stamp of legitimacy to that first category; to a second category, the protection of defense matters; and to a third category, the protection of the integrity of internal discussions within the executive branch, when he said:

It is elementary that the successful conduct of international diplomacy and the maintenance of an effective national defense require both confidentiality and secrecy. Other nations can hardly deal with this nation in an atmosphere of mutual trust unless they can be assured that their confidences will be kept. And within our own executive departments, the development of considered and intelligent international policies would be impossible if those charged with their formulation could not communicate with each other freely, frankly, and inconfidence. In the area of basic national defense the frequent need for absolute secrecy is, of course, self-evident.[21]

A fourth category of protection is that mentioned in *The Federalist*: the protection of intelligence sources and methods. The National Security Act of 1947 specifically requires the Director of Central Intelligence to be responsible for such protection; and in connection with the U-2 incident the Senate Foreign Relations Committee explicitly recognized that, with regard to intelligence operations, "The administration has the legal right to refuse the information."[22]

The executive branch has exercised its right to secrecy through two means. To protect against public disclosure, it has evolved a system of security classification of information. To deny disclosure to Congress, a system of executive privilege has evolved.

Executive classification of material as "confidential" and "secret" can be traced back to the War of 1812. The present system of classification, however, appears to have begun during World War I. Through a series of general orders of the War Department and Presidential executive orders, some supported by statute and others not, an elaborate network of regulations and restrictions accumulated.[23]

By 1970 this rambling accretion of regulations had reached a ridiculous and unmanageable proportion. In 1962 the House Committee on Government Operations found there were "more than a million government employees permitted to stamp permanent security designations on all kinds of documents."[24] The General Accounting Office has estimated that this chaotic system costs the taxpayers between $60 and $80 million a year. And a retired Pentagon security officer, testifying before the House Government Operations Committee, stated that in the Pentagon alone there were over 20 million classified documents and that only 1-5 percent of these legitimately required protection.[25]

On March 8, 1972, after a thorough study within the executive branch, President Nixon issued Executive Order 11652 in an attempt to begin to rationalize the system and reduce the amount of material classified.[26] Signing the document, the President said, "We have reversed the burden of proof. For the first time, we are placing that burden—and even the threat of administrative sanction—upon those who wish to preserve the secrecy of documents rather than upon those who wish to declassify them after a reasonable time."

The President said in that statement, "Clearly, the two principles of an informed public and of confidentiality within the government are irreconcilable in their purest forms, and a balance must be struck between them."[27]

## EXECUTIVE PRIVILEGE

From the very first investigation it undertook in 1792, Congress has found itself in conflict with the executive branch over access to information the Congress believes is needed for its inquiry, and the Executive believes requires protection from disclosure. In that first instance the Select House Committee requested all documents relating to the St. Clair Expedition. President Washington very carefully considered the question at a Cabinet meeting and, according to Thomas Jefferson, decided that "The Executive ought to communicate such papers as the public good would permit, and ought to refuse those the disclosure of which would endanger the public." In that case the President decided that none of the requested papers should be regarded as confidential, and consequently they were turned over.[28]

In 1796, however, President Washington claimed executive privilege for the first time when he refused a House request for correspondence relating to the controversial Jay Treaty with Great Britain.*

The Constitution nowhere confers executive privilege on the executive branch, any more than it confers upon Congress the right to compel disclosure by the Executive. The former is implicit in the powers of the Chief Executive, and the latter in the legislative powers. Both of these powers are firmly rooted in history and precedent.[29]

---

*"In denying the House its request, President Washington advised that 'The nature of foreign negotiations requires caution, and their success must often depend on secrecy; and even when brought to a conclusion a full disclosure of all the measures, demands, or eventual concessions which may have been proposed or contemplated would be extremely impolite; for this might have a pernicious influence on future negotiations or produce immediate inconveniences, perhaps danger and mischief, in relation to other powers.' The necessity of such caution and secrecy was one cogent reason for vesting the power of making treaties in the President, with the advice and consent of the Senate, the principle on which that body was formed confining it to a small number of members." Rehnquist statement in U.S. Congress, Senate, Committee on the Judiciary, *Executive Privilege* (Washington, D.C.: U.S. Government Printing Office, 1971), p. 430.

The decision in this case was made on the rather narrow ground that the House had no role in the treaty process. It should also be noted that the term commonly used for such denial now, "executive privilege," seems to be a recent usage.

The Supreme Court has explicitly recognized the doctrine of executive privilege in the case of *U.S.* v. *Reynolds*; and Chief Justice John Marshall, in *Marbury* v. *Madison*, endorsed the rule that the President is not bound to produce papers or disclose information where *in his judgment* the disclosure would, on public consideration, be inexpedient. In a more recent case, *Barenblatt* v. *U.S.*, the Court expressed its opinion that Congressional power of inquiry "is not without limitations...that it cannot inquire into matters which are within the exclusive province of one of the other branches of government...neither can it supplant the Executive in what exclusively belongs to the Executive."[30]

Congress itself has explicitly and implicitly recognized the existence of the privilege on many occasions. One such evidence is that time-honored formula for resolutions of inquiry. This was the normal way for Congress to obtain information from the Executive until the tremendous expansion of the investigative activity following World War II. Resolutions of inquiry directed to the Department of State in matters of foreign relations always contained the caveat "if not incompatible with the public interest."[31]

In 1807, Thomas Jefferson stated what seemed to be the accepted view of how the judgment of the public interest should be made. "He, of course, the President from the nature of the case, must be the sole judge of which of them the public interests will permit publication. Hence, under our Constitution, in requests of papers, from the legislative to the executive branch, an exception is carefully expressed, as to those which he may deem the public welfare may require not to be disclosed."[32]

The boundaries of these conflicting powers have been the source of continuous conflict. As Senator Fulbright aptly quoted *The Federalist*: "Neither the Executive nor the Legislature can pretend to an exclusive or superior right of settling the boundaries between their respective powers."[33]

The issue has often been quite confused because executive privilege has often been invoked by the Executive not because it desired to keep the information from Congress, but because it knew that the purpose of the investigation being pursued was not to inform the Congress but to make public the material in order to buttress the a priori conclusions of the investigation under way. In military matters this is a consideration of great gravity in the Executive. Just as Robert E. Lee believed the Civil War Investigation Committee to be worth two combat divisions to him, the Executive has feared in recent times that investigations, while pursuing legitimate purposes, can through disclosure furnish the enemy with extremely valuable strategic and tactical combat information. The investigators have, on occasion, admitted this. Chairman J. William Fulbright, for instance, has declared that this is a price that must be paid for an open society.[34] It is to be expected, then, that the Executive can, on occasion, be unwilling to pay that price, which is readily translatable in its mind to a price not only of military and political advantage but also a price paid with the lives of American soldiers.

This kind of problem suggests what more often than not is at the heart of the conflict. Traditionally Congress has been most interested in investigating those subjects that executive departments would just as soon forget, for if they are brought to light, they might cause embarrassment to the administration or to executive officials.[35] It is through this aspect of investigations into executive and administrative activities, methods, mistakes, and inefficiencies that the greatest contribution can be made; as Clinton Rossiter has described it, such investigation serves the purpose of keeping the Chief Executive and his helpers in touch with democratic realities.

The executive temptation to resort early to claims of executive privilege is not surprising in such circumstances. In the face of such frustration there is little Congress can do. As Woodrow Wilson commented:

> Congress stands almost helplessly outside of the departments. Even the special irksome, ungracious investigations which it from time to time institutes...do not afford it more than a glimpse of the inside of a small province of federal administration...it can violently disturb, but it cannot often fathom the waters of the sea in which the bigger fish of the civil service swim and feed. Its dragnet stirs without cleansing the bottom."[36]

In 1969 the frustrations of the Cold War and the bitterness of the lack of success in Vietnam had moved a number of members of the Senate to believe that a serious investigative inquiry into U.S. involvement abroad was required. At the same time the executive branch, under control of a different political party, was engaged in a reevaluation of American foreign policy of its own pursuing a policy of negotiation and Vietnamization in Southeast Asia. The stage was thereby set for a unique period of interaction between the branches in the investigative process.

## THE SYMINGTON SUBCOMMITTEE

On February 3, 1969, Senator J. W. Fulbright, chairman of the Senate Committee on Foreign Relations, announced the establishment of an ad hoc Subcommittee on United States Security Agreements and Commitments Abroad, to be chaired by Senator Stuart Symington. To carry out its evaluation and analysis, the subcommittee hired two staff members: Walter Pincus, a former investigative reporter, and Roland Paul, a former member of the Office of the Secretary of Defense in the Johnson administration. They were promptly given security clearances by the Department of Defense.

This investigation provided the first test of the proclamation by the Nixon administration that it would be an "open administration," and that Congress would have full access to information in the executive branch. In order to give the departments guidance in responding to the Symington subcommittee and all other such requests, a memorandum was sent on February 10 from the White House to all Cabinet members, outlining a policy of full disclosure to Congress and squarely placing the burden of proof on those departments that might be tempted to withhold information from Congress. Procedures were laid out whereby all instances in which an agency wished to decline information requested by a Congressional committee had first to be reported in writing to Bryce Harlow and to John Ehrlichman. This was clearly meant as a deterrent to the expected tendency of the departments to try to protect themselves at the expense of the "openness" of the administration.[37]

The first slight question about such openness was raised on February 25, when the Washington *Post* printed a Flora Lewis account of the Burchinal Memorandum, quoting from top-secret documents that were thought to be in the Symington subcommittee's possession.[38]

The first real issue of access to sensitive information had arisen on February 7, when Senator Symington sent a letter to Secretary of Defense Melvin Laird requesting a copy of the Wood-McClintock Study on Overseas Bases. This study, mentioned in Chapter 4, was an encyclopedic analysis of the entire U.S. overseas base posture, done in the last days of the Johnson administration. It included secret, top-secret, and very sensitive information, and immediately raised questions in the Pentagon as to the advisability of providing this to the Symington subcommittee. After lengthy discussions in the Pentagon, the matter was brought to the attention of the White House, with the suggestion that perhaps another look at the full disclosure policy might be warranted in this case; but that, unless directed to the contrary the Pentagon intended to carry out the instructions on February 10 and turn over the study.

It was decided at the White House that the Wood-McClintock Study would be provided to the Symington subcommittee but that the committee staff would have to study it in the Pentagon rather than turning over the very sensitive parts of the report to the committee itself. The subcommittee staff agreed to the terms, and spent the last week of March studying the Wood-McClintock Report in the Pentagon and taking detailed notes.

Although the situation in Vietnam had been specifically excluded from the scope of the Symington inquiry by the charter of February 3, it soon became clear that the subcommittee had every intention of examining it. On February 18, a long list of detailed questions probing U.S. military involvement from the Indian Ocean to Thai insurgency and European deployments, with all ramifications, was submitted to the Department of Defense. It included detailed questions about the activities of U.S. troops in Southeast Asia. This was the first of a great many exhaustive catalogs of questions submitted to the

Department of Defense and the Department of State, which required the assigning of large staffs in both agencies to work full-time for two years producing responses for the subcommittee, in addition to the long testimony that was to come.

Because of the many sensitive matters involved in the new Symington questions, it was clearly necessary to give full and explicit instructions to the departments on how to comply with these requests. Accordingly, on March 24 the President issued a memorandum for the heads of all executive departments and agencies. It read in part:

> The policy of this administration is to comply to the fullest extent possible with congressional requests for information. While the executive branch has the responsibility of withholding certain information the disclosure of which would be incompatible with the public interest, this administration will invoke this authority only in the most compelling circumstances and after a rigorous inquiry into the actual need for its exercise. For those reasons executive privilege will not be used without specific Presidential approval.

It then went on to lay out specific procedural steps to govern the invocation of executive privilege that required the agency wishing to withhold first to consult the Attorney General and, if the agency head and the Attorney General agreed that executive privilege may be warranted, then to submit a fully detailed recommendation to the President. Only if the President decided that the privilege should be invoked, would information be withheld from Congress.39

This proclamation took the National Security Council staff, the Pentagon, the State Department, and the CIA by complete surprise. They felt that, without further clarification, the directive was far too wide in opening the sensitive files of executive agencies to Congressional inquiry. There was also resentment that the memorandum had been issued by Ehrlichman's office, without any reference whatsoever to the NSC or the departments.

On April 9 the Executive was given further cause for concern. The New York *Times* printed a story by Benjamin Welles disclosing that the Nixon administration had finally furnished the Symington subcommittee with the secret 1,200-page Wood-McClintock Report. Then, with the introduction that "Those who have had access to the study describe its broad conclusions as follows:..." he disclosed classified facts and figures drawn directly from the Wood-McClintock Report.40

In response to this leak, a meeting was held at the Department of State on April 11, in which the White House, the Pentagon, and the CIA all expressed serious reservations about continued openness to the Symington subcommittee. There now were almost daily new requests for information, one of the latest being for the confidential negotiating instructions to General Burchinal in his military discussions with the Spanish. The State Department argued strongly for full compliance, recommending that instead of withholding, the executive branch should work with the subcommittee to tighten its own security. Secretary William Rogers' position was strongly for full cooperation with the subcommittee. The Department of State had also received a further request from the subcommittee staff to provide the subcommittee with its own copy of the Wood-McClintock Report. Rogers was recommending that it be given. NSC and the Defense Department expressed the view that there was good evidence that the subcommittee staff was not undertaking an objective analysis, but was in the process of building a case for attacking the administration for its foreign policy across the board. Rogers was instructed not to deliver the study.

### PINCUS AND PAUL TRIP

By mid-April the subcommittee had been provided with thousands of classified documents and given access to many thousands more in the executive branch. These included internal working documents, negotiating instructions, and background material of a highly sensitive nature.

Early in April the Executive was informed that the subcommittee staff would undertake a three-week trip to Portugal, Spain, Turkey, and Greece on subcommittee business. The staff members were fully briefed, and the U.S. missions in those countries were notified. The instructions that were sent by the Department of State directed the field to give the staff members full access and to cooperate fully with them by providing them with sensitive material and not attempting to hide any problems. State Department optimism on the effectiveness of this approach was not shared by the Defense Department or NSC.

In preparation for their trip, the Symington staff was given a thorough series of briefings in the Office of the Assistant Secretary for International Security Affairs. Despite reservations in the NSC and elsewhere, the official policy was to provide it with copies of the most sensitive unpublished and classified agreements and background papers pertaining to U.S. facilities and operating rights abroad; and this was done. The complete cooperation of the Pentagon in assisting the staff was greatly enhanced by the personal friendships that the staff members had developed in the Office of the Secretary of Defense during the Johnson administration. They departed on April 21. On April 23, the executive branch was given further cause for disquiet when the New York *Times* reported that Senator Symington was considering the declassification of information available to him, on his own authority.[41]

The Executive was made increasingly nervous by the persistent murmurs emanating from the vicinity of the Foreign Relations Committee. In a speech on the West Coast at the beginning of May, for instance, the staff director, Dr. Carl

Marcy, praised the farsightedness of college demonstrators in raising questions about the American role in the world, particularly of its military forces, and pledging that the Senate would move "in a vigorous way" to question President Nixon's policy decisions.[42]

There was further disquiet on May 23, when the Washington *Post* revealed: "A Congressional committee has acquired a secret Pentagon proposal to sink 10 of its 41 Polaris submarines to save money." Details of this study, prepared by Systems Analysis in the Defense Department, were included in the article.[43] This same study had been the subject of discussion in the Symington hearings on Spain, in the context of one argument against the continuing need for the base at Rota.

On May 24, the New York *Times* reported a meeting held "behind the closed doors of the Senate Foreign Relations Committee hearing room by young Senate staff aides for an attack on the defense budget": "...the aides, working through their senators, have demonstrated that they can put the once powerful Senate military establishment on the defensive. Now they are attempting to apply the same tactics against other major items...." And in the same article the first inkling of the results of the Symington staff trip to Europe was suggested: "The subcommittee staff believes that, in a recent trip in Europe, it pinpointed some military bases that have outlived their original purpose and usefulness."[44]

More explicit evidence of the results of the Symington staff trip were not long in coming. On June 14 the Washington *Post* carried two articles (one by Flora Lewis) revealing classified details of military exercises conducted by U.S. and Spanish forces in Spain. both articles identified the two Symington staff members, Pincus and Paul, as the sources of the leaks. Suspicions had been raised in the White House and Pentagon when, during the Pincus-Paul trip, the Spanish Embassy reported that they had been fully briefed, on a classified basis, on these joint exercises and had both expressed their indignation. The NSC staff took morbid pleasure in telling State "I told you so," while warning that this could be only the beginning.[45] It had not escaped notice that the timing of the leak was conveniently two days before debate was to begin in the Senate on the National Commitments Resolution.

Despite these warnings, and over the objections of the NSC, the Department of State insisted that complete openness and full cooperation with the Symington subcommittee should be continued.

Early in June, the subcommittee requested the Department of State to make arrangements for a five-week trip to the Far East for the staff beginning June 25, to include investigations in the headquarters of the Commander in Chief, Pacific, the Philippines, Okinawa, Korea, Taiwan, Japan, Thailand, and Laos. Again complete access to a great deal of highly sensitive information was given to the staff investigators in Washington, and instructions were sent to the field directing embassies and military headquarters to give them all documents requested, up to top-secret, and reminding them that the executive branch policy was to cooperate to the fullest extent possible in assisting the staff members.

## SECOND PINCUS AND PAUL TRIP

The staff investigators left on June 25, and reports from the field soon indicated that they were finding much of interest to them. The first jolt came on July 8, with the Washington *Post* reported that on the previous day Senator Fulbright had revealed the existence of a "secret agreement" that the United States had with Thailand, in the form of a pledge to support Thai forces. "I heard about it only ten days ago and it's *top-secret*."[46] A short time previous to this revelation, the staff investigators were in Thailand and, in accord with the State Department instructions, the embassy staff showed them a copy of the top-secret "Project Taksin" contingency plan. This was in fact not an international agreement as such, but an example of joint contingency planning carried out under the Southeast Asia Treaty Organization. Note was taken of the fact that the staff investigators had spent a considerable amount of time with members of the Thai press corps in Bangkok.[47]

There was considerably more skepticism, then, when immediately upon their return from their Asian trip, the staff investigators, in Senator Symington's name, requested texts of four Presidential letters to the Prime Minister of Thailand. The State Department requested clearance to provide these documents to the staff, but the White House overruled State and instructed it to tell the subcommittee that these were Presidential communications between states, and not appropriate for circulation outside the executive branch. State was instructed that if push came to shove, the President was prepared to invoke executive privilege in order to deny the documents. This decision was taken in the full knowledge that the substance of the documents was not terribly sensitive; rather, to provide Presidential documents would set a wholly new precedent for the remainder of the hearings.

On August 2, the New York *Post* printed a column by Frank Mankiewicz and Tom Braden revealing details of "an extraordinary and secret document, signed on behalf of all of us by Lieutenant General Richard G. Stillwell, Commander of U.S. forces in Thailand." This unauthorized commitment to the defense of Thailand was discovered "when Senate Foreign Relations Committee staffers stumbled across it in the course of investigating a similar agreement with Spain."

On August 11, the committee staff continued the follow-up to their trip by requesting a copy of the Memorandum of Understanding agreed to by President Kennedy and Australian Foreign Minister Sir Garfield Barwick on October

17, 1963, regarding U.S. commitments under the ANZUS Treaty. Once again the State Department strongly recommended turning the document over, and once again the White House instructed State not to do so. State resented this, and argued that providing such documents would do a great deal to help relations with the committee. The White House, however, was adamant.

By late August, the adverse effects of the leak of the "Taksin Plan" had grown considerably. The Thai government was confounded that the administration was unable to protect a document of so sensitive a nature, and it made representations in the strongest terms. The Thai government was joined in its consternation by the White House when, on August 21, Secretary of Defense Laird, without any prior warning, announced that he did not agree with the contingency plan and that it did not have his approval, having been drawn up in 1965. This statement, coupled with the adverse publicity already created, enraged the Thai leadership.

At the beginning of September, Senator Symington informed the Department of State that hearings would open on the Philippines during the week of September 29, focusing on formal and informal commitments, insurgency in the Philippines, nuclear weapons, corruption in the Philippines, and the Philippine contribution to the war in Vietnam.

A meeting was requested by the State Department, and on September 3, Senator Symington met in his office with members of the State and Defense Departments, a session at which he made it clear that he intended to make a major issue of the de facto commitments embodied in so-called contingency plans.

The following Friday, Chairman Fulbright had lunch with Secretary Laird at the Pentagon, and an agreement was reached to provide the committee with access to the "Taksin Plan," at the Pentagon, for their analysis. Laird emphasized to Fulbright that Congress would be consulted before the contingency plan was ever implemented. Fulbright later admitted to the press that he was aware of the contents of the document but was concerned about establishing future precedents for access to such documents.48

## THE EXECUTIVE ORGANIZES

The White House, in the meantime, after having read the thrust of the questions for the Philippine hearings, concluded that a steering group to supervise executive participation in the hearings and, in effect, to limit damage was urgently needed. On September 15, an ad hoc group was set up, consisting of senior members from the White House Legislative Liaison Office, the White House Counsel's Office, and the NSC staff. The President made it known to this group that he was concerned with the possible damage that could be done by the subcommittee and, further, that he had not approved Secretary Laird's making the "Taksin Plan" available to the Foreign Relations Committee, and opposed the providing of any contingency plans as such.

At a meeting in the Cabinet Room on September 15, with the bipartisan Congressional leadership, the President reassured the participants that "Project Taksin" was nothing more than a contingency plan within the framework of the SEATO Treaty, and did not envision any automatic commitment of U.S. troops to fight in Thailand. He then reaffirmed the staunchness of the U.S. alliance with Thailand and the importance that he placed on that relationship.

On September 19, Senator Symington announced on the floor of the Senate that he had scheduled hearings on Laos to begin in executive session on October 14. He declared:

> We have been in war in Laos for five years and it is time the American people know more of the facts...for too long we have permitted our activities abroad to be carried on behind a cloak of secrecy—and often that secrecy veils such activities from the people in this country and their elected officials—not from the enemy.[49]

The real heart of White House concern at this point was not to deny information to the Senators on the subcommittee but, rather, the fear that, once provided to the Senators the information would be made public and used in an attempt to discredit the policies of the administration. The difficulties that this issue would cause in the progress of the hearings became apparent in a preliminary meeting between Ambassador Robert McClintock and the subcommittee staff on September 23. The point was strongly made by McClintock that the Executive did not question the right of Senators to know everything the government was doing; rather, there was a common-sense concern to limit the damaging consequences that would be sure to result to the foreign relations of the United States if certain confidences between governments were breached or if certain kinds of security information or intelligence methods were made public. The subcommittee staff refused to acknowledge that the decision as to what could be made public and what could not belonged to the Executive; rather, it should be the subject of negotiations between them after all the material was provided to the subcommittee. In effect, they maintained that the subcommittee had an equal right to make a determination on degrees of sensitivity and where the public interest could best be served by public disclosure.

On September 24, Ambassador McClintock held the first interdepartmental group meeting and instructed all executive witnesses in the guidelines to be followed in their testimony, as formulated by the White House ad hoc group. He emphasized that information in the following categories was not to be discussed: intelligence collection and processing methods; information on nuclear storage and arrangements; NSC documents; internal working memoranda of the executive branch, including policy recommendations; personnel investigative reports or performance evaluations; military contingency plans; and privileged communications between chiefs of state or between delegated officials of the United States and other governments. McClintock, with tongue in cheek, quoted Baltazar Gracian: "Things which are to be done should not be talked about, and things which have been talked about should not be done," and submitted the conclusions of the interdepartmental group to the White House for approval, which was subsequently given.

On September 25, the President again focused on the upcoming hearings. He had by now been convinced by his staff that they represented a serious challenge to executive prerogatives and responsibilities across the full range of foreign affairs, and that they warranted his close attention and adequate defensive measures. He believed that the hearings would be used as an attempt to mobilize developing isolationist pressures, in order to effect a substantial contraction of U.S. presence around the world. He therefore decided in advance to invoke executive privilege on all contingency plans and to forbid the discussion of intelligence activities and nuclear weapons deployments if these matters were pressed.

Two days later, the Department of State issued a warning to its posts in the Far East to prepare for possible adverse publicity.

## THE HEARINGS BEGIN

On the day that the hearings opened, September 30, the White House convened a meeting of senior administration principals to settle the policy for the conduct of the hearings, in light of the President's decisions of September 26. In attendance were Attorney General John Mitchell, Secretary Laird, Undersecretary Elliot Richardson, Henry Kissinger, Director of Center Intelligence Richard Helms, John Ehrlichman, Kenneth BeLieu, Ambassador McClintock, Egil Krogh, Colonel Alexander Haig, and Richard Allen. A consensus was achieved that the basic issue in the hearings was the confrontation between the Executive and the Senate over the direction of U.S. foreign policy, that there was the secondary consideration of a Democrat-controlled committee developing political issues for the 1970 campaign, and that there was very real danger that substantial damage could be done to our foreign relations with the countries involved. All present at the meeting recognized, however, that the President strongly preferred to cooperate fully with Congress; and that factor should operate unless there was clear danger of damage to foreign relations. The President's guidance was further clarified in the meeting. While the CIA, for instance, had been exempted from testifying on Laos, it had to be decided how far other agency representatives should testify as to CIA activities. And while the President had prohibited the providing of contingency plans, the subcommittee already had a number of contingency plans, and a blanket denial would look rather embarrassing. At this meeting it was established that rather than have witnesses invoke executive privilege, they would, when confronted with requests falling within the Presidential prohibitions, simply request that they be permitted to refer the question back to their agency.

A procedure for dealing with the many requests still coming from the subcommittee staff for material falling within the prohibitions was developed. Under this principle, agencies were instructed that where such material could well result in damage to U.S. foreign relations if given to the subcommittee, they were to deny the material for administrative reasons and, while taking all deliberate time, refer the matter to ever-higher levels for decision until, after weeks or months of such administrative action, the matter would go to the President for a final determination on executive privilege. In the meantime, of course, the subcommittee would not have the information. The participants also took note of the intention of the subcommittee staff to hold press briefings after every day's hearings. It was further decided in this meeting that rather than deny the discussion of intelligence matters, this restriction would be changed to allow the Directors of the CIA, the National Security Agency, and the Defense Intelligence Agency to make themselves available to the subcommittee for testimony under special security protection while maintaining the prohibition on any other employees of those agencies testifying.

## SYMINGTON MEETS THE PRESIDENT

After the first day of hearings on September 30, it became evident that there was trouble. Accordingly, on October 1, the President invited Senator Symington to visit with him to discuss the hearings. The meeting took place in the Oval Office. The President and Senator Symington agreed that no contingency plans or nuclear weapons deployments would be discussed in the hearings, and the President agreed to allow the Director of the Central Intelligence Agency to appear before the subcommittee to discuss matters of a sensitive intelligence nature. There was a tentative sign of relief in the executive branch but, as always, the knotty problems of interpretation lay ahead.

There were smirks in the White House when, on October 3, Tass international service highlighted Senators Fulbright and Symington for opening their inquiry into American military commitments abroad. Tass quoted Jack Anderson as disclosing in *Parade* magazine the existence of 402 large and 1,917 small bases beyond U.S. territory. The executive officials assumed that those numbers had been drawn directly from the still secret Wood-McClintock Report.[50]

At the daily interdepartmental group meeting on October 3, a troublesome breach developed between the Defense and State Departments over which was to dog the executive branch response to the hearings for the rest of the year. It arose over who should take the principal role in testifying on military operations in Laos. State in effect did not want to take the rap. The administration feared the Laos hearings more than the Philippine hearings because of the oft-stated intentions of the staff and the subcommittee members that they were "going to try to lift the lid" on American involvement in Laos.51 As Ambassador G. Mc-Murtrie Godley put it, the committee had seemed to become obsessed with a kind of reverse domino theory, whereby they were convinced that because the United States had gotten heavily involved in Vietnam, any kind of U.S. involvement in any Southeast Asia country would inexorably become "another Vietnam."

On October 7, the meeting of principals was reconvened in the White House Situation Room. The results of the President's meeting with Symington were reviewed, and the completed Philippine hearings were debriefed. The consensus was that the eight guidelines originally stipulated should be reasserted and firmly applied for the next round of hearings.

In the course of the Philippine hearings an interesting question had been raised as to whether an official testifying for the executive branch may refuse to give his personal opinion on a policy matter. The law on this, as on most aspects of executive privilege, is not definitive. A 1912 federal statute provides:

> The right of employees, individually or collectively, to petition Congress or a member of Congress, or to furnish information to either house of Congress, or to a committee or member thereof, may not be interfered with or denied.52

It is also a misdemeanor for a witness before a Congressional committee to "refuse to answer any question pertinent to the issue under inquiry.53 Neither statute, however, deals with a case where the witness does not wish to give his opinion. The White House group directed that executive branch witnesses should not give their personal opinions on matters of executive policy. The Department of State objected to this interpretation, and said that the law required them to instruct their witnesses to give their personal opinions. The Justice Department, however, disputed that interpretation; and the final ruling of the White House meeting was that there was to be no personal opinion given in testimony.

On October 13, the New York *Times* printed an article reporting on the four days of closed-door hearings held by the Symington subcommittee.

> Information obtained by the subcommittee was said to show that the United States had to underwrite at least part of the cost of maintaining Philippine troops in Vietnam and to increase its military assistance to the Manila Government.

One Senator, not named, was quoted in the article as saying, "Do we tell ourselves and the world that they are mercenaries?"54 This leak appeared to the

White House to be a confirmation of its fear that the subcommittee was going to be used as a major forum of attack against the administration's Vietnam policy. The next day an article appeared describing the intention of the members of the subcommittee as being to force a public acknowledgment of the American operations in Laos.[55]

On October 10, Senator Symington informed the State Department of his intention to begin hearings on Thailand a month later, and requested a list of individuals to be returned from Thailand to testify.

At the interdepartmental group meeting of October 15, one of the major witnesses from the Philippine hearings, Mr. Robert E. Usher, the Philippine Desk Officer, recounted to the future witnesses some of the lessons derived from the experience of his testimony (an experience that McClintock referred to as "The Fall of the House of Usher"). He warned that the subcommittee confronted witnesses with leaked newspaper accounts and asked them to confirm the substance of these articles for the public record. This put them in the very difficult position of not being able to deny such leaks and therefore assisting in the unintended declassification of the sensitive material.

On October 16, the level of executive paranoia was driven still higher by a leak in the Washington *Post* quoting "sources close to the Symington subcommittee" in disclosing that the administration wanted to prevent the subcommittee from disclosing U.S. support of PHILCAG (the Philippine contingent in Vietnam) before the Philippine election.[56]

During this period difficulties again developed between the State and Defense Departments over the conduct of the hearings. The State Department had been unpleasantly surprised at the rough handling it had received in the Philippine hearings and, concluding that Symington was really out for blood, had decided that the Defense Department should take the leading role in the Laos hearings. Secretary Laird refused to allow a Defense Department principal to do so. State believed that Defense wanted to have it take all of the heat. The White House knew that Symington wished to develop the theme that military presence per se draws the U.S. into commitments, and therefore it was thought important to emphasize the administration's policy that the country team was always subordinate to the ambassador. State was therefore directed to have Ambassador William Sullivan, formerly Ambassador to Laos, take the leading role in the hearings, with junior officers from the military permitted to testify under him.

On October 17, a meeting of the White House group of principals, chaired by John Ehrlichman, was again convened in the Situation Room. At this meeting it was agreed that the "fig leaf" of silence on U.S. activities in Laos was still important vis-à-vis the Soviets, and therefore there should be no public acknowledgment through the hearings. It was agreed that while leaks from the subcommittee were probably inevitable, they were not nearly so damaging as pronouncements backed by the authority of a government witness and confirmed on the record. It was further agreed that Ambassador Sullivan would be the leading witness with Defense Department witnesses in support, and would take the leading role in insuring that the testimony was fully censored before publication by the subcommittee.

Note was also taken at the meeting of yet another leak, suspected by some to have come from the subcommittee, that appeared that morning in Jack Anderson's column in the Washington *Post*, quoting secret documents from the Military Advisory Group in Taiwan. The subcommittee staff members were believed to have had access to those documents, and with no further proof many in the executive branch jumped to the conclusion that they had leaked the material.[57]

## LEAKS CONTINUED

Paranoia rose to a fever pitch when, on each of the next two days before the hearings began on October 20, the Washington *Post* carried stories drawing on classified information regarding numbers of CIA personnel in Laos and bombing sortie rates that, with no further evidence, were immediately ascribed to the subcommittee by the executive branch officials.[58] The day that the hearings opened, the *Post* quoted Senator Symington as saying that he and his staff "have become convinced that the secrecy surrounding our relations with that country has gone on far too long." He stated that it was a travesty to deny that Americans were participating in the fighting in Laos.[59]

The first three days of the hearings on Laos seemed to confirm the worst fears of executive officials. On the morning of the third day the *Post* printed a story reporting that the executive sessions had revealed that "The CIA is said to employ Green Berets on detached duty to lead some Lao units."[60] No one questioned where the leak may have come from. The same day the Washington *News* editorialized:

Despite the administration's wishes, the subcommittee's findings will be published (or leaked) fairly soon. They will show that the United States increased military aid to Manila and is paying part of the cost of maintaining the Filipino battalion in Vietnam.[61]

In the meantime negotiations were being carried on between Symington and Ambassador McClintock on the declassification of the Philippine transcript. A deal was struck whereby Symington agreed to delay the publication of the transcript until after the Philippine elections (November 11), in return for the State Department agreeing to make no substantial cuts in the transcript. Symington rubbed in a little salt by announcing his deal on the floor of the Senate on

October 23.[62] That also was the only way the White House found out about the deal.

On October 26 and 27 the New York *Times* ran long articles revealing details of the "secret war in Laos." Although the datelines on these articles were Vientiane, and most of the information probably could have been gathered by an enterprising reporter there, many executive officials nevertheless ascribed the stories to further leaks from the subcommittee.[63]

In reviewing the transcript of the Philippine hearings that had finally been approved by the State Department for publication, it was realized that it included confirmation by officials of the executive branch that the United States was paying the bill for the Philippine, Korean, and Thai contingents in Vietnam and also contained remarks uncomplimentary to the Philippine government by executive branch officials. Since the transcript was to be released on November 11, with Senator Symington holding a press conference, it was decided by the White House to preempt him and have the State Department announce, in the course of its press briefings, the facts that were to be revealed in the published hearings. This the State Department refused to do, because it was feared that Symington would be extremely upset at being thus upstaged. At the same time Senator Fulbright held a confidential background session for the press on October 28 at the Capitol, and released details drawn from the executive hearings on the extent of U.S. involvement in Laos, including the fact that the United States was spending some $150 million a year to arm and support 36,000 Meo tribesmen in Laos, that the CIA was running the war, and that the Meo tribesmen were being supported by U.S. Air Force operations based in Thailand. The next day, articles appeared in the Washington *Post* and the New York *Times* revealing this material.[64]

In the meantime the State Department, fearing the reaction of the Philippine government to the publication of the transcript, requested permission from the subcommittee to show a copy of the transcript to President Ferdinand Marcos pior to its publication. The subcommittee adamantly refused to allow the transcript to be shown to Marcos before its press conference on November 13, and the State Department, unbeknown to the White House, acquiesced.


## THE TURNING POINT


On October 30, Senator Symington called Secretary Laird's assistant and apologized for Senator Fulbright's release of the classified information that had appeared in the papers the previous day. Symington then called Ambassador McClintock and warned him that unless the State Department was liberal in its declassification of the Laos transcript, Senator Fulbright would hold his own public hearings on Laos to get it on the record. In the same telephone call

Symington expressed his determination to see that the figures on support to the Philippine battalion were included in the published report. This subsequently led to an open breach between the White House and the State Department when the latter agreed to the declassification despite being directed emphatically to the contrary by the White House. On this date the President himself became convinced that serious damage could well result from a continuation of the policy of cooperation. This decision was occasioned by the receipt of a dramatic cable from the U.S. Ambassador in the Philippines, Henry Byroade, embodying his reaction to reading the full transcripts for the first time. He warned in great detail that the impact of the publication of hearings in their present form would be an unmitigated disaster for U.S. interests in the Philippines and for the future of U.S.-Philippine relations.

The President and the White House staff's hostility to the Foreign Relations Committee was now very high, and secondarily there was great resentment at the unwillingness of the State Department to stand up to the committee over the declassification of the transcripts. The White House felt that the sanctity of confidential agreements with all governments and U.S. ability to enter into them in the future were directly threatened.

Disturbing reports arrived at the same time from Bangkok that the Thai government was beginning a serious review of its relations with the United States because of what the Bangkok *Post* described as the pressure being generated by some Senators away from honoring commitments under SEATO.[65]

On October 30, Secretary Rogers testified for three and a half hours in closed session before the full Foreign Relations Committee. In an effort to ameliorate some of the impact of the Laos hearings, he acknowledged to the press immediately following the hearings that U.S. involvement in the "secret war" was common knowledge. He also pointed out that Congress was quite familiar with developments in Laos. This latter statement was disputed by Fulbright, who met separately with the press and denied that Congress had known what was going on.[66] Rogers was also lashed by Fulbright about the administration's continued refusal to provide him with a copy of the "Taksin Plan." The following day the Department of State issued a statement backing Rogers' position, pointing out that since 1963 Congress had been briefed fully on the situation developing in Laos and that all members who had any interest were well aware of U.S. activities.[67]

The White House requested the Central Intelligence Agency to examine its records of briefings in the Senate since 1963. According to the CIA records, 67 members of the Senate had been fully briefed on a classified basis regarding CIA activities in Laos. Some of these briefings had been in committees and subcommittees, and others had been individual ones requested by members.

On October 31, a predictable result of the dropping of the "fig leaf" took place when a note was delivered from the Soviet Foreign Minister to the U.S. government protesting U.S. military intervention in Laos.

On the evening of November 4, Secretary Rogers spoke with the President about the hearings; and while the President expressed his deep concern about them, he agreed to Rogers' urging that the figures for U.S. support to PHILCAG be made public. That same day the State Department delivered 48 sensitive papers concerning U.S. activities in Thailand and Thai activities in Vietnam to the subcommittee in preparation for the Thai hearings, which were to run November 10-14.

The next day, while Secretary Rogers made a final review of the Philippine and Laos transcripts, the interdepartmental group met to instruct witnesses and review potential problems. White House representatives again urged the State Department to preempt the publicity following the appearance of the PHILCAG information when the transcript would be released on November 12—again in vain.

The Thai government continued to indicate that it would be very upset if the hearings produced inordinate publicity about U.S. support arrangements for Thai troops in South Vietnam. It was pointed out to them, however, that they themselves had been fairly open about putting those arrangements on the public record in Thailand through numerous newspaper articles and government press conferences.

On November 7, Senator Symington informed the Defense Department that hearings would begin on Taiwan on November 24. On the same day Secretary Laird, unknown to the White House, finally yielded to committee demands for the "Taksin Plan," sending copies to the Foreign Relations Committee. Not unexpectedly, Senator Fulbright, upon reviewing it, immediately announced to the press that he considered it a U.S. commitment and that it should have been submitted to the Senate as a treaty.[68]

The opening hearing on Thailand on November 10 turned out to be the most tempestuous to that date. As instructed, the State Department witnesses refused to discuss contingency plans; and under heated cross-examination, the confidential meeting between Senator Symington and the President was revealed, to the surprise of many present, not the least being Senator Symington, who had not mentioned the meeting to Fulbright. Under further pressure, Ambassador McClintock invoked executive privilege for the first time.

## THE EXECUTIVE DIGS IN

On November 10, at the other end of Pennsylvania Avenue, the President decided that more effective measures were needed to limit the damage of the hearings. He directed the establishment of a formal White House Working Group, making it responsible for the formulation and enforcement of policy guidelines for all agencies with regard to the Symington hearings. There was subsequently much distress at the White House when the day's events in the hearings were recounted, and the first meeting of the White House Working Group was hastily called for the next morning.

The meeting was chaired by John Ehrlichman and attended by Kissinger, BeLieu, Haig, Krogh, Assistant Secretary of State Marshall Green, and NSC staff. The President's extreme unhappiness with the course of the hearings was reported, and his wish reiterated that the State Department must be prepared to take the full burden of conducting the testimony of all executive branch witnesses and insuring that the damage would be limited. It was pointed out that the interdepartmental group at State charged with this was to report directly to the White House Working Group, and that the Secretary of State did not make final decisions in this matter. Procedures for instructing witnesses in declining to discuss matters were agreed to, and it was emphasized that under no circumstances was executive privilege to be invoked or referred to by witnesses in so declining. They were to say simply that they had been instructed by the Secretary of State not to discuss those matters, and that the committee members should take the questions up with the Secretary.

The State Department's interpretation that the declassifying of transcripts was a matter for negotiation and joint agreement with the committee was emphatically refuted. The President's firm belief that this was an executive branch prerogative and not a subject for deals or compromise was reiterated. For the third time State was directed to make public the fact of U.S. support for the Philippine, Thai, and Korean contingents in Vietnam in order to preempt Senator Symington's headlines. For the third time there was no result.

It was further decided that it was impossible for Ambassador McClintock to act as chairman of the interdepartmental group and liaison with the subcommittee, since he was about to be nominated by the President to another embassy and thus was in a vulnerable position to confront the committee over Symington subcommittee matters. Therefore, he should be replaced.

There was further grinding of White House teeth on November 11, when the Baltimore *Sun* printed an article, quoting "subcommittee sources," disclosing that some of the information that will remain classified in the Philippine transcript

> ...concerns exploitation of U.S. servicemen in the areas surrounding Clark Air Force Base and the theft of equipment from the installation... there is an organized ring of thieves operating at the base ...said one highly placed source who said the report detailed the operation.... "Someday all of this is going to come out."[69]

And the following day an article appeared in the Washington *Post* discussing reconnaissance over mainland China, a subject that was discussed in the hearings on November 12.[70] During this period the Department of State carefully prepared the Thais for coming jolts through successive briefings of the Thai Ambassador in Washington and Foreign Ministry officials in Bangkok.

On November 14, Ambassador McClintock was replaced as chairman of the interdepartmental group by John Stevenson, the legal adviser to the State Department, who chaired his first meeting on November 18, in preparation for the Symington hearings on Taiwan that were to commence November 24.

In conjunction with the Thai hearings the subcommittee staff had repeatedly requested a copy of a National Security Council study, "Foreign Internal Defense Policy," that had been completed earlier in the year. The Department of State concluded that this paper would only be used against the administration if it were turned over to the subcommittee, and in any case the White House Working Group was adamant that no NSC documents whatsoever be given to the committee. The policy of "administrative denial" was therefore applied, without any suggestion that executive privilege was being invoked. The State Department took the position that any members of the subcommittee would be briefed on this subject upon request, but not staff, and no documents would be turned over. Despite the keen staff interest, the matter was never escalated to the members of the subcommittee itself.

On November 19, the President evidenced his growing unhappiness in a statement on the occasion of the signature of the National Science Foundation Act. In reaffirming his March 24 memorandum restricting executive privilege, he added a major qualification:

> At the same time there must be some limits on what information can be reported. Voluminous reporting of detailed day-to-day activities of an agency can be unduly burdensome without providing any significant assistance to the Congress in discharging its legislative responsibilities. More importantly, premature disclosure of information can seriously impair the ability of executive branch agencies to carry out effectively their responsibilities...I think that the Congress and the executive branch agencies appreciate the importance of striking a working balance between the needs of Congress for information and those of the agencies for candid and free communication in carrying out their responsibilities. I interpret statutory provisions to keep the Congress fully and currently informed with respect to all of the activities of executive branch agencies and the intent of Congress in enacting such legislation to be consistent with the proper division of powers between the Congress and the executive branch.[71]

On November 18, after a delay caused by a last-minute struggle over cost figures on PHILCAG, the Symington subcommittee released the Philippine testimony. As expected, it resulted in headlines about the "mercenary" issue of the United States paying the support costs for the Philippine unit in Vietnam. All of the major disputes between the White House and State Department over what could or could not be included had been resolved in favor of publication. Detailed costs per sortie or air strike, and a complete breakdown of payment amounts to the Philippines for their construction battalion in Vietnam, were highlighted.

Moreover, Senator Fulbright used the occasion to launch a major attack on the administration's Vietnam policy:

> This seems to me to be the ultimate in corruption for us to make deals like this in pursuit of an illusory policy all designed to prove to the world that we have great support in Vietnam which we do not have at all....We pay Korea and Thailand exorbitant prices for what they furnish, and the trouble is you have here a built-in resistance to any ending of the war. They do not want the war to end, I would think, with the kind of income they are getting for these troops.

The Washington *Post* headlined its story "Panel Told of Secret Filipino Pay"; The New York *Times* front-paged "U.S. Paid 39-Million To the Philippines for a Vietnam Unit"; the Baltimore *Sun* concentrated on another revelation, headlining "U.S. Airmen Anti-Huk Effort in Philippines"; the Washington *Star* headlined "U.S. Paid Its Allies for Vietnam Units Senators are Told." The articles pointed out that the tone throughout the hearings was one of suspicion and hostility toward the executive branch: "A prosecuting attorney's approach was often evident."[72]

## REACTION ABROAD

The reactions of the Philippine, Thai, and Korean governments were predictable and immediate. They were outraged at the characterization of their soldiers as mercenaries, and hinted that if the U.S. government was so contemptuous of those forces in South Vietnam, they might be withdrawn in the very near future.

The reaction in the White House to these headlines was equally predictable and more immediate. The White House was determined that from now on, it must deal with the subcommittee on the basis of all-out confrontation, and that this kind of onslaught against the administration's relations abroad, and specifically against its Vietnam policy, could not be permitted to happen again.

The following day the Communist Pathet Lao's clandestine English-language radio gleefully broadcast the U.S. newspaper accounts of U.S. clandestine activities.[73]

The revelations and charges by the Symington subcommittee created a storm in Manila. The President's office issued a statement that said: "The Philippines has received no fee nor payments of any kind in support of the PHILCAG or its personnel, nor has there been any grant given in consideration of sending the PHILCAG to Vietnam." In the Philippine Congress, the House majority leader declared: "In view of these grave distortions and slanderous misrepresentations, it is about time we considered dismantling U.S. military bases in the Philippines." And President Marcos, after meeting with the Foreign Policy Council, announced his intention to withdraw the Philippine battalion from Vietnam.[74]

The Symington subcommittee had drawn its first blood.

The next meeting of the White House Working Group, on November 21, had something of an atmosphere of a combat command post. New instructions to witnesses were agreed to, warning all witnesses that they were being pitted against highly knowledgeable and intelligent men basically hostile toward the administration's policies; and while they were to maintain their composure and give all due respect, they were to consider themselves in a directly adversary relationship. Responses to be used in avoiding the answering of questions on prohibited subjects, such as nuclear deployments, contingency plans, and National Security Council documents, were refined. The NSC staff quoted Thomas Jefferson: "that the Executive ought to communicate such papers as the public good would permit, and ought to refuse those, the disclosure of which would injure the public; consequently were to exercise a discretion."

In preparing for the Taiwan hearings, there were several obvious problems that had to be dealt with. Because the head of the Military Assistance Group in Taiwan, Major General Richard G. Ciccolella, was particularly outspoken and several documents in which uninhibited views were revealed had been leaked, there was no objection raised when General Ciccolella was advised to go immediately into Walter Reed Hospital for three weeks to recuperate from a back operation, thus causing him to miss the hearings.

In a conversation with John Stevenson, Senator Symington advised the executive branch that they should deal directly with him and not with Senator Fulbright. He had been very unhappy over the hearing on November 17 which Senator Fulbright had taken over and turned into a full committee hearing. He then expressed his determination to have the executive branch testify on nuclear weapons deployments and, further, stated that he would not accept the deletion from the printed record of the figures for U.S. bombing in northern Laos.

The hearings were held on November 24-26, and from the outset the atmosphere was strained. As instructed, Ambassador Walter P. McConaughy declined to discuss intelligence matters, deferring to the agency directors. This caused an immediate uproar, with Senator Fulbright threatening to make an immediate public statement on the matter and to retaliate by refusing to confirm any more ambassadors.

Resentment increased again when, on November 26, the Washington *Post* printed a story revealing that Senator Fulbright had "told the Senate that the surveillance flights over China had been quietly suspended in March 1968, and then resumed the following October. He noted that shortly after the resumption of spy flights the Communist Chinese reportedly shot down a U.S. airplane." With no further evidence, it was immediately concluded that the information came from the subcommittee staff, who had been fully briefed on the subject matter during their visit to Taiwan.[75]

On December 1, the New York *Times* printed an article, quoting "informed Congressional sources," revealing that "it had cost the United States about $1 billion to obtain the deployment of a Thai division to fight in South Vietnam." The article contained much detail that seemed to have been drawn from the classified transcript of the Symington hearings on Thailand.[76]

Reports reached Washington the next day that Foreign Minister Thanat Khoman and the Thai government were so furious that they were seriously considering withdrawing from SEATO. Meanwhile, the Philippine press was filled with commentary urging abrogation of the base agreements with the United States, quoting Fulbright to show that the bases were not in the Philippine interest but, rather, served only American purposes (and the price therefore should be considerably raised) and variously lamenting the disloyalty of the United States to her small allies.

On December 6, the Washington *Star* revealed that USIA had been running the Thai government counter-insurgency propaganda operations. Since this had been a major point of discussion in the Symington hearings, the executive branch added this to its growing list of subcommittee sins.[77]

The American Ambassador in the Philippines, Henry Byroade, attempted to calm the Filipinos in a hard-hitting speech that did not endear him to the Foreign Relations Committee chairman. He said that the Senate testimony

> ...included some statements about the Philippines which I agree were unfortunate and uncomplimentary. But I ask you to consider the source....They were made by but two out of 535 members of our Congress....These remarks...put the Philippines in a distinguished company which includes past American Presidents, Secretaries of State and a number of other world leaders.[78]

In his televised press conference on December 8, the President took the opportunity to do some damage limitation himself. In response to a question about U.S. payment for Thai and Korean troops in Vietnam, he responded:

> ...with regard to the billion dollars that allegedly has been paid to
> Thailand, the amount is, of course, far less than that. But quite can-
> didly, yes, the United States is subsidizing the Thai troops. We also
> are subsidizing the South Korean troops. We are doing exactly what
> we did in Western Europe immediately after World War II when we
> subsidized virtually all of Western Europe, due to the fact that they
> could not maintain forces themselves for their own defense. These
> are newly developing countries; they are unable to maintain their
> forces for their defense, and therefore we think that subsidy is cor-
> rect. And I could only say this: It seems to me it makes a great deal
> of sense. The Thais are in Vietnam as volunteers, and if they are
> willing to go there as volunteers I would much rather pay out some
> money to have them there than to have American men fighting there
> in their place.[79]

On December 12, the Peking-based insurgent radio "Voice of the People of Thailand" delightedly broadcast an article castigating the Thai and the U.S. governments for their secret military deal brought to light by the U.S. Senate.[80]

In the meantime, the negotiations between the State Department and the
subcommittee staff on the declassification of the Laos testimony had reached a
deadlock. Senator Fulbright threatened to delay the Defense Appropriations
Bill, in an attempt to force a relaxation of the executive branch position. "Protesting that the 'cloak of secrecy' was making a 'mockery of the power of Congress,'" he proposed a filibuster when the defense bill reached the floor later in
December.[81]

On December 13, the Hanoi Domestic Service broadcast a commentary on
"human traitor Nixon buying Thai blood for war." The broadcast dwelt upon
the Congressional revelations of the $1 billion spent for a five-year agreement to
get 10,000 Thai troops to fight in Vietnam along with those of South Korea,
Australia, New Zealand, and the Philippines.[82] The same day in Thailand, the
Bangkok *World* published an article recommending withdrawal of the Thai
troops from Vietnam, the imposing of rent on the bases used by the United
States in Thailand, and the imposition of import duties on U.S. goods.

Two days later the Symington hearings achieved their second concrete
result with the passage of the Cooper-Mansfield amendment to the Military
Appropriations Bill. The amendment had been introduced in various forms since
the preceding summer, and sought to prohibit U.S. involvement in Laos or Thailand. The NSC staff had opposed the amendment, not because it was contemplated to involve U.S. ground forces in either country, but because it opposed
signaling the North Vietnamese that we would under any circumstances deny
ourselves any military option in Southeast Asia. Through the maneuvering of

executive lobbyists and supporters in the Senate, the amendment had been successfully sidetracked until December 15. At that time Kissinger was preoccupied on other matters, and the NSC staff member covering the problem was out of the country. Since both Secretary Laird and Secretary Rogers favored the amendment, the only signals received by the administration's leaders in the Senate were "no opposition." Accordingly this became the executive branch position on the original version, which read as follows:

> Section 643. None of the funds appropriated by this act shall be used for the support of local forces in Laos or Thailand except to provide supplies, material equipment, and facilities, including maintenance thereof, or to provide training for such local forces.

The final version passed by a vote of 73-17 after it had been modified by Senator Frank Church to read as follows:

> Section 643. In line with the expressed intention of the President of the United States, none of the funds appropriated by this act shall be used to finance the introduction of American ground combat troops into Laos or Thailand.[83]

Making the best of it, the White House the next day endorsed the Senate resolution after the weekly Tuesday morning Republican Congressional leadership meeting with the President. Press Secretary Ronald Ziegler said the White House regarded the prohibition as an "endorsement" rather than a curbing of administration policy.[84]

The effect of passage of the amendment was again predictable and immediate in Bangkok. The Bangkok *World* headlined "Senate Limits U.S. Troop Aid to Thailand," and the Bangkok *Post* headlined "U.S. Bars Combat Troops from Thailand, Laos."

## THE LAOS TRANSCRIPT

Of special concern in the declassification of all of the transcripts was the protection of the U.S. Ambassadors' frank testimony, disclosure of which would compromise their future dealings with the countries concerned. While Symington had given firm assurances that he would cooperate in withholding such testimony from publication, getting agreement on what constituted that kind of material proved to be very difficult.

On December 21, the Peking-based insurgent radio "Voice of the People of Thailand" revealed that the United States was giving the Thanom government a battalion of Hawk antiaircraft missiles in exchange for the Queen Cobra Regiment being sent to Vietnam to act as U.S. mercenaries. Without any further evidence, this too was added to the leaks blamed upon the subcommittee.[85]

The White House made some New Year's resolutions of its own on January 1, after reading several headlines in the morning papers, such as that in the Chicago *Tribune*—"Senate Leak Hurt U.S.-Asian Ties"—in which "sources" in Southeast Asia were quoted giving evidence of injury to the future of U.S. relations in that area as a result of the unilateral declassification of material from the hearings of the Symington subcommittee and the personal elaborations of some of the committee members.[86]

The next day there were many questions at the State Department's daily briefing about the status of the Lao and Thai transcripts. The State Department responded that the Laos transcript had been completed and returned some time ago to the committee, but the Thai transcript was still under review. It was not pointed out that the subcommittee had still not accepted the deletions made by State in the Laos transcript.

On January 4, Vice-President Agnew was in Bangkok, where Thai leaders expressed their concern over the impact of the Symington hearings. Agnew responded to the Thai leaders, "Some of the people back home are so anxious to make friends of our enemies that sometimes they seem ready to make enemies of our friends."[87]

In preparation for the Japan hearings scheduled for January 26, a further refinement of instructions for the avoidance of the executive privilege nettle were given to prospective witnesses. When asked to discuss the prohibited subjects, such as nuclear weapons, contingency plans, or NSC documents, the witnesses were told to respond:

> I have been instructed by my department not to deal with this matter.

If pressed, he was then to respond:

> If you wish to pursue the subject I shall be pleased to refer it to my department.

When asked if he was invoking executive privilege, he was to respond:

> Under the President's directive of March, 1969, a decision to invoke executive privilege requires a specific Presidential determination. I am merely informing you that under my department's regulations no officer may disclose classified information, even to a congressional committee, without being authorized to do so. I have been so authorized with respect to this particular item.

When asked who gave him such instructions, he was requested to respond:

> I have received my instructions on behalf of the head of my department.

If pressed, he was then to respond:

> That question concerns the internal workings of the executive branch. I am not authorized to discuss it.

Meanwhile, as the deadlock over the Laos transcript continued, Senator Fulbright continued to read newspaper accounts of the U.S. activities in Laos into the record and to endorse them as "almost exactly the same type of material...which the Department is refusing to clear for publication in the committee's hearings...."[88]

On January 21, Ehrlichman chaired another meeting of the White House Working Group. It was agreed that John Stevenson would attempt to reach agreement with Senator Symington on reaffirmation of the prohibition on the discussion of nuclear weapons deployments, contingency plans, and other matters. He was also to reaffirm that intelligence operations, matters under active policy review, and other sensitive subjects were to be treated under special security procedures, with only one transcript to be held by the executive branch.

The following day, Stevenson met with Senator Symington and his staff. Symington refused to accept the restriction on nuclear weapons testimony, denying that he had reached any such agreement with the President. While objecting to the special restrictions for ambassadors testifying on intelligence matters, Symington reluctantly agreed to that procedure. As to the discussion of contingency and operational military plans, Symington indicated that he would construe the meaning of the term very narrowly. He then said casually that of course while he would abide by these ground rules, he could not vouch for what other Senators might ask.

The hearings on Japan and Okinawa began on January 26, with Undersecretary Johnson as the principal witness, and continued through January 29. Johnson had previously spoken with Senators Mansfield, Fulbright, and Symington on matters of a sensitive nature that he did not want pressed. To the surprise of the skeptics in the White House, the hearings went relatively smoothly and in a pleasant atmosphere. On the second day of the hearings, however, the newspapers applied further salt to the executive wounds. The Washington News disclosed that U.S. air missions into Laos were up 100 percent over the year before, and that some days as many as 750 bombing sorties were flown from the seven bases in Thailand. It was immediately concluded that the leak came directly from the top-secret Laos transcript still being negotiated. The Post reported Senator Mansfield as threatening that although a Senate committee did not

ordinarily take it upon itself to release secret transcripts, "it has been done....
Either you get agreement or the Congress, on its own, will have to assume the
responsibility by releasing those parts which will not do damage to national
security."[89]

The hearings, meanwhile, were getting attention in some odd places. On
January 29, a Bulgarian broadcast in English recounted an article by Wilfred
Burchett detailing the exposés of U.S. activities in Southeast Asia brought
about by the Symington subcommittee hearings.[90]

In a news conference on January 31, the President responded to a question
about Senator Mansfield's threat to unilaterally declassify the Laos transcript
and about disclosing more of U.S. involvement in Laos by saying:

> I answered that same question in my press conference approxi-
> mately a month ago in this room, and I will not go beyond that
> answer at this point except to say that the North Vietnamese have
> 50,000 troops in Laos and thereby threaten the survival of Laos. Our
> activities there are solely for the purpose of seeing that the Laotian
> Government which was set up by the Laotian accords and—at their
> request for the purpose of seeing that they are not overwhelmed by
> the North Vietnamese and other communist forces.[91]

On February 4, Fulbright tried another psychological approach. He said
that high administration officials had told his committee that Laos "is even more
important than Vietnam." Further, American military involvement was deepen-
ing to the point where the United States "may soon have to decide whether to
go all the way in Laos—that is to make it another Vietnam—or to get out."
The State Department still remained adamant, however, at White House insistence, in its position on the deletions from the Laos transcripts.[92]

On February 5, the "Voice of the People of Thailand" radio in Peking
quoted an AP dispatch dated January 28, revealing that the United States was
paying for, equipping, and training 12,000 Thai mercenaries fighting in Laos.[93]

Four days later, a member of the Foreign Relations Committee, Senator
Albert Gore, charged that the committee had gathered ample evidence that the
U.S. participation in the war in Laos had been "secretly but greatly escalated."
He spoke on the basis of the Symington hearings, some of which he had attended, and declared that "I would not rule out the possibility of exercising my
prerogative as a senator to discuss the hearing record on the floor." It was noted
that in 1968, during an argument over secret hearings on the Gulf of Tonkin incident, Senator Wayne Morse had unilaterally made public classified messages
and documents and had read them into the record.[94]

On February 11, the Peking Domestic Service joined in denouncing U.S.
military bases abroad, noting that the growing pressure on the U.S. domestic
scene for withdrawal was echoed around the world, where

...anti-U.S. demonstrations have erupted one after another. Angry shouts of "down with U.S. imperialism!" and "Yankee go home!" are resounding in the air and U.S. aggressors are becoming rats running across streets with everyone yelling: "Kill them"....U.S. imperialist number two chieftain Spiro Agnew, the "god of plague and war," who recently went to the Asian and Pacific region to carry out plots, has hurried back to America in utter disgrace amidst the anti-U.S. waves whipped up by the masses of people....Under the strong opposition of the world people as well as the American people, U.S. imperialism put on a display of trickery in 1969 by announcing with crocodile tears that it was prepared to consolidate, close down, or reduce the number of its overseas military [bases]. This, however, is an utterly misleading statement. These military bases which U.S. imperialism announced it would close down are either obsolete or those which U.S. imperialism is forced to withdraw.[95]

A development that the Executive did nothing to thwart was the sudden growth of open hostility between the Armed Services Committee and the Foreign Relations Committee over what was perceived by Senators John Stennis, Margaret Chase Smith, Henry Jackson, and Peter Dominick as a direct encroachment of the Symington subcommittee upon the jurisdiction of the Armed Services Committee. The bitterness was of course related not only to the Symington hearings but also to the role of the Foreign Relations Committee in leading the attack on the ABM system the previous summer and again in 1970, as well as its relentless attacks upon the administration's policy in Vietnam. Several members of the Armed Services Committee began to threaten to introduce a resolution requesting investigation of those committees that exceed their jurisdiction.[96]

## THIRD PINCUS AND PAUL TRIP

Early in February the State Department was informed that the subcommittee staff would undertake an extensive trip to the NATO area to prepare for hearings on NATO and on nuclear weapons deployments. The department, as usual, prepared instructions for the embassies to be visited, outlining the intentions of the staff and the subject matter of their interest, and advising complete openness and cooperation. This time, however, the White House insisted on clearance of the cable and substantially revised it to warn the posts that they could expect trouble and that they should err on the side of caution in the withholding of information from the staff. The specific restrictions formulated by the White House Working Group and the State Department interdepartmental group were reiterated as to the kinds of documents and information that should not be provided, and that when any doubt existed, the matter was to be referred back to Washington.

The White House was very concerned about the effects of the Symington subcommittee upon the NATO alliance. It was determined not to permit the process that took place in the Far East investigations to be repeated in NATO. Accordingly, the White House dispatched a staff member to all of the military and embassy posts that the Symington staff would be visiting. He was instructed to brief the senior American officials on the procedures used by the staff and by the subcommittee, and the dangers entailed, and to advise them to take appropriate measures to limit potential damage while providing all information that the subcommittee was legitimately entitled to. State was not informed of this mission for fear that it would tell the committee.

On February 3, Senator Symington wrote to the Secretary of State, pointing out the many newspaper accounts of U.S. activities in Laos, suggesting that this was presenting a misleading picture to the American people, and urging that the consideration for preserving the form of the 1962 accords should be rejected in favor of the American public's right to know what was going on. On February 16, Symington took the same arguments to the floor of the Senate.

The following day, the White House Working Group resolved several sticky issues that were expected to appear in the Korean hearings the following week. The first involved charges that had been made against the Korean divisions in Vietnam of brutality against the South Vietnamese civilians. It was decided to take this matter head-on and explain how such reports had been handled. Copies of the reports on such allegations prepared by outside research groups, the leaking of which had recently precipitated publicity, were not to be given to the subcommittee. It was further decided that executive witnesses should not be required to testify on reports prepared by nongovernmental groups.

On February 16, Senator Symington engaged in a little psychological warfare against the executive restrictions upon testimony concerning nuclear weapons deployments. He told the Senate:

> Recently I have received some extraordinarily disturbing information, which to the best of my knowledge was not known to any member of the Senate, and which could have major impact, not only on our future relationship with various countries—including the other superpower—but also on our national security.

He indicated this had to do with the deployment of U.S. nuclear weapons overseas, but neither the Joint Congressional Committee on Atomic Energy nor the State Department nor the Defense Department professed to know what he was talking about.[97]

Further goading the executive branch, Symington gave an interview to his hometown newspaper, the St. Louis *Post-Dispatch*, in which he declared that the United States could abandon well over half of its 429 major military bases abroad, that the defense budget could be cut by one-fourth, that the "wrong people" were making vital decisions on American foreign and defense policy, and that "the place that is least important to us probably is the Far East."[98]

There was much exchanging of I-told-you-so's in the White House when, on February 18, the anti-American riots that had developed with the deterioration of U.S. relations with the Philippines following the Symington revelations, culminated in a mob of 2,000 Filipino youths attaching the U.S. Embassy with stones and fire bombs.[99]

On February 20, the White House Working Group resolved a long-standing problem resulting from the Symington request of the previous summer for a memorandum between President Kennedy and Australian Foreign Minister Sir Garfield Barwick regarding the ANZUS agreement. The State Department had responded to persistent requests from Senator Symington by urging the White House to allow the memorandum to be transmitted. The White House Working Group finally decided, however, that as a government-to-government document and a Presidential document, it was not appropriate to provide to the committee; but since the substance of the memorandum was, if anything, helpful to the administration case, a separate memorandum outlining the complete substance of the actual document should be provided to the committee on a classified basis. Thus the information was given but the sanctity of government-to-government exchanges was protected.

That same day, the subcommittee staff was given extensive briefings by the Department of State for its upcoming trip to the NATO area. It became apparent to the State Department briefers that the staff members intended no more tender treatment for NATO than they had given to the Asian allies.

The Korean hearings were held February 24-26 with Ambassador William J. Porter as the lead administration witness. While not containing any unforeseen surprises, they did not go as smoothly as the hearings on Japan and Okinawa. Meanwhile, Senator Symington continued his protracted conflict over the Laos transcript on the floor of the Senate.[100]

Throughout February there were daily articles in the U.S. press from correspondents in Southeast Asia that revealed more and more details of American involvement in Laos. On February 28, the Washington *Post* carried a story reporting that since Senator Symington had been unable to persuade the administration to declassify part of the Laos transcript, he had decided to put into the *Congressional Record*, with his blessings of authenticity, an article by T.D. Allman. This article recounted a number of facts that the administration was insisting remain classified in the Laos transcript. A St. Louis *Post-Dispatch* article revealed that "corruption is siphoning off rice and American money in Laos."

The details of this corruption were said to have been found by senators investigating U.S.. involvement in Laos. And the New York *News* contained the revelation that the United States was paying for several thousand Thai soldiers fighting in Laos.[101]

Still more was released by Symington on February 28 in a speech in St. Louis. He said that the United States had been "escalating heavily" its bombing around the Laos Plain of Jarres. "During some months in 1969, U.S. air attacks in that area doubled as against those of the same month in 1968 and in other months they tripled.[102]

In the meantime, in Laos, the North Vietnamese had launched their annual counterattack across the Plain of Jarres in mid-February; and by the end of the month they had retaken the Plain and the situation had returned to where it had been the previous summer. During this counterattack the U.S. Air Force had greatly increased its sortie rate, giving direct air support to the Laotian army and the irregular army of Vang Pao. The retaking of the Plain by the North Vietnamese had occurred much more quickly than had been anticipated, and there was growing concern in Washington that the North Vietnamese might not stop at the southern edge of the Plain but move toward Vientiane and toward Luang Prabang, the royal capital. For the first time in the war, U.S. B-52 strikes were called in against North Vietnamese and Pathet Lao positions. Despite numerous news reports about the B-52 strikes, Secretary Laird refused to confirm their use and implied that this was not the case in an appearance on "Meet the Press."[103]

The heightened publicity about the war in Laos brought a new surge of leaks on March 2. On the "CBS Morning News" it was reported that staff members of the Symington subcommittee had revealed to UPI that nuclear installations in Europe and in Korea were exposed and were in danger of being captured in the event of hostilities. The Symington staff had visited such sites in Korea and were given classified briefings in Europe. Also, the *Nation* magazine published an article recounting the stories about General Richard Ciccolella in Taiwan, as well as classified details of the suspension of the Formosa naval patrol and the March 1968 suspension of reconnaissance flights over China. These had all been contentious issues with the subcommittee. On the same day, on the floor of the Senate, Senator Mansfield declared that the United States was "up to our necks" in Laos and that it "cannot be camouflaged any longer." He said that U.S. bombing in Laos was heavier than it was in North Vietnam, "and that there could now be as many as 20,000 sorties a month."[104]

On March 4, the Communist Pathet Lao clandestine radio gleefully broadcast an endorsement of Senator Fulbright and Senator Mansfield's revelations in Laos.[105] The same day Senator Fulbright declared that he was "scared to death" because some unnamed executive officials had told him that Laos was more important than Vietnam. When asked at the State Department afternoon briefing whether anyone at State had frightened Senator Fulbright lately, the Department spokesman said that he did not know who had frightened the Senator.106

The next day, the Washington *Post* leaked a story that the exposed nuclear weapons about which Senator Symington had hinted the previous month were in fact storage areas for nuclear bombs, nuclear artillery pieces, and Honest John missiles in the custody of the U.S. Army's Seventh Division.

During the first week of March the Thai government changed its position on disclosure of the role of Thai bases and recommended that there was no further reason to keep secret the use of the bases in support of operations in Laos and Vietnam.

On March 6, yet another of the points at issue in declassifying the Laos transcript was made moot by the publication in the Washington *Post* of an accurate account of the death of 12 Americans at a communications facility in Laos called Phou Pha Thi. The subcommittee was of course blamed.

The White House, meanwhile, had been responding to these varied pressures by reexamining its position on public disclosure. After a National Security Council meeting on February 7, the President decided to make public the details of U.S. activities in Laos. Accordingly, after a week of drafting and redrafting by the NSC staff, a statement by the President on Laos was released from the Key Biscayne White House on the afternoon of March 6. The statement gave a historical survey of U.S. involvement in Laos, beginning with the Kennedy administration and ending with an explanation of the current facts.

> In recent days, however, there has been intense public speculation to the effect that the United States involvement in Laos has substantially increased in violation of the Geneva accords, that American ground forces are engaged in combat in Laos and that our air activity has had the effect of escalating the conflict.
>
> Because these reports are grossly inaccurate, I have concluded that our national interest will be served by putting the subject into perspective through a precise description of our current activities in Laos.
>
> These are the facts:
> —There are no American ground combat troops in Laos.
> —We have no plans for introducing ground combat forces in Laos.
> —The total number of Americans directly employed by the U.S. Government in Laos is 616. In addition, there are 424 Americans employed on contract to the Government or to Government contractors. Of these 1,040 Americans, the total number, military and civilian, engaged in a military advisory or military training capacity numbers 320. Logistics personnel number 323.
> —No American stationed in Laos has ever been killed in ground combat operations.

—U.S. personnel in Laos during the past year has not increased while during the past few months, North Vietnam has sent over 13,000 additional combat ground troops into Laos.

—When requested by the Royal Laotian Government, we have continued to provide military assistance to regular and irregular Laotian forces in the form of equipment, training and logistics. The levels of our assistance have risen in response to the growth of North Vietnamese combat activities.

—We have continued to conduct air operations. Our first priority for such operations is to interdict the continued flow of troops and supplies across Laotian territory on the Ho Chi Minh Trail. As Commander in Chief of our armed forces, I consider it my responsibility to use our air power to interdict this flow of supplies and men into South Vietnam and thereby avoid a heavy toll of American and allied lives.

—In addition to these air operations on the Ho Chi Minh Trail we have continued to carry out reconnaissance flights in North Laos and fly combat-support missions for Laotian forces when requested to do so by the Royal Laotian Government.

—In every instance our combat air operations have taken place only over those parts of Laos occupied and contested by North Vietnamese and other communist forces. They have been flown only when requested by the Royal Laotian Government. The level of our air operations has been increased only as the number of North Vietnamese in Laos and the level of their aggression has increased.[107]

Thus the Symington subcommittee had achieved its third concrete result; the extent of U.S. involvement was now a matter of public record. The committee, however, somewhat understandably resented the fact that its transcript did not achieve that goal but was preempted by the President.

As it turned out, however, the Presidential statement and the background briefing given by Dr. Kissinger on the same day to further explain it opened a Pandora's box of troubles. Proper consideration had not been given to the fact that it is virtually impossible ever to get a precise and accurate number for anything out of the Pentagon bureaucracy. The remainder of the month was to see a series of corrections of numbers of personnel and of casualties that strained the credibility of the Presidential statement. And far from relieving the pressure of Congressional and press attention, it precipitated a new wave of critical press comment.[108]

Immediately following the President's statement, the State Department relented on the disputed items in the Laos transcript, with the execption of some limited categories, such as information that could endanger the lives of U.S.

military personnel, Thai operations in Laos, and exact statistics for the period prior to January 20, 1969, that were found to be totally unreliable.

Senator Fulbright, appearing on "Meet the Press" on March 8, said that Mr. Nixon had not told the full story, and that he himself was surprised to learn from secret testimony of large, unbudgeted spending and of the extent of CIA involvement in Laos.[109] Fulbright followed up on March 11 by introducing a resolution in the Senate that would require affirmative action by Congress for any further use of U.S. armed forces in or over Laos.[110] The Communist clandestine Radio Pathet Lao had now taken a real interest in the activities of the Senate, and repeatedly broadcast accounts of the denunciation of U.S. policy by U.S. Senators.[111]

On March 10, a meeting was held of the White House Working Group that turned into a heated showdown between the Secretary of State and the rest of the President's advisers. Rogers began the meeting by saying that he was to have a final meeting with Senator Symington the following day over the Laos transcript, and that he believed there was no further basis for insisting on deletions from it. Laird immediately disagreed, saying that he would have no problem in dealing with his committees but that "the SFRC gang" was completely against the administration. Ehrlichman reaffirmed the President's feeling that the important thing was not what had already leaked out and what would become public in the future but, rather, the method by which the facts became public. There was still good reason for keeping the imprimatur of the executive branch from such revelations. Rogers responded that the material would become public in any case, and that it was his understanding that the President wanted to disclose everything unless there was an overwhelming reason not to. He personally could see no reason for withholding the numbers of Air Force sorties in Laos. Laird pointed out that the publication of numbers and costs of our bombing in Laos would immediately be used by administration enemies on the Hill to pressure for legislation to cease all bombing. Rogers responded that the military, as everyone knew, liked to bomb for its own sake. He recalled that during World War II the Air Force used to bomb Guam just for fun, even though they knew there were no Japanese there. Laird had grave reservations about the public release of statistics of any kind regarding Laos, and especially on casualties, because of the impossibility of getting reliable figures from the Pentagon bureaucracy. He pointed out that each day he got new statistical reports that contradicted those he had been given the day before.

The meeting finally agreed, however, that reliable records were available from the beginning of the Nixon administration, and that the administration could stand on the record of statistics from that date forward. They agreed, over the objections of Rogers, that it would be unwise to go beyond the information made public in the President's March 6 statement and the Kissinger background session.

On the matter of nuclear weapons testimony, Rogers said it was his understanding that the restriction on testimony was to apply only to the Philippines; and he warned of grave consequences from Fulbright and Symington if they did not get their way on such testimony. Ehrlichman pointed out that the President most certainly intended nuclear weapons to be barred from testimony in all the Symington hearings, and not just the Philippines. Bryce Harlow pointed out that historically there had always been different treatment for nuclear weapons deployments in testimony before the Congress, and he felt that the public would overwhelmingly support the President in refusing to allow testimony before the Symington subcommittee because of the extreme sensitivity of these matters. The meeting adjourned in agreement, over Rogers' objections, that there should be no further discussion of nuclear weapons before the Symington subcommittee.

Some days after the meeting, the Justice Department reminded the members of the White House Working Group that the President had a clear right to withhold information from Congress concerning military and foreign affairs in the broadest of terms if, *in the President's judgment*, such disclosure did "not comport with the public interest." He pointed out, further, that provision of nuclear weapons information to the Joint Committee on Atomic Energy did not constitute any reason for the Executive not to refuse a request from a different committee. He also reminded the White House Working Group of the long-standing Justice Department position that a decision to invoke a claim of executive privilege, and the limitations of such invocation, were essentially policy questions and not legal questions.[112]

On March 11 and 13, the special security used for the testimony of the intelligence directors was breached for the first time, when Senator Fulbright used the conformation hearing for an AID official to get on the record the reports that AID was being used as a cover for CIA agents in Laos.[113] Shortly afterward a "Huntley-Brinkley Report" stated that Richard Helms had testified to this effect in a top-secret session before the Fulbright Committee, revealing that CIA men had been using AID as a cover for their activities in Laos.[114] The next day the New York *Times* carried a story reporting that Fulbright, following a top-secret hearing before his committee, revealed to the press that he had confirmed that the CIA was using AID as a screen for its operations in Laos. Fulbright blamed this dissimulation on the National Security Council.[115]

On March 15, Senator Symington reflected on some of the motivations behind his pursuit of the hearings on "Face the Nation:"

> I have crossed the Rubicon of my thinking with respect to the whole operation in the Far East. It's breaking the back of the American economy. It's taking the money we need—we all know we need so badly—here at home for education and water and air pollution control, and crime, and things that we need here at home....

This Vietnamization, to me, is rather ridiculous because we've had—they talk about 550,000 people out there. The truth is there have been at least 800,000 people out there, directly involved in Vietnam, counting the people in Thailand and in the fleet and the thousands of people in Japan and the Philippines, and Guam, and Okinawa...now if the South Vietnamese Government today can't do it with 800,000 of the finest Americans who ever lived, how can they do it without those Americans? That's why I'm not a believer in Vietnamization as against the success of negotiation.

Question: Senator, we hear a lot of talk about corruption out in Southeast Asia....

Symington: I have a report, which unfortunately is highly classified, from the GAO, and we will now proceed to try to get that report declassified, like we're trying to get the Laos hearings, the Taiwan hearings, the Thailand hearings, the Japanese hearing, declassified. It will be, ultimately, and it's a pretty shoddy story. I'd rather not go any further than that....

The greatest problem today, as I see it, in this country, is the growing secrecy about our policies that involve the future of our children and our country. And this whole question of secretiveness that has developed in recent years about what we're doing with respect to our relationships with countries with whom we are not at war could result in the destruction of the United States. Because if we're going to, for example, put nuclear weapons all over Europe it would be a relatively difficult matter to explain that, or to prevent their being captured if a government suddenly overturned in Europe. It's that type and character of information that I think American people have the right to know about. And not only do they not know any of the details—and there are some details they should not know—don't misunderstand me—but the proper committees in the Senate are not informed on these subjects and...well we're asking for a lot of information, and we're getting a lot more than we did before.[116]

On March 16, the New York *Times* reported that Senator Symington had revealed that the Philippine government had misused funds provided by the United States to help support the Philippine military detachment in South Vietnam.[117]

On March 13, the State Department provided the Symington staff with the revised changes in the Laos transcript, according to the instructions of the White House Working Group. Symington refused to accept these, and in several calls to the department, he pressed for immediate review at the highest levels. The working level at the State Department fully agreed with Symington for a variety of reasons, and urged the Secretary to take it up with the President.

With the increasing criticism and pressure building in Congress and the press on U.S. activities in Laos, the White House and the NSC became quite concerned and resentful that there were no answering voices to defend the administration's point of view. The NSC was urged to participate in a counteraction to mobilize some support and neutralize increasingly debilitating criticism. This was made urgent when, on March 17, word reached the White House of the overthrow of Sihanouk in Cambodia. Bryce Harlow immediately called a meeting at the White House of all of the leading Senate Republicans who were in town.

A senior official of the NSC began the meeting with a briefing on the situation in Laos. He emphasized that the President and the administration had been fully candid with Congress and that nothing had been held back. He deplored the discrepancies in figures, especially for casualties in Laos, and blamed this on the impossibility of getting straight answers from the military. He said that they could rely that it was a fact that there had been, in any case, fewer than 50 Americans killed on the ground in Laos and that there had been no U.S. combat units operating in Laos except occasional spillover in the border area. The official gave a full and, according to participants, persuasive argument for continuing U.S. activities in Laos, both assistance and training in support of the Laotian army, and in using air strikes against the North Vietnamese. He expressed optimism over the course of the war in South Vietnam and the success of Vietnamization. He told the Senators that he expected real negotiations to be achieved in 1970.

On Cambodia, the official assured the Senators that the United States had no prior knowledge of the removal of Sihanouk and, in fact, expressed skepticism that Sihanouk would be gone for very long. He assured the Senators that the United States intended to pursue a policy of neutrality toward Cambodia and that nothing was being done to give encouragement to Lon Nol.

The effect of this exposition was immediate. Several of the Senators present lamented that they had been far too lax in allowing the debate to go by default. They then turned the meeting into a strategy session on how to take the offensive for the administration in the Senate and to counteract Symington and Fulbright.

On March 14, Foreign Minister Thanat succumbed to temptation and blasted Fulbright and his resolution.

> Senator Fulbright's resolution openly denouncing U.S. defense policy is aimed at seeking popularity with certain uninformed sectors of the U.S. population and has in effect given aid and comfort to the enemy. Such a resolution will have the effect of prolonging the war in Southeast Asia and compromising its security.[118]

Secretary Laird reaffirmed on March 20 that, despite whatever Rogers had agreed with the committee, he adamantly refused to allow the release of the cost and number of sorties flown over Laos and certain other matters, since all of these would be of material assistance to the North Vietnamese. The day before, he had publicly made a strong defense of continued U.S. bombing in Laos, saying that he would recommend continuing it even if the Communists took over the whole country.119 The same day, White House spokesman Ziegler confirmed that there was some Thai involvement in Laos but that press reports of two battalions were "grossly exaggerated."120 The President confirmed Thai participation in his press conference of March 21, but referred detailed questions to the governments of Thailand and Laos.

On March 27, Secretary Rogers sent a letter to Symington in which he disavowed any role in insisting on maintaining the classification on sortie numbers and other matters at issue. This was viewed by the White House as a stab in the back.

By the end of the first week of April, the Laos transcript problems still had not been resolved, despite daily meetings at the working level between the subcommittee staff and State and Defense personnel, and several telephone calls between Symington and both Rogers and Laird. Nevertheless, at the end of that week the subcommittee sent its transcript to the printers. Symington had expressed the intention to publish the Laos transcript on April 15. It had not escaped notice at the White House that this date coincided with a massive antiwar demonstration to take place at the White House and the Capitol.

By April 7, the subcommittee had gotten galley proofs of the Laos transcript. Late that afternoon a reporter for Knight newspapers called one of the principal witnesses in the Symington hearings, telling him that he had a partial transcript of the hearings and requesting an appointment to discuss them with him. This was disturbing because there were still numerous items in the galley proofs that it had not been agreed to declassify. Nevertheless, the galley proofs were not marked by the subcommittee as classified.

On April 13, Senator Symington informed the administration that a new series of hearings on U.S. relations with Europe, Africa, and the Near East would begin on May 18, focusing on NATO. The same day, State Department staff members met with Senator Symington in an attempt to resolve the last disputes over security deletions. Symington accepted most of the deletions still at issue, but informed the State Department people that unless he heard directly from Secretary Rogers or Laird by noon the next day, he would refuse to delete a number of unsettled items. One matter at issue was the reference in the transcript to the total of U.S. operations in Laos as costing over "a billion dollars." This figure was thought to be exaggerated and damaging by the Executive, and the White House was adamant in insisting that the figure be kept classified. Consequently, the White House instructed State to inform Symington before noon on April 14 that this issue was to be kept classified. State refused, on the ground that there was no foreign affairs reason to do so; and no one called Symington by noon of the fourteenth.

Upon receipt of a copy of the galley proofs, the U.S. Embassy in Vientiane was distressed to find that the very matters most likely to cause friction with the royal Lao government had not been deleted.[121]

On April 17, the Philadelphia *Inquirer* carried a story by the reporter who had contacted State and informed it that he had a copy of the transcript in which it was revealed that there existed a secret "understanding" between the United States and the Soviet Union. He went on to give details drawn from the classified galleys that reportedly had come into his hands.[122]

That same day Senator Symington held an advance press conference to beat the drums for the publication of the transcript, which was to be made public the following Monday. He denounced the administration for keeping some matters classified, and then released a letter to him from his staff member Walter Pincus, revealing six areas of information, such as "use of bases in Thailand for air strikes in Laos," that Pincus believed the American people had a right to know.

On April 19, the transcript was made public; and the great wave of adverse headlines that the administration feared was realized, with special attention to the "over a billion" cost and the sortie rates and sortie costs.[123]

It was also found, upon examination of the published transcript, that after five months of negotiation the subcommittee had gone ahead and included six different instances of material that it had agreed to delete. These matters were, not unnaturally, among the more politically juicy, including references to American guerrilla activities, percentage rate increases in air strikes, and a discussion of navigational aids.[124]

Meanwhile, on April 21 the President had decided another sensitive matter on the question of the Symington request for the Kennedy-Barwick memorandum. He determined that the committee should be given access to it, and that Assistant Secretary of State Abshire should carry the document to the Hill and show it to Senator Symington and any other member of the Foreign Relations Committee who would like to see it. The document, however, was not to be left in the possession of the committee and no copies were to be made of it. This precedent came to be the accepted procedure for such sensitive documents during the remainder of the Nixon administration. Not unexpectedly, the Communist Pathet Lao Radio rejoiced over the publication and gave considerable air time to its broadcast.[125]

## NUCLEAR DEPLOYMENTS

Further carrying out his policy of conciliation, Secretary Rogers called Senator Fulbright on April 20 to tell him that he would be pleased to arrange a full briefing for the committee on nuclear deployments abroad, and it was accordingly set up for May 21. This was done despite the clear directive from the White House Working Group that nuclear weapons deployments were to be discussed only through the Joint Committee on Atomic Energy and not with the Symington subcommittee.

On March 26, Senator Symington supplemented the release of his testimony with an implied confirmation of a series of dispatches by reporters in Laos, adding much detail to the subcommittee transcript. He had all of the articles read into the record.126

On April 27 the New York *Post* revealed that

> Senate investigators have uncovered details of an arrangement whereby the Royal Thai government has been reaping multimillion dollar profits by charging the U.S. Army exorbitant rates for transporting American arms through the Southeast Asian kingdom.

The day before, the President had settled the matter of nuclear weapons briefings for the subcommittee. After discussions with Secretaries Rogers and Laird, as well as Kissinger and Ehrlichman, he authorized the preparation of a joint briefing for the committee, to be agreed upon by State and Defense; that only one transcript would be allowed, and that would be held by the Department of Defense.

The Symington practice of endorsing and then reading into the record news reports from Laos, giving them a stamp of legitimacy, now was being followed by Senator Mansfield.127

The first Harris Poll taken after the publication of the Symington transcript showed the worst fears of the executive branch being realized. By a substantial 56-26 percent, a majority of the American people, according to the Harris survey, said that they believed the President "has not told the real truth about the situation" in Laos. Over 70 percent of the public was worried that "Laos and Cambodia will turn into another Vietnam." By 59 to 30 percent, Americans favored "staying out of Laos and Cambodia altogether." These results showed the sharp turnaround that the Symington publicity had worked on U.S. public support since the previous November.128

On May 8, Symington convened the subcommittee for a special hearing on Taiwan in order to hear Major General Richard Ciccolella, whose convalescence could no longer be extended. The controversial Ciccolella had been exhaustively briefed and, perhaps because of this, the hearing went more smoothly than was expected.129

If the executive branch was distressed at the course of the Symington hearings, it was evident that Senator Fulbright was not entirely pleased. On May 18 he held hearings on ambassadorial nominations, one of which was that of Robert McClintock, formerly the chairman of the Symington interdepartmental group, who had been nominated to be Ambassador to Venezuela. Fulbright took the occasion to engage in a bitter attack on the cooperation of the administration and the Department of State with the subcommittee. He attacked McClintock for having specifically instructed a witness not to testify on certain subjects before the Symington subcommittee. Despite McClintock's defense that he was acting under instructions, Fulbright viewed this as an example of the contempt of the administration for Congress and dismissed the witness with the remark that he was not disposed to recommend confirmation. Fulbright also bitterly criticized the failure of the administration to bring back Ambassador G. McMurtrie Godley from Laos to testify before the committee. The White House Working Group had recommended that the State Department definitely not do this, as he was needed during the dry-season offensive going on in Laos. McClintock's nomination languished unacted on, for many many weeks, until Fulbright finally relented and allowed it to go through.

On May 20, the nuclear weapons briefing was rescheduled for May 27, at Senator Fulbright's request. Ronald Spiers, Director of Political-Military Affairs in State, was to be the principal witness. The same day, the White House Working Group formally advised Secretary Rogers that the restrictions on this testimony were a matter of Presidential concern, and that certain sensitive topics were not to be discussed. Agreement on what was within and what was without the White House guidelines for the nuclear briefing proved difficult to achieve; and as late as the eve of the briefing, State and Defense had not agreed.

The start of the briefing was delayed for about an hour and a half on May 27, while the committee met in executive session to decide whether it would accept the requirements of one transcript to be retained by State. When it finally began, the chairman reluctantly agreed to the stipulation, on the understanding that the committee could have the transcript for its use on thirty minutes' notice at any time. The briefing lasted for two hours and went very smoothly, with Spiers seeming to satisfy the committee in the detail of his answers. Partial credit for this success belonged to the excellent performance of the administration witnesses on the preceding two days. On May 25, and 26, the subcommittee had held its hearings on U.S. forces in Europe, with General David A. Burchinal and General James H. Polk, Commander of the U.S. Army in Europe, as principal witnesses.[130]

As a result of the hearings on Europe, Senator Fulbright developed a new issue with the State Department. He threatened to hold up the extension of the Foreign Military Sales Act unless the cable of instructions sent by State regarding the Symington staff trip to Europe during the past winter were given to the committee. Symington and Fulbright were both very disappointed at the lack of pay dirt brought back by the staff. They of course did not know of the very special precautions taken by the executive branch, and of the detailed accounts of their staff's discussions and interests while they were in Europe that had come back to the executive branch. Later in the summer, in return for an appropriate concession, Assistant Secretary David Abshire provided the committee with a copy of the cable of instructions.

On June 5, the subcommittee distributed the published transcript of the Thailand hearings through a procedure that had now become standard. It distributed the copies to the press with an embargo on publication until June 8. In handing out the reports, the subcommittee staff held a press conference in which it carefully drew the press' attention to the items more embarrassing to the Thais, in order to highlight the case it wished to make that the Thais would not have sent any forces to Vietnam without U.S. insistence and U.S. financial support.

As expected, then, on June 8 the papers were full of derogatory headlines over the issue of U.S. support to Thai troops in Vietnam and related matters.[131] In a column in the Washington *Post*, Chalmers Roberts reported:

> Walter Pincus, the subcommittee's chief consultant, read newsmen sortie figures for raids in North Laos alone, increasing from 20 in the year 1964 to 32 per day by September, 1968, to "over 100" per day in 1969.

He also reported that since the administration insisted on keeping classified all references to reports that Thai troops have been serving in Laos, Symington inserted a newspaper report that 5,000 had been sent to Laos in the uniform of the Royal Laotian Army.[132] It was recalled by the Office of the Secretary of Defense that on April 28, the subcommittee staff had called Laird's office to request authorization to publish that sortie rate information in the Symington transcript for Thailand. He was told by the Assistant Secretary of Defense that these figures must remain classified, and that was the administration's final position.

On June 10 Fulbright sent Rogers a letter thanking him for the Spiers brief on nuclear weapons, but saying that the committee now intended to go into nuclear weapons deployment on a country-by-country basis and would require Mr. Spiers or other knowledgeable witnesses for more detailed information.

While there were the predictable press stories and commentary in Bangkok, reaction to publication of the Thai transcript was not quite so serious as might have been the case had the Laos transcript not drawn some of the lightning earlier and had the administration not had time, through Ambassador Leonard Unger, to prepare the Thais and to discount the inevitable publicity.

Prior to the July 4 recess, Secretary of State Rogers agreed with Senator Fulbright to call Ambassador Godley home from Laos and to provide him as a witness before the Foreign Relations Committee on July 21. On July 7, upon learning of this commitment, the President directed that Godley not be called home, but that CIA Director Helms testify in his stead.

On July 2, Foreign Minister Thanat lashed out at the U.S. Senate, denouncing "some Western politicians" for "hounding, harassing, and persecuting" member governments of SEATO to serve "domestic personal gains" during the inaugural session of the SEATO Ministerial Council in Manila. He said that more disturbing than the Communist attacks on SEATO

> ...are blows repeatedly dealt to it by political circles in certain western countries...for reasons of internal politics, particularly the opposition to involvement in Asia on the one hand and the current struggle between the executive and the legislative branches of government on the other, some western politicians have thought it convenient to use an international matter to serve their domestic political gains.[133]

His attack was met with "hear, hear" at the White House. This was followed by consternation when, unexpectedly, Secretary Rogers heatedly defended the Foreign Relations Committee in a clash with Thanat on the closing day of the ministerial conference.[134]

Relations with Thailand continued to deteriorate throughout the rest of the summer, with the Prime Minister variously suggesting that the United States was on the verge of a national mental breakdown, that it could no longer be relied upon as an ally, and that as a result "it seems relations between Thailand and the United States will evolve toward a more selective basis."[135]

After the July 4 recess, a new deadlock had developed over the declassification of the Taiwan transcript, but another problem had been resolved when Secretary Rogers got agreement from the President to allow Ambassador Godley to return from Laos and to testify in executive session. But still another sticky problem, Fulbright's wish to continue the question of nuclear deployments on a country-by-country basis, approached another stalemate when Secretary Laird adamantly refused to participate in such hearings and State declined to participate alone. Since Secretary Rogers was out of the country, it was assumed that Fulbright would await his return to take up the matter with him; but it was felt that time and the legislative backlog were working for the success of another application of "administrative denial."

On July 15 the final session of the NATO hearings was concluded without incident.[136] The following day the White House Working Group instructed the Department of State that if the Godley testimony was to go forward, the most stringent security measures must be taken, and that the President was personally concerned. It reaffirmed that there was to be only one transcript of Godley's testimony, and that must be held by the Department of State. No part of the transcript was to be declassified or published; and if the committee did not agree to these conditions, the President wanted to review the matter. By this time the senior officers at State referred to the directives from the White House Working Group as the "Ehrlichman Diktat."

Also on July 16, final agreement was reached on the publication of the transcript on China, but the subcommittee staff insisted on using the same device used on the Laos transcript by including a letter from the staff pointing out those matters that had been kept classified.

On July 17 the subcommittee held a hearing on Spain in which only committee staff were witnesses, making a predictable record.[137] Three days later the subcommittee had another busy day. Assistant Secretary David Newsom testified in secret session on Morocco and Libya. Afterward the subcommittee held a press conference releasing copies of the Taiwan transcript, not to be published until the following morning.[138]

On July 25 a reporter from the New York *Times* called the Department of State, requesting information about the existence of a secret U.S. naval communications base in Morocco. And three days later the *Times* published a detailed article identifying, locating, and describing the function of the communications base near Kenitra. Disclosure of this private agreement with Morocco to maintain such facilities caused considerable difficulties in the Arab world, and domestically for the Moroccan government; it also had a very detrimental effect on U.S. relations with that country. The article began, "A Senate Foreign Relations subcommittee has discovered...."[139]

Meanwhile, the publication of the Taiwan transcripts brought the usual amount of adverse publicity, this time focusing on the existence of bases on Taiwan that were capable of handling U.S. B-52's.[140]

On July 21, Ambassador Godley "briefed" the Symington subcommittee on Laos, after a stormy delay in which the subcommittee first accepted the State Department conditions that there be one transcript, held by the department, and then, in a turnabout, refused to have any transcript and instead called the session a briefing rather than a full hearing. The briefing itself was a useful exchange and went relatively smoothly; but when it was concluded after two and one-half hours, Senators Fulbright and Symington blasted the administration for imposing such supersecret ground rules:

> This is obviously a calculated move on the part of the Executive not to cooperate in the traditional manner with the Committee on Foreign Relations...this is an effort to neutralize if not destroy any influence that the Committee on Foreign Relations has.

CBS News reported that the State Department admitted that it was ordered to carry out those instructions by the White House.[141]

The following day, a member of the Symington staff called the State Department to inform it that the full committee was deeply dissatisfied with the precedent, and that State might expect to find Senators making speeches on the floor that would draw on the supersecret testimony of Ambassador Godley.

On July 25 the New York *Times* carried an article revealing that the United States had pledged to support the defense system of Spain and to make its defense policies compatible with those of Spain in return for rights to continue using the bases. This disclosure followed the classified briefing of the Foreign Relations Committee on the Spanish agreements by Undersecretary Alexis Johnson.[142]

Later in the month, Senator Symington took his argument on nuclear weapons deployments to the people, arguing that the executive branch had made commitments with foreign countries that could bankrupt the nation and harm the national security, and that some of them resulted from "clandestine agreements" for the storage of nuclear weapons on foreign soil.

On July 31 Jack Anderson's column carried quotations from the top-secret, no-transcript briefing by Ambassador Godley ten days earlier.[143]

Meanwhile, in Morocco the storm began to break with such banner headlines as "Is There Secret Agreement Between Morocco and U.S. for Installation of American Forces at Sidi Yahia?" and "Moroccan People Demand Explanation and Appeal for Clarification."[144]

On August 3, Senator Fulbright announced his opposition to the just-concluded Spanish Base Agreements and proceeded to reveal much information of a classified nature about the agreements that had been given to the Foreign Relations Committee in executive session by Undersecretary Johnson on July 24, and in the previous Symington subcommittee hearings. He referred to U.S. payments to Spain of approximately $400 million, including fighter planes and warships in return for the base rights; he also cited statements made in confidence by Undersecretary Johnson and statements by General Earl Wheeler. The next day, in a very uncharacteristic belligerency, the State Department issued a statement criticizing the breach of security and acknowledging privately that its criticism was directed specifically at Fulbright for his speech the previous day.[145]

The following week, Senator Symington gave his rationale for that kind of disclosure, saying:

> Public disclosure is a truly vital safeguard against government adoption of positions and policies of unknown and potentially dangerous implication....the executive branch, as the party in original possession of pertinent information, will inevitably prevail unless the legislative branch, with the help of public opinion, can obtain disclosure....Only the Congress can cut through executive secrecy.[146]

In this atmosphere, nonetheless, Senator Fulbright continued to be perplexed by the administration's refusal to provide the committee with more information on sensitive nuclear weapons deployments. In a letter of August 9, he complained at the nonresponsiveness of the department:

> ...you do not provide the slightest enlightenment as to what those judgments are, what problems are perceived or even the basic facts as

to what redeployments are proposed...of course, the procedure you have described does not involve the participation of the Foreign Relations Committee in the consideration of the foreign policy issues involved.

The Fulbright-Symington doctrine of disclosure gained popularity in Congress. On August 10 the New York *Times* reported the release by Congressman Allard Lowenstein of a classified USIA poll that had been given to the Senate Foreign Relations Committee, with the clear understanding that its classification must be maintained. The poll disclosed that confidence in the U.S. abroad had declined as a result of the Cambodia operation.[147]

In response to what appeared to the White House as more and more of a hemorrhage of national security information, the President directed on August 11 that in dealing with the Foreign Relations Committee, there were to be no compromises and no conciliatory gestures whatsoever.

During the month of July the Mission of Thailand to the United Nations in New York tried to fight back a little by issuing a press release defending that nation's contribution to the Vietnam War and reprinting copies of two letters sent by U.S. citizens to Senators Fulbright and Symington deploring their attacks on Thailand. This measure greatly upset Senator Fulbright, who promptly addressed a letter to the Secretary of State, demanding to know if this action by the Thai Mission was not in contravention of the Charter of the United Nations.[148]

On August 17 the Department of State, upon reviewing the galley sheets prior to the publication of the Symington transcript on Japan, found that the subcommittee staff had refused to delete sections of testimony relating to classified operations in Laos. The Legal Advisor's Office immediately called the Symington staff to point this out. It was told that the committee would publish the material anyway, since in *its* view there seemed to be no good reason for not doing so.[149]

The next day the White House Working Group resolved the outstanding conflicts over the Ethiopia transcript by directing that the precise substance, but not identified as the verbatim text, of the relevant security agreements be released as part of the transcript. These included the so-called Herter, Bundy, Gilpatric, and Rusk commitments.

On August 23, *Parade* magazine printed a story revealing that "The scandalous truth is that approximately $4 million of the $32 million earmarked by the U.S. for payment of non-combat Filipino troops in South Vietnam was skimmed by various Philippine Government officials." These allegations appeared to have been drawn from a still-classified report prepared by the GAO at the request of the Symington committee. It was in the hands of the Symington subcommittee.

On September 2, Secretary Laird finally got around to replying to Fulbright's letter of June 10, regarding the pursuit of country-by-country hearings on nuclear weapons deployments. In the reply he dismissed the idea out of hand, pointing out that the discussion of such sensitive matters as nuclear weapons involving operational and contingency plans and command and control procedures are already available to Congress through the Armed Services and Appropriations Subcommittees and the Joint Atomic Energy Committee.

Symington released the transcript of the Korea hearings on September 12. As usual, the papers were subsequently filled with headlines about mercenaries, Korean brutality, and corruption. An added twist was the accusation made by the Senate subcommittee staff that, via-à-vis North Korea, it was the United States that was "the more threatening side."[150]

The subcommittee published the report on the hearings on Ethiopia on October 18, producing the usual front-page headlines, this time about secret pacts for the support of the Ethiopian army, and that U.S. military equipment was being used against the Eritrean Liberation Front.[151] The administration had insisted that the functions performed at the U.S. communications station at Kagnew be deleted from the published transcript. Subsequently, however, a New York *Times* account outlined the specifics of those functions.[152]

The subcommittee published its report on the hearings on Morocco and Libya on October 31. In the usual headlines about secret commitments being disclosed, the subcommittee staff was quoted as pointing out that the executive branch had insisted on deleting the formal admission that the United States was operating communications facilities in Morocco and that that branch had refused to budge on this until after the leak to the newspapers on July 28, describing the testimony given in secret session.[153]

Publication of the transcript naturally added considerable fuel to the fire that had begun with the August leak in Morocco, with considerable adverse press comment that led to a reassessment by the government of Morocco and, ultimately, a drawdown of U.S. presence and renegotiation of the agreements.[154]

On November 22, the subcommittee released its report on the NATO hearings. the headlines this time concentrated on Symington's charges that "We put these [nuclear] weapons all over the world, and in my opinion at least in some places we do not guard them properly, and that is based on actual experience plus letters of protest I received." Symington and his staff strongly implied that the incidents had been related to the 1967 coup d'état in Greece.

## FINALE

On November 24, the Symington subcommittee held its last hearing in the Ninety-first Congress with an open session with Carl Kaysen, former deputy to McGeorge Bundy in the Kennedy White House as principal witness. The hearing concentrated primarily on the war in Southeast Asia.[155]

The *Christian Science Monitor* of December 7 carried an article reporting details of an incident that reportedly took place in Greece, where a nuclear weapons site was surrounded by Greek troops during the coup. It reported that a NATO contingency plan called "Prometheus" was activated. The article said, "The authority is a subcommittee of the Foreign Relations Committee."

When it was learned that the final report of the Symington subcommittee was near completion, the Department of State called Senator Symington to request an opportunity to review the galleys for security. Symington refused, because he said that the committee was very concerned that there be no premature disclosure of the substance of the report.

On December 21, Senatory Symington released the final report of the subcommittee, which summed up the many charges and concerns expressed by the committee over its two-year life, in 2,500 pages of cleared testimony. No major recommendations were made, but the subcommittee indicated that its records were expected to be the foundation of an effort the following year to cut appropriations for bases overseas, including the U.S. troop presence in Europe; to further scale down the defense budget; and to reduce the overall size of the armed forces.[156]

Thus, the Symington subcommittee concluded its two years of operation to the accompaniment of vast sighs of relief from the other end of Pennsylvania Avenue. The effects of the hearings, however, were far from over.

## CONCLUSIONS

In establishing the Symington Subcommittee on Commitments, it was the intention of the Senate Foreign Relations Committee to undertake "a detailed review of the international military commitments of the United States and their relationship to foreign policy."[157] The charter of the subcommittee reflected a concern deeply felt in the committee, that there had developed an "imperial" presidency and complementary defense/military apparatus with a policy life of its own. The concern of course had its source in the Vietnam War, and the frustrating role of the committee in its conduct. The passion and bitterness of this latter issue came to influence the inquiry of the committee to an increasing extent as the hearings proceeded.

But the concern of the committee and of a wide segment of the Senate had a deeper source than the war alone. Consensus over the larger role of the United States in the world had disintegrated, and with it also a commonly held conceptual framework.

From its announcement, the executive branch viewed the inquiry with some unease. But the new administration, as was seen in Chapter 5 was at first determined to live up to its campaign pledge of an "open administration." The pessimism of the NSC and the Pentagon was not shared in the Oval Office, and their recommendations to restrict the subcommittee's access to information were overruled by the President. Access to thousands of pages of sensitive material was promptly provided to the subcommittee and its staff. To cooperate with the results of their inquiry, the Executive offered to follow the procedures used in the 1951 hearings on the Korean War, and provide a referee to declassify the transcript daily, on the spot.[158]

This period of optimistic cooperation, as we have seen, did not live through the spring of 1969. It came to grief over the perennial corollary of democratic government: leaks. Leaking of course has never been a phenomenon unique to Congress; but as more and more material involving Spanish bases, Southeast Asia, and nuclear weapons deployments, known to be in the hands of the subcommittee and its staff, found its way into the press, the conclusion was quickly reached in the Executive that the subcommittee was the source and, further, that it was a calculated policy on its part. No investigation was ever undertaken, nor any measures to prove the source of the leaks. Once the hearings began, the number of embarrassing relevations was seen in the Executive as a very serious hemorrhage. Actually, the nature of closed Congressional hearings makes some disclosure inevitable, regardless of precautions. No Senator can leave one of these secret sessions without running a gauntlet of reporters. If he does not give them some tidbit, however innocent he might believe it to be, he will incur the wrath of the press gallery—and no member can afford that. After gathering the succession of such crumbs from departing members, the press normally has at least one, and usually several, solid stories.[159]

Nor is this unique to one committee. A member of the House Foreign Affairs Committee said with dismay, in 1970, "I have really been shocked to see how some of my colleagues walk out of a closed meeting of the committee and tell the press all about it."[160]

Thus the irreconcilable conflict between the public's right to know and the government's responsibility to protect certain kinds of information became a central consideration of the investigative process—at both ends of Pennsylvania Avenue.

The Executive became convinced, by early summer of 1969, that the subcommittee and its staff had abandoned all semblance of objectivity and were embarked on a systematic campaign to discredit the Executive's policies in Europe, and to undermine its efforts to achieve "peace with honor" in Vietnam.

The subcommittee, it was felt, was attempting to generate public opposition through leaking only derogatory information, and by attempting to create the public impression that the Executive had hidden scores of secret commitments from Congress.

Accordingly, the Executive organized itself internally to fight the subcommittee every step of the way, and to limit damage to U.S. policy (and the domestic image of the administration) as much as possible.

The results of this two-year interaction were many. If one objective of the hearings was to diminish public support for executive policies, particularly in Vietnam, it was achieved.

The successive charges by the subcommittee, with accompanying media attention, of the "secret war in Laos"; "mercenaries" in Vietnam; U.S.-financed corruption in the Philippines; provocation in Taiwan; secret military commitments in Spain, Korea, Thailand, and Ethiopia; secret bases in Morocco; and careless and excessive nuclear deployments all further eroded the votes in Congress that would have supported the executive policies.

Perhaps more significant, the cumulative effect on public opinion was to obscure, confuse, and discredit the Executive's foreign policy. There was a general impression left that "very substantial military commitments have been made in secret to other countries without the knowledge of American taxpayers or their representatives in the Congress.[161]

The effects upon U.S. relations with the nations involved in the revelations were in some cases significant. North Vietnam apparently followed the hearings with much interest. The Communist propaganda radios in Southeast Asia gave considerable attention to the charges of the subcommittee. It is the judgment of the senior State Department intelligence analyst on North Vietnamese affairs that the hearings were a significant factor in establishing the judgment in Hanoi that the U.S. Congress would not sustain the U.S. government negotiating position then being secretly put forward by Henry Kissinger.[162]

In the Philippines, reaction to the charges was strong. The U.S. Embassy was stoned, the Philippine battalion withdraw from Vietnam, and the price for renewal of U.S. base rights was raised. In the judgment of the U.S. Ambassador at the time, Philippine relations and cooperation with the United States had not recovered four years after the hearings.[163]

The impact of the hearings upon Laos seems to have been minimal. Senior U.S. Air Force commanders feared, however, that the leaking of certain U.S. rules of engagement during the hearings resulted in tactical changes by the North Vietnamese that contributed to greater aircraft losses.[164]

In Thailand, the reaction to the Symington charges was more restrained than in the Philippines, but seems to have resulted in a major policy decision to seek improved relations with the Soviet Union and China, and a significant reduction in cooperation with the United States, particularly with regard to Thai support of the Lao and the Cambodian governments.[165]

The hearings had little impact on U.S. relations with South Korea, Japan, Taiwan, Greece, Turkey, Ethiopia, Libya, or Portugal. The adverse effect of the hearings upon the Moroccan government was noted above.

The effect of the hearings upon NATO was minor, partly because of effective executive countermeasures; and partly because it was seen as part of the larger Senate effort to pass a mandatory troop cut, the Spanish hearings similarly were part of a larger effort treated elsewhere.

Because of the excessive confrontation, hostility, and bitterness that developed between the branches during the inquiry, there was virtually no voluntary modification of executive policy formulation. To be sure, the creation of new objective facts through the process, as noted above, resulted in de facto modifications of policy; in some cases they were significant, but in not one instance (with the possible exception of Spain) did the investigative process influence the Executive voluntarily to change its mind. It need hardly be said that the Symington subcommittee was, at the conclusion of its work, judged by the Executive to have been a total disaster.

The operations in Laos and Thailand were open secrets, well-known to Congress and reported in the press for years prior to the hearings. But the mileage the subcommittee was able to derive from those issues points up a central question. How far can the executive branch proceed alone in pursuit of policy, however wise and just, if Congress is not a knowing participant and, most important, if the policy may not be articulated and defended freely to the American public?

The Symington hearing process demonstrated the lack of wisdom, time after time, of the Executive's pursuit of sound policy without the support of informed consensus. It performed this function far better than floor debate would have, because it brought to the dialogue the leading protagonists and policy operators to squirm in the realization that their policies and actions were quite sound, yet they themselves appeared as perfidious schemers.

There is a danger inherent in the "secrecy and dispatch" essential to the conduct of foreign policy, and that is the elitist fallacy that because the public and Congress can never have the information resources available to the policy elite, Congress and the public therefore cannot be trusted to make policy judgments. Further and most important, unless executive policy is supported by a public judgment that it is reasonable it cannot succeed, (that is, consensus). The executive branch must, therefore, provide the public with all long-run intentions. A price in confidentiality and in time required to articulate positions publicly must be paid.

## NOTES

1. U.S. Congress, Senate, Judiciary Committee, *Congressional Power of Investigation* (Washington, D.C.: U.S. Government Printing Office, 1954), p. 2.

There is a fundamental difference, however, between the power of investigation in the British Parliament, where there is a unitary government of parliamentary supremacy; hence its powers to investigate the Executive are by definition unlimited, since it is investigating a branch of itself. The situation is considerably different with a government of separated powers, as in the United States.

2. Woodrow Wilson, *Congressional Government* (Boston: Houghton Mifflin, 1913), p. 303.

3. U.S. Congress, Senate, Committee on Government Operations, *Councils and Committees* (Washington, D.C.: U.S. Government Printing Office, 1972), pp. 31-44.

4. Joseph Harris, *Congressional Control of Administration* (Washington, D.C.: Brookings Institutions, 1964), pp. 251, 252; *Guide to the U.S. Congress* (Washington, D.C.: Congressional Quarterly, 1971), p. 245.

5. *Guide to the U.S. Congress*, p. 248.

6. Ibid., p. 248.

7. Nelson M. McGeary, *The Development of Congressional Investigative Power* (New York: Columbia University Press, 1940), p. 7.

8. Harris, *Congressional Control*, p. 253.

9. Harry T. Williams, *Lincoln and the Radicals* (Madison: University of Wisconsin Press, 1941), p. 63.

10. *Guide to U.S. Congress*, p. 257.

11. Harris, *Congressional Control*, p. 255.

12. *Guide to U.S. Congress*, p. 259.

13. Harris, *Congressional Control*, p. 260.

14. *Guide to U.S. Congress*, p. 259.

15. Interview with Professor Charles Burton Marshall, March 1974; Harris, *Congressional Control*, p. 262.

16. *Guide to Congress*, p. 248.

17. Ibid., p. 249.

18. Cited in Arthur Schlesinger, Jr. *The Imperial Presidency* (Boston: Houghton Mifflin, 1973), p. 332.

19. John Jay, "Federalist No. 64," *The Federalist Papers* (New York: New American Library, 1961), p. 392.

20. Cited in U.S. v. Curtiss-Wright Export Corp., 299 U.S. 304, 319 (1936).

21. New York *Times* v. U.S., 39 Law Week 4879, 4884 (1971).

22. U.S. Congress, Senate, 86th Cong., 2nd sess., S. Report. 1761, p. 22. Cited in "Statement of William H. Rehnquist, Assistant Attorney General, Office of Legal Counsel, Department of Justice," in U.S. Congress, Senate, Committee on the Judiciary, *Executive Privilege: The Withholding of Information by the Executive* (Washington, D.C.: U.S. Government Printing Office, 1971), p. 420. Hereafter referred to as *Executive Privilege*.

23. U.S. Congress, Senate, Committee on Foreign Relations, *Security Classification as a Problem in the Congressional Role in Foreign Policy* (Washington D.C.: U.S. Government Printing Office, 1971), p. 4.

24. Cited in Arthur Schlesinger, Jr., "The Secrecy Dilemma," New York *Times Magazine*, February 6, 1972, p. 12.

25. Ibid., p. 8.

26. U.S. President, *Public Papers of the Presidents* (Washington, D.C.: Office of the *Federal Register*, 1974), Richard M. Nixon, 1972, p. 403. For a comprehensive discussion of the classification problem, see Schlesinger, *Imperial Presidency*, pp. 331-76.

27. New York *Times*, March 9, 1972, pp. 11, 12.

28. *Guide to the U.S. Congress*, p. 254.

29. *Executive Privilege*, p. 421.

30. U.S. v. Reynolds, 345 U.S. 1 (1953); Marbury v. Madison, 5 U.S. 137 (1803); Barenblatt v. U.S. 360 U.S. 109 (1959).

31. *Executive Privilege*, p. 431.

32. U.S. Department of Justice, *Memorandum Reviewing Inquiries by the Legislative Branch During the Period 1948-1950 Concerning the Decision Making Process and Documents of the Executive Branch* (Washington, D.C.: U.S. Government Printing Office, 1959), p. 37.

33. *Executive Privilege*, p. 420. For an entirely different interpretation of executive privilege see Raoul Berger, *Executive Privilege* (Cambridge, Mass.: Harvard University Press, 1974). This shrill polemic, voluminously but very selectively documented, presents a highly tendentious argument that executive privilege does not exist.

34. Detroit *News*, March 3, 1971, p. 9.

35. Burton Sapin, *The Making of United States Foreign Policy* (New York: Praeger, 1966), p. 59.

36. Woodrow Wilson, cited in Dean Acheson, *Present at the Creation* (New York: W.W. Norton, 1969), p. 100.

37. Based on interview with Bryce Harlow, March 1969.

38. Washington *Post*, February 25, 1969, p. 17.

39. Based on an interview with Bryce N. Harlow, April 1969.

40. New York *Times*, April 9, 1969, pp. 1, 12.

41. New York *Times*, April 23, 1969, p. 6.

42. Ibid., May 6, 1969, p. 46.

43. Washington *Post*, May 23, 1969, pp. A-1, A-20.

44. New York *Times*, May 24, 1969, p. 1.

45. Washington *Post*, June 14, 1969, pp. 1, 25.

46. Ibid., July 8, 1969, p. 3.

47. Based on interviews conducted in Bangkok, July 1970.

48. Reuters, September 10, 1969.

49. U.S. Congress, Senate, 91st Cong., 1st sess., September 19, 1969, *Congressional Record*, p. S10981.

50. *Foreign Broadcast Information Service*, October 3, 1969.

51. Washington *Post*, October 6, 1969, p. 7.

52. 5 U.S.C. sec. 7152.

53. 18 U.S.C. sec. 142.

54. New York *Times*, October 13, 1969, p. 15.

55. Washington *Star*, October 14, 1969, p. 15.

56. Washington *Post*, October 16, 1969, p. 5.

57. Ibid., October 17, 1969, p. D-17.

58. Ibid., October 18, 1969, p. A-2.

59. Ibid., October 20, 1969, pp. A-1, A-11.

60. Ibid., October 22, 1969, p. A-11.

61. Washington *News*, October 22, 1969.

62. U.S. Congress, Senate, 91st Cong., 1st sess., October 23, 1969, *Congressional Record*, p. S13103.

63. New York *Times*, October 26, 1969, p. 1, and October 27, 1969, p. 3.

64. Washington *Post*, October 29, 1969, p. A-1; New York *Times*, October 29, 1969, p. 1.

65. Bangkok *Post*, October 27, 1969, p. 1.

66. Washington *Star*, October 30, 1969, p. 7.

67. Baltimore *Sun*, October 31, 1969, p. 2.

68. Washington *Post*, November 8, 1969, p. A-5.

69. Baltimore *Sun*, November 12, 1969, p. 1.

70. Washington *Post*, November 13, 1969, p. A-8.

71. U.S. President, *Weekly Compilation of Presidential Documents*, November 24, 1969, p. 1628.

72. U.S. Congress, Senate, Committee on Foreign Relations, *Commitments*, I (Washington, D.C.: U.S. Government Printing Office, 1971), 1-363.

73. *Foreign Broadcast Information Service*, November 20, 1969, p. I-1.

74. New York *Times*, November 20, 1969, p. 13.

75. Washington *Post*, November 26, 1969, p. 2.

76. New York *Times*, December 1, 1969, p. 1.

77. Washington *Star*, December 6, 1969, p. 5.

78. Washington *Post*, December 7, 1969, p. A-39.

79. New York *Times*, December 9, 1969, p. 16.

80. *Foreign Broadcast Information Service*, December 13, 1969.

81. Washington *Post*, December 12, 1969, p. A-2.

82. *Foreign Broadcast Information Service*, December 14, 1969.

83. U.S. Congress, Senate, 91st Cong., 1st sess., December 15, 1969, *Congressional Record*, p. S16751.

84. New York *Times*, December 17, 1969, p. 1.

85. *Foreign Broadcast Information Service*, December 22, 1969.

86. Chicago *Tribune*, January 1, 1970, p. 1.

87. New York *Times*, January 4, 1970, p. 12.

88. U.S. Congress, Senate, 91st Cong., 2nd sess., January 20, 1970, *Congressional Record*, p. S198, and January 21, 1970, p. S262.

89. Washington *News*, January 27, 1970, p. 1; Washington *Post*, January 27, 1970, p. 6.

90. *Foreign Broadcast Information Service*, January 30, 1970.

91. U.S. President, *Public Papers of the Presidents*, Richard M. Nixon, 1970, p. 43.

92. Washington *Post*, February 5, 1970, p. 2.

93. *Foreign Broadcast Information Service*, February 5, 1970.

94. Washington *Post*, February 10, 1970, p. A-2; UPI 158, February 9, 1970.

95. *Foreign Broadcast Information Service*, February 11, 1970.

96. Washington *News*, February 12, 1970, p. 2.

97. New York *Times*, February 17, 1970, p. 11.

98. St. Louis *Post-Dispatch*, February 19, 1970, p. 2.

99. Washington *Post*, February 19, 1970, p. 1.

100. U.S. Congress, Senate, 91st Cong., 2nd sess., February 25, 1970, *Congressional Record*, p. S2367; Washington *Post*, February 26, 1970, pp. A-1, A-18.

101. Washington *Post*, February 28, 1970, p. A-12; St. Louis *Post-Dispatch*, February 28, 1970; New York *News*, February 28, 1970, p. 6.

102. Washington *Star*, March 1, 1970, p. 16.

103. Washington *Post*, March 2, 1970, p. A-18.

104. "CBS Morning News", March 2, 1970; Joseph Goulden, *Nation*, March 2, 1970; U.S. Congress, Senate, 91st Cong., 2nd sess., March 2, 1970, *Congressional Record*, p. S2729; Washington *Post*, March 2, 1970, p.4.

105. *Foreign Broadcast Information Service*, March 4, 1970, p. I-1.

106. Washington *Star*, March 4, 1970, p. 1.

107. New York *Times*, March 7, 1970, p. 10.

108. Chicago *Tribune*, March 7, 1970; New York *Times*, March 7, 1970, p. 30; Washington *Post*, March 8, 1970, pp. D-1, D-4, D-6; Washington *Star*, March 9, 1970; Washington *News*, March 9, 1970.

109. "Meet the Press," March 8, 1970.

110. S. Res. 368, 91st Cong., 2nd sess., March 11, 1970.

111. *Foreign Broadcast Information Service*, March 12, 1970, p. I-1.

112. Based on interview with Assistant Attorney General William Rehnquist, March 1970. Also see Rehnquist statement in *Executive Privilege*, U.S. Congress, Senate, Committee on the Judiciary, p. 420.

113. Washington *Post*, March 12, 1970, p. 8.

114. "Huntley-Brinkley Report," March 13, 1970.

115. New York *Times*, March 14, 1970, p. 11.

116. "Face the Nation," March 15, 1970.

117. New York *Times*, March 16, 1970, p. 9.

118. *Foreign Broadcast Information Service*, March 18, 1970, p. J-1.

119. Washington *Post*, March 20, 1970, p. 1.

120. Baltimore *Sun*, March 21, 1970, p. 1.

121. Based on interviews conducted in Vientiane, Laos, July 1970.

122. Philadelphia *Inquirer*, April 17, 1970, p. 1.

123. Philadelphia *Inquirer*, April 20, 1970, p. 1; New York *Times*, April 20, 1970, p. 8; Washington *Post*, April 20, 1970, p. A-1; Washington *Star*, April 20, 1970, p. 1; Chicago *Tribune*, April 21, 1970, p. 1.

124. U.S. Congress, Senate, Committee on Foreign Relations, *United States Security Agreements and Commitments Abroad* (Washington, D.C.: U.S. Government Printing Office, 1971), I, 380, 483, 490, 502, 504, 556.

125. *Foreign Broadcast Information Service*, April 23, 1970, p. I-1.

126. U.S. Congress, Senate, 91st Cong., 2nd sess., March 26, 1970, *Congressional Record*, p. S4650.

127. Ibid., p. S6835.

128. Chicago *Tribune*, May 7, 1970.

129. U.S. Congress, Senate, Committee on Foreign Relations, *Commitments*, I, 1061.

130. Ibid., II, 2015-2301.

131. Washington *Post*, June 8, 1970, p. 1; Washington *Star*, June 8, 1970, p. 1; Chicago *Tribune*, June 8, 1970, p. 1; Washington *Post*, June 10, 1970, p. A-23.

132. Washington *Post*, June 8, 1970, pp. A-1, A-8.

133. New York *Times*, July 2, 1970, p. 7.

134. New York *Times*, July 4, 1970, pp. 1,3.

135. Washington *Post*, July 16, 1970, p. 19; Baltimore *Sun*, July 19, 1970, p. 1; New York *Times*, July 31, 1970, p. 7.

136. U.S. Congress, Senate, Committee on Foreign Relations, *Commitments*, II, 2128.

137. Ibid., II, 2388.

138. Ibid., I, 918-1146.

139. New York *Times*, July 28, 1970, p. 4.

140. Washington *Post*, July 21, 1970, p. 1; Washington *Star*, July 21, 1970, p. 3.

141. New York *Times*, July 22, 1970, p. 3; "CBS Evening News," July 21, 1970.

142. New York *Times*, July 25, 1970, p. 2.

143. U.S. Congress, Senate, 91st Cong., 2nd sess., July 28, 1970, *Congressional Record*, p. S12258.

144. *Al-Alam*, August 1, 1970, p. 1.

145. Washington *Star*, August 4, 1970, p. 6; New York *Times*, August 4, 1970, p. 1.

146. New York *Times Magazine*, August 9, 1970, pp. 7, 64, 65.

147. New York *Times*, August 10, 1970, p. 5.

148. U.S. Congress, Senate, 91st Cong., 2nd sess., August 12, 1970, *Congressional Record*, p. S13276.

149. U.S. Congress, Senate, Committee on Foreign Relations, *Commitments*, II, 1359, 1373.

150. Washington *Post*, September 12, 1970, pp. 1, 9; Washington *Post*, September 15, 1970, p. 20; Baltimore *Sun*, September 13, 1970, p. 1; Baltimore *Sun*, September 15, 1970, p. 4. Also see U.S. Congress, Senate, Committee on Foreign Relations, *Commitments*, II, 1519-1768.

151. New York *Times*, October 19, 1970, p. 1; Washington *Star*, October 19, 1970, p. 2; Washington *Post*, October 19, 1970, p. 1. Also see U.S. Congress, Senate, Committee on Foreign Relations, *Commitments*, II, 1881-1958.

152. New York *Times*, November 19, 1970.

153. Washington *Post*, November 1, 1970, p. 3; New York *Times*, November 1, 1970, p. 3.

154. *Al-Alam*, November 5, 1970, p. 1; and November 7, 1970, p. 1; *L'Opinion*, November 7, 1970, p. 1; *Istiqlal*, November 7, 1970, p. 1.

155. U.S. Congress, Senate, Committee on Foreign Relations, Subcommittee on U.S. Security Agreements and Commitments Abroad, *United States Security Agreements and Commitments Abroad: Broader Aspects of U.S. Commitments* (Washington, D.C.: U.S. Government Printing Office, 1971).

156. Ibid., II, 2415, Also see Washington *Star*, December 21, 1970, p. 4.

157. U.S. Congress, Senate, Committee on Foreign Relations, *Commitments*, II, 2303.

158. Francis Wilcox, *Congress, the Executive and Foreign Policy* (New York: Harper and Row, 1971), p. 104.

159. Ibid., pp. 112-13.

160. Cited in ibid., p. 113.

161. "NBC Sunday Night News," December 20, 1970.

162, Interview with senior analyst on North Vietnamese affairs, Bureau of Intelligence and Research, Department of State, June 1970.

163. Interview with Ambassador Henry M. Byroade, November 1973.

164. Interviews with senior U.S. Air Force commanders, Udorn, Thailand, and Saigon, Vietnam, August 1970.

165. Interviews with senior U.S. Embassy officials, Bangkok, Thailand, July 1971.

# CHAPTER

# 6

## THE AUTHORIZATION/
## APPROPRIATIONS PROCESS:
## THE CAMBODIA SUPPLEMENTAL

The "power of the purse," including power over expenditures as well as taxation, is the most far-reaching and awesome power granted to the federal government by the Constitution. It is the source and substance of all activities of the federal government and of the machinery of government in all its branches. In the most unambiguous grant of power contained in the Constitution, the framers clearly intended to impart the "power of the purse" to Congress alone.

In all democracies the "power of the purse" is the normal prerogative of the legislature, but in no other democracy has the legislature such power to subject executive budget proposals to such detailed review and such extensive revision in the relating of appropriations directly to policies, programs, and activities of the executive departments.[1]

Article I, section 8, clause 1 provides:

> The Congress shall have power to lay and collect taxes, duties, imposts and excises, to pay the debts and *provide for the common defense* and general welfare of the United States; but all duties, imposts and excises shall be uniform throughout the United States.

Thus the very power to tax is tied, inter alia to the need to "provide for the common defense."[2]

More explicit grants of power over defense affairs are contained in Articles 12, 13, and 14 of section 8:

> Article 12: To raise and support armies, but no appropriation of money to that use shall be for a longer term than two years;
> Article 13: To provide and maintain a navy;

Article 14: To make rules for the government and regulation of the land and naval forces;[3]

These three clauses imply a great deal more than they make explicit; and, as we shall see, it is only since about 1950 that they have been translated into detailed influence by Congress. While the two-year appropriation limit for the army was inserted because of the colonial fear of standing armies, it later became the basis for an entirely different use of the appropriation process: the molding of both defense posture and defense policy.

Section 9, clause 7, is at once an implicit recognition of the Executive's powers of expenditure and also the most important single restriction on Presidential power found in the Constitution:

7: No money shall be drawn from the treasury but in consequence of appropriations made by law; and a regular statement and account of the receipts and expenditures of all public money shall be published from time to time.[4]

That the framers intended this "power of the purse" to be used extensivly in the area of foreign and defense affairs cannot be doubted. In "Federalist No. 58," Madison wrote:

[The House] alone can propose the supplies requisite for the support of government. They in a word hold the purse—that powerful instrument by which we behold...the people gradually enlarging the sphere of its activity and importance, and finally reducing, as far as it seems to have wished, all the overgrown prerogatives of the other branches of the government. This power over the purse may, in fact, be regarded as the most complete and effectual weapon with which any constitution can arm the immediate representatives of the people, for obtaining a redress of every grievance, and for carrying into effect every just salutary measure.[5]

In the "Twenty-fourth Federalist," Hamilton said:

...the whole power of raising armies was lodged in the *legislature*, not in the *executive*;...there was to be found in respect to this object an important qualification even of the legislative discretion on that clause which forbids the appropriation of money for the support of an army for any longer period than two years—a precaution which upon a nearer view of it will appear to be a great and real security against military establishments without evident necessity.[6]

And in the "Twenty-sixth Federalist," he stated:

> The legislature of the United States will be *obliged* by this provision, once at least in every two years, to deliberate upon the propriety of keeping a military force on foot; to come to a new resolution on the point; and to declare their sense of the matter by formal vote in the face of their constituents.[7]

In 1789 it was perfectly reasonable to expect that Congress was entirely capable of handling the military and defense responsibilities involved in the exercise of the "power of the purse." The sizes of armies, the methods of warfare, and the simple problems of primitive logistics were all issues well within the ken of the legislators of the day. Through their own investigations and judgment, they could be expected to determine the kinds of armed forces required for the republic's defense and the diplomatic policies best to serve the young republic's interests. Indeed, the largest challenges of the time seemed to be the lower-level questions of food, forage, horses, and musket balls.[8]

The first appropriation act of the new Congress, however, did not include the kind of detailed itemizing that appeared later; instead, it provided lump sums for four general categories: $216,000 for the civil list, $137,000 for the Department of War, $190,000 to discharge warrants previously issued by the Board of Treasury, and $96,000 for pensions to disabled veterans.[9]

With the Appropriation Act of December 23, 1791, however, Congress began the process of narrowing executive discretion by the introduction of a "that is to say" clause. For example, approximately $500,000 was appropriated for the War Department—"that is to say," $102,686 for pay of troops, $48,000 for clothing, $4,152 for forage, and so on. Two years later the process had gone to the level of such minutiae as an item of $450 for firewood, stationery, printing, and other contingencies.[10] Thus the period of lump-sum appropriations was short-lived, and did not reappear until the later periods of war.

The solidifying of the Congressional "power of the purse" over military and foreign affairs, like all other aspects of the money power, was determined largely during the monumental struggle between the first Secretary of the Treasury, Alexander Hamilton, and his Federalists, on the one hand, and the Democrats and supporters of Thomas Jefferson, on the other, who swiftly gained ascendancy in the House of Representatives. The details of that struggle are outside the scope of this study; but by the time Hamilton had been driven from office and Jefferson had assumed the Presidency in 1801, Congress and, most important, the House of Representatives had established a determined grip on the spending power of the executive branch.[11] Shortly after Jefferson took office, he warned Congress that it would be prudent to appropriate "specific sums to every specific purpose susceptible of definition."[12] He was less scrupulous, however, in his adherence to the constitutional provision that "no money shall be drawn from the Treasury but in consequence of appropriations made by law" when he agreed to accept France's offer to sell Louisiana for $15 million, even though no such sum had been authorized or appropriated. Later in 1807, while Congress was in recess, Jefferson ordered the purchase of military supplies for an emergency created by the attack made by a British vessel on the American ship *Chesapeake*. "To have awaited a previous and special sanction by law would have lost occasions which might not be retrieved," said Jefferson to Congress when it had convened.[13]

In 1820, when an attempt was made by Congress to reiterate the prohibition on unauthorized commitments, there was an interesting exception made for contracts for subsistence and supplies for the army and navy. This exception reflected a certain sanctity in these appropriations that lasts to the present day and, indeed, must be considered a qualification to the Congressional "power of the purse" over the military.[14]

In 1837, the House further solidified its position by passing a rule providing that "No appropriation shall be reported in any general appropriation bill or be in order as an amendment thereto, for any expenditure not previously authorized by law...."[15]

By 1860 the House Ways and Means Committee had become the most powerful body in Congress. Its tight control over the purse dominated all other committees and gave it a special status under the House rules. It controlled House proceedings, and its chairman was second only to the Speaker in influence. The problems of government finance up to this period however were quite different from those to be encountered from this point forward. Total expenditures as late as the period 1846 to 1853 averaged less than $50 million annually for the entire federal government.[16]

The Civil War of course brought about a tremendous change. The federal budget, for instance, climbed from $63 million in 1860 to $1.3 billion in 1865. During the war itself, the military forces continued to enjoy the benefit of largely unspecified lump-sum appropriations. The authority of the executive branch to transfer funds from one account to another, however, was repealed, and a requirement instituted that each agency must return all unexpended funds to the Treasury; further, the obligation of funds in excess of existing appropriations was specifically prohibited. At the same time, the House transferred some responsibilities of the Ways and Means Committee, which heretofore had handled all supply as well as revenue bills, to two new standing committees, the Committee on Appropriations and the Committee on Banking and Currency.[17]

As was noted elsewhere, the exigencies of war often have led to the ignoring of established appropriations procedures. After the firing on Fort Sumter, while Congress was adjourned, President Lincoln, for instance, directed his Secretary of the Treasury to spend $2 million for "military and naval measures necessary for the defense and support of the government..." even though there was neither authorization nor appropriations.[18]

In 1876 the appropriations power was greatly augmented by a rules change in the House that allowed substantive riders to be attached to appropriations bills. Thus, the appropriations process came to include general policy as well as financial matters. This action is of arguable constitutionality and has never really been settled. Edward Corwin raises the question of whether Congress, by such riders, is constitutionally entitled to lay down conditions that bind the President if he signs the appropriation, and decides inconclusively that "A logically conclusive argument can be made on either side of this question which, being of a 'political' nature, appears to have been left to be determined by the tussle of political forces."[19]

In 1855, in reaction to the greatly increased power of the Appropriations Committee, jurisdiction over the supply bills for the army, navy, and consular and diplomatic service were taken away from it and dispersed to the legislative committees of jurisdiction. A similar dispersion took place in the Senate.[20] This spreading of responsibility led almost immediately to a loss of Congressional control and to considerable confusion. The Appropriations Committee had a fairly unified control and policy oversight, while most of the legislative committees, "having intimate and for the most part cordial relations each with a particular department, launched out into an unrestrained competition for appropriations, the one striving to surpass the other in securing greater recognition and more money for its special charge."[21]

The disorganization in Congress during this period was exceeded by relative chaos in the executive branch. There was no central budgetary authority in the executive branch; the chief of each agency simply submitted his own estimates, usually padded in the expectation of cuts, to the Secretary of the Treasury, who then transmitted them to Congress. The President had virtually nothing at all to do with the process.[22] Woodrow Wilson wrote in 1885 that the United States had "a financial policy directed by the representative body itself, with only clerical aid from the Executive."[23] Moreover, such spending control as was exercised by the legislative committees during this period seems to have been more apparent than real, judging from the practice of deficiency appropriations, or "supplementals," that were routinely submitted if the original budget request or final appropriation did not meet the needs of the executive department.[24]

The Budget and Accounting Act, drawn up in 1920 with the active encouragement of President Wilson and signed into law in 1921 by President Harding, directed the President to prepare and transmit to Congress each year a budget showing federal revenue and expenditures for the previous and current years, and an estimate for the following year. It further set up the Bureau of the Budget to carry out this function for the executive branch. It set up also the General Accounting Office, under a comptroller general, to assist Congress in its oversight function of the budgetary process.[25]

In anticipation of passage of the Budget and Accounting Act, the House of Representatives on June 1, 1920, restored full jurisdiction to the Appropriations Committee for all supply bills, which it had originally been granted in 1865. It set up ten subcommittees, of five members each, with jurisdiction over one or more agency budgets. The Senate followed suit.

The newly reconstituted Appropriations Committee went at the first Harding budget with a vengeance, taking 20,000 pages of printed testimony and reducing the budget by more than $300 million. The chairman of the Appropriations Committee immediately took on a tremendous new prestige. "For the first time since Joseph G. Cannon had been tumbled from the throne of Blaine and Reed, there was an individual in the House who could put on his hat and walk to the other end of Pennsylvania Avenue and talk to the President of the United States eye to eye and man to man in the plain blunt language of yes and no."26

The exigencies of World War II brought a return to the lump-sum appropriations practices of all previous wars. While surveillance and some line-item supervision was exercised by the Appropriations Committees, the successful hiding of the Manhattan Project illustrates the rather gross scale of the categories appropriated.

In 1946, an extremely far-reaching organization was effected by the Legislative Reorganization Act, under which each legislative committee was charged to "exercise continuous watchfulness of the execution by the administrative agencies concerned of any laws, the subject matter of which is within the jurisdiction of such committee." It required the formation of a Joint Committee on the Legislative Budget, composed of members of the House Ways and Means and Appropriations Committees and the Senate Finance and Appropriations Committees. This joint committee under Republican control in 1947, set ceilings on appropriations and expenditures well below the Truman budget submission.

One significant contribution of the 1946 act was its provision for the hiring of professional committee staffs on a supposedly nonpolitical career basis. This was a considerable step forward—for instance, in 1945 the staff serving the Foreign Relations Committee consisted of one clerk serving on a half-time basis, an assistant clerk, a secretary, and the part-time services of another secretary.27

That first attempt at a legislative budget in 1947 died in conference. In 1948, the attempt succeeded in passage; but when its projected $10 billion surplus turned into a $1.8 billion deficit, it became somewhat discredited. When the Democrats took control of the Eighty-first Congress, it was pronounced a failure and buried. Although the provision remained part of the law, it was never thereafter attempted.28

By 1950, however, the size of the federal government, and especially its defense establishment, had become so vast and complicated that it really was beyond the capability of one committee, let alone one subcommittee or several to oversee fully. In 1952, for example, Carl Vinson, chairman of the House

Armed Services Committee, urged acceptance of the Defense Appropriation Bill just as it was reported out by the Appropriations Committee, saying: "They [the subcommittee] deserve the support of every member of this house because they are in a far better position to know the needs and necessities of national defense than you and I, who have not given...the bill the complete and detailed study it should have.[29] Vinson, who first came to the House of Representatives in 1914, and who served as chairman of the Naval Affairs Committee under Franklin Roosevelt and later as chairman of the Armed Services Committee, had enormous influence over defense policy, primarily through his control of the authorization process after the 1959 reforms. When asked about the report that he might resign his seat to become Secretary of Defense at one point, Vinson replied: "I would rather run the Pentagon from here."[30]

After several years of reflection in retirement, however, Vinson had a somewhat different perspective. He said that the role of Congress "has come to be that of a sometimes querulous but essentially kindly uncle who complains while furiously puffing on his pipe but who finally, as everyone expects, gives in and hands over the allowance, grants the permission, or raises his hand in blessing, and then returns to his rocking chair for another year of somnolence broken only by an occasional anxious glance down the avenue and a muttered doubt as to whether he had done the right thing."[31]

In 1959, in a little-publicized action, Congress did more to gain real influence over the defense establishment, and hence the strategic doctrine of the executive branch, than it had done in the 170 previous years.

Until 1959 there had been permanent legislation of a general nature authorizing appropriations for research and development, aircraft, and other items. These general authorizations served as open-ended permission to request appropriations for these programs without further specific legislative action on the part of the Senate and House Committees on Armed Services.

In 1959, under the sponsorship of Senator John Stennis of Mississippi, Congress passed an act requiring annual authorizations for important weapons systems and activities before any funds could be appropriated. This act (section 4-12 [b] of Public Law 86-149) prohibited the appropriation of funds for the procurement of aircraft, missiles, or naval vessels until a legislative authorization from the Committee on Armed Services had been passed. In the years since the 1959 act, research, development, test, and evaluation; tracked combat vehicles; the strengths of reserve components; all "other weapons"; naval torpedoes; and the active-duty strength of the armed forces have been added to this authorization requirement.[32]

Thus, today, the annual military authorization bill and the annual military appropriations bill provide that the Committees on Armed Services and the Committees on Appropriations hold detailed "posture" hearings, undertaking in each one a sweeping review not only of the military hardware and the dollars requested, but of the entire range of U.S. military and strategic policy as well as

the international policital situation that is used by the administration as justification for the requests. During the course of these hearings, all of these committees and subcommittees go into some detail as to the international climate, foreign policy assumptions of the executive branch, and worldwide military commitments. Each of these bills then provides the opportunity for detailed explora-
tion of the more contentious issues during floor debate. This is of course more
extensive in the Senate than in the House, and always more extensive in both
houses on the authorization bill than on the appropriations bills.[33] The authorization bill has come to be the central focus of attention because amendments
and restrictions may be attached to the authorization bill by simple majority
vote, whereas it takes a two-thirds vote to do so on an appropriations bill.

In the Hearing Room of the House Armed Services Committee, witnesses
find themselves confronting, in addition to the members and chairman of the
committee, an impressive walnut plaque bearing in gold letters the words from
Article I, section 8, subsection 14: "The Congress shall have power to make
rules for the government and regulation of the land and naval forces." One
who had occasion to sit many, many hours before that walnut plaque, former
Army Chief of Staff General Omar Bradley, concluded from the experience that
"The military policy of the United States is shaped by Congress, because...Con-
gress controls the appropriations which in the final analysis...control the military policy...."[34]

Another who had occasion to spend hundreds of hours before that walnut
plaque, former Secretary of Defense Robert McNamara, in reflecting upon the
process, thought that

> ...the greatest power of all, of course, is the power of Congress to
> state to the public and bring to bear the pressure of the public upon
> any administration which is failing in any way to provide adequately
> for the national defense....the role of Congress is, as I have observed
> it, to lay out the problems as the congressional representatives of the
> people see them...and in many, many cases Congress has changed
> the initial decision of the executive branch with respect to such
> appropriations.[35]

Underlying the whole process, in the view of William Elliott, is the assumption "that the Congress may always repudiate any major shift in military posture
and, whatever may be the wisdom of such a repudiation, there can be no denial
of the constitutional rights of Congress in this connection.[36]

The implications for Congressional exercise of the war powers of this far-
reaching power of the purse in defense affairs was treated in Chapter 3. The
Johnson and Nixon administrations both had laid heavy emphasis upon the
participation by Congress in the prosecution of the war and, hence, its legitimi-
zation through the appropriations process. For instance, on May 4, 1965,

President Johnson, in requesting a special appropriation to meet the mounting costs of the war, told Congress that this was "not a routine appropriation. For every member of Congress who supports this request is also voting to persist in our effort to halt Communist agression in South Vietnam."[37]

In 1970 and 1971, a series of cases on the constitutionality of the war confirmed the legitimizing role of military appropriations and other collaborative legislation. In the case of *Orlando* v. *Laird* and *Berk* v. *Laird*, district courts upheld the principle that even in absence of an explicit authorization for hostilities, Congress had ratified the escalation of the war by its votes on military appropriations, on renewal of the draft, and on other "joint action" or "mutual participation."[38] The following year, the First Circuit Court of Appeals ruled in the case of *Massachusetts* v. *Laird* that in a situation of prolonged but undeclared hostilities, in which the executive branch "continues to act not only in the absence of any conflicting congressional claim of authority but with steady congressional support, the Constitution has not been breached."[39]

The situation was quite the contrary, however, in the absence of such collaboration through appropriation. For instance, in the summer of 1973 the courts seemed about to take a contrary view, as would seem to have been justified, regarding the legitimacy of pursuing the bombing campaign in Cambodia. Every military appropriation bill from October 1970 on contained a clause expressly forbidding direct military support for the government of Cambodia except in connection with the withdrawal of U.S. troops from Southeast Asia and the release of prisoners of war. These conditions were fulfilled in March, 1973, and thereafter the appropriations argument alone could no longer support the executive policy. As will be seen later in this chapter, however, this situation was avoided, perhaps inadvertently, by Congressional authorization for combat air support in the course of the debate on the Cambodia Supplemental.[40]

The period following World War II brought a great increase in Congressional influence through the appropriations process, not only in defense but also in diplomatic and foreign political affairs. The greatest single catalyst to this process was the executive branch policy of containment, resulting shortly after the war in the proposing of massive assistance programs through the "Truman Doctrine," "Point 4," and the Marshall Plan. Because of the formidable opposition to such bold policies that was certain to be encountered in Congress, the executive branch embarked on an unprecedented policy of consultation and cooperation with Congress before and during the sending up of these requests. This was the great era of "bipartisan foreign policy." One result was that Congress was brought into the policy-making process in the area of foreign assistance as it had never been on any foreign policy issue. The years since have shown that this was a permanent admission to the process, not a passing opportunity. The history of the foreign assistance programs in its many incarnations provides a record not merely of Congressional participation but, indeed, of Congressional dominance. The policy impact in many cases went far beyond the mere shape or size of assistance programs themselves. In 1956, for example, the Eisenhower administration decided to withdraw from the Aswan Dam Project for a variety of reasons. At least one observer, however, described the impending action by the Senate to cut off any aid to Egypt as a determining factor in a decision that was to have grave repercussions for U.S. interests in the Middle East for many years.[41]

As Arthur Schlesinger put it shortly after the end of the Kennedy administration:

> In the realm of hemisphere affairs, Monroe could promulgate a doctrine, Theodore Roosevelt wave a Big Stick and Franklin Roosevelt become a Good Neighbor without reference to Congress; and if Congress disapproved, there was little it could do. But the Alliance for Progress, since it needed appropriations, was at the mercy of Congress every step along the way. No one wished to change the system; but it was hard to deny that contemporary Presidents, hedged around by an aggressive Congress and an unresponsive bureaucracy, had in significant respects notably less freedom of action than their predecessors.[42]

The Congressional hold over appropriations for foreign assistance, moreover, drew into the policy process the pull and haul of the many interest groups and lobbyists finding opportunities in such legislation as agriculture, coal, shipping, maritime labor, machine labor, and machine tools, each of whom managed to obtain certain conditions and restrictions on the legislation, according to their need.[43]

A less dramatic but sometimes more pervasive appropriations hold over international diplomatic and political affairs is exercised by the authorization and appropriations for the Department of State. Since 1971, however, the Senate Foreign Relations Committee and the House Foreign Affairs Committee have followed the example set by the Armed Services Committee 15 years before and now have required an annual authorization bill for the Department of State, USIA, and AID. Each of the bills produced since that time has proved to be what the executive branch describes as "a Christmas tree" of restrictive amendments.

In the course of this process, then, the authorizing and appropriating committees currently exercise four distinct but closely related types of control over foreign and defense policy. First, they determine whether any funds will be committed for a policy proposed by the Executive. Second, they decide the amount of funds to be allocated for such a commitment and, within such allocation, what parts of the program will be funded high and which low or not at all. In the case of the defense posture, this is tantamount to molding the defense posture and, hence, to determining the parameters of the strategic doctrine available to the administration. Third, they shape the nature of U.S. participation in international organizations and in defense organizations. Fourth, they review and pass upon the administrative and policy procedures of the departments in the carrying out of programs under their jurisdiction. In the case of USIA, for instance, this gives Congress control over the image projected abroad of the United States and of the public affairs policy of the executive branch.

The hearings of the appropriations subcommittees and of the Armed Services Committees and the reports published by the committees contain many examples of policy decisions and administrative directives. Though many of these are actually written into the acts themselves, it is not necessary to do so, since verbal instructions to the responsible secretaries can normally secure commitments that are just as binding.[44]

A typical appropriation act is written in technical, legal, and often abstruse language and contains a vast body of statutory authorizations, provisions, restrictions, and conditions. They may typically include statements of the activities or objects for which each line item might be spent; allocations to or limitations on expenditures for subitems under each line item; restrictions or limitations on the number and prices of items to be purchased; prohibitions of the use of such purchased items for certain activities; directives concerning internal administration; and other substantive legislation. The 32 regular and special appropriation acts for fiscal 1960, for instance, required 248 pages of fine print, totaling approximately 100,000 words.[45]

The informal webs of "understandings" between the committees and the executive chiefs over whom they have jurisdiction are one of the most important and effective powers of the authorizing and appropriating committees. These understandings, usually developed a short period after the accession of a new incumbent to the Cabinet post, are in effect promises to the committees that lump-sum appropriations, such as they are, will be spent in exactly the manner desired by the committee.[46]

The chairman and senior members of these committees are usually formidable overseers. Coming from safe districts as a rule, these members often have served decades on the same subcommittees and committees, and are usually better-informed about certain aspects of their departments and their budgets, which they have been reviewing for more years than the Cabinet officers themselves.[47]

The relationship between the Joint Committee on Atomic Energy and the appropriations committees, on the one hand, and the Atomic Energy Commission, on the other, is a good example. The Appropriation Act of 1970, for instance, makes available a lump sum of $1.9 billion to the commission. Despite the lack of detailed breakdowns and individual line items, there is a very detailed and solid understanding between those committees and the commission as to how those appropriations are to be spent.[48]

## LIMITATIONS

There are of course limitations on the effectiveness of the appropriations power as well. The sheer complexity of the process is one formidable shortcoming among others that include the many different types of appropriation bills in which funds are voted, the confusing terminology, the technical jargon such as NOA (new obligational authority), delivery ceilings, expenditure ceilings, and carry-overs. The amount appropriated for any fiscal year does not indicate even approximately what the actual expenditures will be for a program. An appropriation authorizes a department to incur obligations, but the spending may be spread over several or even many years. In addition, there are the annual supplemental appropriations and deficiency appropriations that often are huge, and their relationship to programs voted earlier is often very difficult to ascertain.

Another problem is conflict among committees themselves. In many instances the Appropriations Committee of, say, the House will seek to impose policies on a department that are in direct contradiction to those favored by the legislative committee of the same or the other house. The executive branch therefore sometimes finds itself subject to conflicting instructions and no clear legislative policy guidance.

Because of these and other problems, there has grown up a perennial problem of delay. It is now the norm that the authorization and appropriations process for the major agencies of the executive branch is rarely, if ever, completed before the end of the second quarter of the fiscal year in which the legislation is intended. During this interim period the executive branch must operate on continuing resolution authority. In these cases it is faced with a situation described in 1825 by the Secretary of Navy, who reported to Congress that for nearly half of the year his department acted in "perfect ignorance of the law under which it is bound to act." As a result, "The law is necessarily, not complied with, because it is passed after the act is performed."[49] Legitimate questions have been raised, moreover, whether all of this effort, especially on such bills as the State Department authorization and the foreign assistance bills, is really worth it. A high percentage of the leadership of the committees is often tied up for months in conflicts between and among committees and between the committees and the executive branch over these appropriation and authorization bills. A good case can be made that the scarce time of these committees and their members could be used much more advantageously.

One of the most controversial of the limitations on the appropriations power exercised by the executive branch is the Presidential impoundment of appropriated funds. The policy has a long history, beginning in 1803, when President Jefferson declined to spend money for gunboats, and was exercised from time to time by his successors. In 1941, President Roosevelt carried it to new dimensions by systematically impounding funds appropriated for public works not directly related to the war effort. In 1949, President Truman created a furor by impounding appropriations for the Air Force, and President Kennedy did the same when he refused to spend $180 million appropriated for the RS-70 bomber in 1961. In 1967 alone, President Johnson impounded a total of $5 billion. President Nixon carried impoundment to its greatest extreme to date, impounding a total of $15 billion by 1973.[50] Congressman George H. Mahon, chairman of the House Appropriations Committee, said, "The weight of experience and practice bears out the general proposition that an appropriation does not constitute a mandate to spend every dollar appropriated....I believe it is fundamentally desirable that the Executive have limited powers of impoundment in the interests of good management and constructive economy in public expenditures."[51] That all of Nixon's impoundments could be justified seems doubtful. William Rehnquist, then of the Department of Justice and later appointed to the Supreme Court, advised in 1969 that "With respect to the suggestion that the President has a constitutional power to decline to spend appropriated funds, we must conclude that the existence of a broad power is supported by neither reason nor precedent...." He found it difficult "to formulate a constitutional theory to justify a refusal by the President to comply with the Congressional directive to spend.[52]

A quite pervasive limitation on the detail that the appropriation power may determine is the wide variety of contingency and transfer authorities permitted by most appropriations bills. Reprogramming, for instance, is a procedure allowed for the shifting of funds within an appropriations item; and the transfer authorities normally permit the President to take funds that have been earmarked for one class of appropriations and apply them to another. Contingency funds have often been used for purposes not even contemplated by Congress when it appropriated the money. For instance, in 1961, President Kennedy established the Peace Corps by executive order. He financed the agency by the use of contingency funds drawn from the Mutual Security Act until Congress finally appropriated funds for the agency seven months later.[53]

Appropriations for the Defense Department and for foreign assistance have been especially generous in permitting the transfer of funds and the use of contingencies. It was such a transfer authority, as we shall see, that President Nixon used to extend financial assistance to Cambodia after the fall of Sihanouk and before the passage of the Cambodia Supplemental that is the subject of this chapter. By the time of the passage of the Supplemental, it included $100 million to restore funds that the President had already diverted to Cambodia from other programs.

By far the most significant restraint on the appropriations power is the de facto limit imposed by ongoing hostilities. During such hostilities, while opposition to nearly any other legislation is within the rights of a Senator, voting against defense appropriations is a kind of civil disobedience for members, described by one critic as "a congressional version of not paying taxes."[54] No member can afford to be characterized by his enemies back home as taking the guns away from our boys on the battlefield. As noted in Chapter 3, for instance, in 1967 an Associated Press survey reported that 40 out of 48 responding Senators opposed President Johnson's policy in Southeast Asia; but later that year only three of these Senators actually voted against a $12 billion supplemental appropriation for the war.[55] One of those who did vote against it, Senator Ernest Gruening of Alaska, later recalled that President Johnson had said to him, "I don't care what kind of speeches you make as long as you don't vote against the appropriations."[56] Gruening did, and was defeated at the next election.

During any hostilities, moreover, lump-sum appropriations become the order of the day. During the Civil War, Congress appropriated $50 million to pay volunteers, $26 million for subsistence, and $76 million to cover a wide assortment of items, all of these to be divided "as the exigencies of the service may require." During World War I, Wilson received $100 million for "national security and defense," to be spent at his discretion, and $250 million to be applied to construction costs under the Emergency Shipping Fund.[57] There was of course the example in World War II, whereby the Manhattan Project was funded for several years from funds appropriated for "expediting production." Appropriations for the project totaled well over $2 billion, and members of the House Appropriations Committee told one observer that about $800 million had been spent on the project before they even knew about it.[58]

While it is a mixed picture, it cannot be denied that since 1945 there has been a sustained Congressional effort to shape foreign and defense policy through appropriations that has resulted in a significantly greater dependence of foreign and defense policies on appropriations, with the result that the executive branch has lost influence to Congress. The vast growth of the tools needed for defense, the size of the foreign affairs and defense establishment, and the extent and utility of economic and military foreign assistance have drawn Congress inextricably into policy formulation to an extent it has never before enjoyed. Indeed, in most cases it can exert a controlling influence over both defense and strategic doctrine as well as foreign political and military commitments. In organizational terms, the interaction between substantive policy making and the budgetary process is drawing the personnel of Congress and the personnel of the executive branch into a process by which the abstractions of policy are translated into specific programs and action. It is this interaction process to which we now turn in examining the events surrounding the administration's request for supplemental assistance for Cambodia in 1970.[59]

## THE CAMBODIA SUPPLEMENTAL

The circumstances surrounding the deposing of Prince Sihanouk and the beginning of U.S. involvement with the Lon Nol government were treated in Chapter 3. It was pointed out that the U.S. government had absolutely no involvement in Prince Sihanouk's removal as head of state, and greeted the event with both disappointment and skepticism. The day after the coup, a senior National Security Council official informed a group of Republican Senators that the policy of the administration would be to maintain strict neutrality, and there was no intention to become involved in Cambodia. (See the account of this meeting in Chapter 3.) The administration maintained a wait-and-see attitude for the next four weeks. During this period, however, it became apparent that the Lon Nol government was determined to put as much military pressure as possible upon the North Vietnamese in Cambodia. The reaction of the North Vietnamese, as outlined in Chapter 2, was to move out of the sanctuaries and undertake actions against the Cambodian army. The judgment was made that in conjunction with this effort, the North Vietnamese were also attempting to secure a corridor of territory to the Gulf of Siam in order to reestablish the supply lines that had been lost to them with the fall of the port of Sihanoukville.

By the middle of March, a number of officials in the NSC and in the Pentagon had concluded that the U.S. government had no choice but to take action. The Cambodian forces were losing ground rapidly, and the prospect loomed of the North Vietnamese gaining de facto control of all of Cambodia. Without the restraining influence of Sihanouk on the North Vietnamese, such a situation was judged intolerable.

In mid-March, then, for the first time voices were heard recommending immediate assistance to the Cambodian army. Moreover, the long-standing desire of the Joint Chiefs of Staff to take direct action against the Cambodian sanctuary areas was given serious consideration. The development of the policy culminating in the decision to launch the incursion into the sanctuary areas on April 30 was of course closely intertwined with the decision to give grant military assistance to the Cambodian armed forces. It is the latter decision and its implementation that concern us in this chapter.

The issue was crystallized when, early in April, the Lon Nol government formally requested substantial assistance in the form of military weapons, supplies, and ammunition. Through most of April, this request and its implications were the subject of vigorous policy dispute within the executive branch. Not surprisingly, the Joint Chiefs argued for a prompt and favorable response. The civilian Pentagon officials were more cautious in their recommendations, and the officials of the Department of State were not favorably disposed to responding to the request. The latter department was highly sensitive to the repercussions that the granting of such assistance would bring about in Congress. It shared, moreover, a very real concern about the wisdom of any actions that would widen U.S. involvement in Indochina. The National Security Council staff saw developments in Cambodia as a direct and perhaps mortal threat to its projected schedule of Vietnamization and, consequently, to the strategy for the secret negotiations then going on in Paris. It favored the provision of military supplies to the Cambodian government without delay. The dispute continued into the last week of April and was finally resolved by the President himself after a full meeting of the National Security Council.

The Senate Foreign Relations Committee left no doubt as to its view of the wisdom of granting such assistance. On April 27, Secretary Rogers met in executive session with the committee and explained to it the nature and size of the Cambodian request, without indicating whether he endorsed or opposed the request. Immediately following this secret session, Senator Fulbright informed the press that the committee was nearly unanimous in its opposition to providing any military assistance to Cambodia, for fear of leading to a "widening war" in Indochina. He reported that the committee had been informed that the Cambodian government wanted enough American equipment to supply "an entire army," including "rifles and guns and half-tracks and trucks and jeeps and helicopters and airplanes...Spam and all that goes with it." Fulbright reported that "The committee was virtually in agreement—and very firmly in agreement against sending assistance to Cambodia under the circumstances."

## AID BEGINS

During the last week in April, the South Vietnamese government, with the knowledge and assistance of the American Embassy, sent a quantity of captured AK-47 automatic rifles to the Lon Nol government. Fulbright said that the committee opposed even such minimal assistance.[60]

Three days later the President announced on nationwide television that he had ordered the U.S. Army to attack the sanctuary areas of Cambodia, and that under the discretionary authority available to him under the Foreign Assistance Act, he was ordering the dispatch of arms and ammunition to the Cambodian government.[61] In the furor that followed the announcement of the Cambodian incursion, the issue of assistance to the Lon Nol government was virtually forgotten. Under the Foreign Assistance Act, the President had available funds to be used at his discretion. Measures were immediately taken to begin the shipment of weapons, ammunition, and some trucks and vehicles. The funds available were sufficient to deal with the limited needs of a Cambodian army still only about 45,000 men strong. The size and duration of assistance that would ultimately be required was unknown to the executive branch. While the bitter debate proceeded in the Senate on the Cooper-Church amendment, this issue was not directly focused upon. Through the summer, funds and stocks were utilized from the military assistance programs and the magnitude of the future needs began to take shape. The Cambodian army was rapidly expanded to over 100,000 personnel by the end of the summer. By that time nearly $40 million worth of material had been provided, and it had become clear that the actual need for the coming year would be in the magnitude of several hundred million. The administration could now not avoid the challenge of going to Congress for authorization of a program of such magnitude.

In the second week of September, Secretary of Defense Laird sent the President a memorandum strongly urging immediate action on a Supplemental authorization request for almost a billion dollars for various foreign assistance programs, to include almost $250 million in military and budgetary support for the Cambodian government. Shortly thereafter he met privately with the President, and the President decided to accept Laird's recommendation to proceed immediately with the Supplemental request. After the President's decision there was nearly a month of interdepartmental maneuvers that eventually resulted in agreement between the State and Defense Departments and National Security Council as to the size of the program. Both the State Department and the Budget Bureau had objected to the size and the nature of the Cambodian program. On October 8, the President decided to delay the submission of the request to Congress until after the November elections, for which Congress was due to recess the following week. It must be remembered that this was the first "lame duck" session of Congress in many years, and no one held very high prospects for achieving anything at all.

On October 12, a meeting was held at the White House to organize a special strategy group to plan the presentation and the defense of the Supplemental when the Congress returned in November. Assistant Secretary of State David Abshire was given primary responsibility for handling the presentation, while the National Security Council staff and William Timmons were to be responsible for coordinating the activities of all of the agencies in directing the legislative battle that was to come.

During October the challenge of obtaining Congressional authorization for aid to Cambodia grew to become the highest priority matter of foreign policy in the administration. Interagency groups were hard at work reaching agreement on final dollar figures and on the shape of the legislative package. Other groups in the White House and State were drafting and redrafting the Presidential message that would accompany the presentation. The NSC-Abshire group was preparing a strategy for the legislative battle, with briefings and target lists of vulnerable and swing Senators, plus detailed analyses of what approaches were likely to be fruitful with each target Senator.

By November 1, a complete package was ready to go to the President for his final decision on details and dollar figures. The National Security Council and State Department recommended that the President call a joint session of

Congress and present his prepared message in person, thus providing a clear demonstration of the highest possible priority.

The President's domestic advisers and Secretary Laird argued against such a high-level course of action, recommending instead that the Presidential message be sent to Congress with the legislation and that the main presentation be made through a meeting with the key bipartisan leadership, followed by meetings with the members of the Foreign Relations and Armed Services Committees of both houses.

By the end of that week, a sizable coordinating group had been set up in the State Department, under the leadership of Assistant Secretary Abshire. Rogers had made available personnel from all appropriate bureaus in State and had given Abshire first call on the senior sub-Cabinet officers of the department. A number of briefing teams were put together, including personnel from the Pentagon and Joint Chiefs, and they refined their presentations in preparation for going into action as soon as the message was sent.

With Congress silenced by its absence, the interagency process went forward with remarkable speed. By the middle of the second week of November, a complete game plan had been assembled and presented to the President by the National Security Council-undersecretary's committee, which had been assigned overall responsibility for pulling the package together. All agencies had finally agreed that it would be unwise to proceed with the scenario involving an address to a joint session of Congress, and instead settled on a course of action involving the launching of the campaign by the President at a bipartisan leadership meeting to take place on November 18. The Presidential message had been prepared, and numerous briefing papers and position papers for handouts on the Hill were ready in packages. These papers and the President's message focused on the Nixon Doctrine as the keystone of American foreign policy, and the supplemental as the first direct application of the Nixon Doctrine in its purest form. The importance of funds for military assistance to Israel was the part of the package stressed first, then the necessity to increase assistance to Korea following the previously announced withdrawal of 20,000 U.S. troops from Korea, and finally the need to enable the continued withdrawal of U.S. forces from Indochina through helping the Cambodians to carry the burden of their own defense.

Abshire had taken special care to coordinate the approach with Senator Gale McGee, the only member of the Foreign Relations Committee known to be favorable to the request. Abshire was especially concerned that the timing of the presentation not interfere with the Foreign Assistance Appropriations Bill that was due for markup as soon as Congress returned.

Another essential element of the presentation was the scheduling of a breakfast meeting between Congressman Otto Passman of Louisiana and the Secretary of State and the senior department officers as soon as Congress returned. Passman, as chairman of the Foreign Assistance Subcommittee of the House Appropriations Committee, was the central figure on the House Appropriations side.

The briefing teams that had been assembled were each assigned specific target Senators, with suggestions of the primary concerns and interests of each. In addition to the Senators themselves, key staff members were targeted and a schedule of briefings was arranged to commence immediately following the White House presentation.

## THE SUPPLEMENTAL TAKES FORM

While seeming to be a simple, straightforward request, the presentation was actually quite complicated, involving numerous separate documents that had a number of separate committee jurisdictions. In addition to these formal documents, there were the many materials prepared for press releases, ghost-written speeches for administration supporters on the floor, Congressional hand-outs, and position papers, all of which fell under the responsibility of Abshire's coordinating group in State.

To follow the initial blitz, and in addition to the briefing team follow-ups, Abshire had prepared a detailed strategy for the briefings of those Congressional leaders who would inevitably be absent from the White House briefing. He set up a detailed schedule for a series of breakfast meetings to be hosted by the Secretary or Undersecretary at the Department, during which geopolitical briefings—to highlight the importance of the Supplemental and to put it in perspective—would be presented to small groups of Senators.

It had always been the practice that the specific figures for the foreign assistance programs for each country were kept classified because of the difficulties that one country comparing its share with another's inevitably produced. In this case it was strongly recommended that all of the country figures in the Supplemental be declassified, so that they could be fully discussed in the floor debate that was essential to passage of the Supplemental request.

By November 12, the press had got hold of the story and the outlines of the package were front-page news. Later that morning a strategy session was held by the White House group. Dr. James Schlesinger, then Assistant Director of the Budget Bureau for International Affairs, explained the technicalities of the budget request and possible damage that could be done by restrictive amendments. After admonishing all present to hold the information close, so that the Hill was not informed prematurely of the details and the strategy, Timmons was distressed to hear from Secretary Laird's legislative assistant, Richard Capen, that Laird had already provided the briefing papers to the Armed Services Committee.

On November 13, the President signed the Presidential Determination to transfer $50 million from other accounts to pay for assistance to Cambodia. Speaker John McCormack and Senator Richard Russell, Chairman of the Senate Appropriations Committee, were briefed on the details and the rationale for the signing. At a meeting of the working group that afternoon in Timmons' office, it was decided that there would be no further separate handling of publicity for the Presidential Determination, rather, it would be lumped in with the presentation of the Supplemental scheduled for the following Wednesday, in order to give Congress the fewest number of separate targets.

## THE BATTLE BEGINS

On Monday, November 16, Congress reconvened for its "lame duck" session. A good example of the complete isolation of the foreign policy process in the White House from the management and domestic side run by H.R. Haldeman was provided that afternoon. While the foreign affairs advisers to the President—since the National Security Act of 1947 set up the National Security Council as a separate entity—have always been a bit apart from the rest of the White House apparatus, Haldeman had carried the separation to considerable extremes. He reportedly had a deep distrust of "eggheads" and intellectuals. During the 1968 campaign Haldeman had methodically demoted all of the candidate's advisers who were concerned with substantive policy issues and relegated them about five levels below the junior account executives and advance men whom he had brought in to take over the campaign.

After the election, Haldeman and his associates carried this distrust of anyone with a graduate degree into management of the White House staff. He and his associates particularly distrusted the National Security Council staff, not only because they were intellectuals but also because a number of them had been recruited from the previous administration and were suspected of being registered Democrats. As a result, Haldeman moved swiftly to isolate those people from the rest of the White House staff. The privileges for the National Security Council staff in the White House Mess were withdrawn, and their access to the west wing of the White House was restricted. These physical separations reflected even deeper differences in intellectual approach, and resulted in increasingly numerous disputes between the National Security Council and Haldeman and his staff.

On the morning of November 16, the National Security Council was informed by Dwight Chapin, Haldeman's assistant for scheduling, that Haldeman had decided to cancel the Wednesday meeting for the President to present the legislative package to the Congressional leadership, because Haldeman felt that the President was too busy to take the time. Upon hearing this, the National Security Council staff expressed the view that account executives from J. Walter Thompson were not necessarily fully qualified to run the government, and that eventually they could bring the administration to a bad end. It was not until a senior National Security Council official intervened directly with the

President that Haldeman was overruled and the leadership briefing was rescheduled for ten o'clock on Wednesday, November 18.

On November 18 the leadership met with the President; and because of the advance press attention, they were well aware of the subject of the briefing. The President began the meeting by briefly explaining the status of the situations in the Middle East and in Southeast Asia. He stated his intention of requesting appropriations for Israel, Jordan, and Lebanon in the Middle East, to enable them to maintain their defense capabilities. He informed them that in East Asia, he was requesting $155 million for Cambodia in order to facilitate the continued success of Vietnamization, and a further $65 million for South Vietnam. He explained his submitting the request during the post-election session rather than waiting for the new Congress by the potentially explosive situation in the Middle East and by his concern that no further instability be injected into Vietnamization and the current schedule for troop withdrawals from Vietnam.

The President then called on a senior adviser to explain the requests in more detail. In his brief remarks the official emphasized that the primary consideration was the implementation of the Nixon Doctrine. He emphasized the importance of carrying out the pledges of the U.S. government to provide the tools for those nations that had the will power to carry the burden of their own defense. He pointed out that under the Nixon Doctrine, the administration had already reduced overseas military personnel by 300,000 as of the following spring, and that 68 U.S. military installations on foreign soil had been closed and 44 others reduced. He then reviewed the operations in the Cambodian sanctuaries in May and June, and concluded that they had greatly impaired the enemy's ability to fight in South Vietnam and had directly resulted in a dramatic reduction of U.S. casualties back to pre-1965 levels. He praised the Lon Nol government for a remarkable job in mobilizing its manpower effectively in a very short period of time, to the point where the Khmer army numbered 135,000 men, compared with only 35,000 as of March 18. There was now the problem of having more soldiers than arms and equipment to outfit them. The majority of those present expressed support for the President's actions, but the expected critics expressed their opposition in no uncertain terms. The President closed the meeting by emphasizing that it was important that the Congress give full consideration to the measure without delay, and that it consider the package as a whole and not break down its components for separate consideration. The total requested was $1,035 billion.

Senator Mike Mansfield, responding for the opposition, told the President that the measure had no chance for passage unless there were a number of assurances given to the Senate, such as an increase in troop withdrawals, an ironclad pledge that no U.S. troops would be involved in the Middle East, and a promise of further troop withdrawals from Korea. If those pledges were made by the President, then action would be possible before the end of the Ninety-first

Congress. Senator Fulbright expressed his grave reservations, saying that this measure represented a very serious enlargement of U.S. commitments in Southeast Asia.

The following morning, the President repeated the performance at a meeting with the House leadership. The reception of the House members to the same presentation was quite supportive, bordering on enthusiastic.

Following the preordained game plan, President Nixon met that afternoon privately with Senators Mansfield and Scott to discuss the legislation on an off-the-record and informal basis. At the same time Secretary Rogers and Assistant Secretary Abshire met with Senator George Aiken to enlist his support as a special defender of the legislation for the department. That afternoon the supplemental foreign assistance bills were received by the Senate Foreign Relations Committee and the House Foreign Affairs Committee. That evening Secretaries Laird and Rogers jointly made a presentation to 43 members of the leadership of both the House and the Senate, answering questions and explaining details of the legislation.

## THE KEY TO SUCCESS

On November 20, Abshire embarked on what he perceived as the key to success of the administration's effort to pass the Supplemental, gaining the support of Senator John Sherman Cooper of Kentucky. On that evening Abshire and Secretary Rogers met with Cooper for several hours in a relaxed and social atmosphere. They explained the situation in Southeast Asia as the administration saw it, and how important the passage of the Supplemental was to the continued progress of Vietnamization. While they did not gain Cooper's agreement, he listened.

The wisdom of such careful attention was demonstrated the following day, when Cooper unexpectedly endorsed the "protective reaction" strikes that the administration had just launched against North Vietnam in retaliation for its shooting at reconnaissance aircraft. He told the press that he believed the action to be necessary to protect intelligence aircraft. In contrast with Cooper, the supposed main supporter of the administration on the committee, Senator George Aiken, the ranking Republican, denounced the U.S. action taken without any consultation with Congress. He asked, "Why should we expect to fly planes unmolested over North Vietnam all the time? I expect we wouldn't like for them to fly over us."[62] Overall the "protective reaction" strikes were a considerable, though temporary, setback to the administration's effort on the Supplemental.

The State Department was mobilized for this legislative offensive in a manner perhaps not equaled before or since. On November 23, Rogers approved Abshire's recommendations for the setting up of a coordinating group, chaired by Abshire, to deal with all aspects of the administration's presentation of the Supplemental. The group was given a staff and offices at the State Department. Rogers formally named Deputy Assistant Secretaries James Wilson, Roger Davies, Colgate Prentice, George Aldrich, William D. Blair, Thomas R. Pickering, and Arthur A. Hartman to work on the coordinating group. In addition AID, the White House Legislative Liaison Office, the National Security Council staff, and the Office of the Secretary of Defense designated members of the group. Because of Abshire's close relationship with the National Security Council, the White House designated the group to have overall responsibility for the administration in handling the Supplemental.

On November 24, the situation in the Senate seemed to deteriorate. Senator Aiken called Abshire and told him that he was for the Cooper-Church amendment being attached to the Supplemental because, in his view, it conflicted in no way with the Nixon Doctrine. That afternoon Aiken made a major speech on the floor, calling for more consultations between Congress and the executive branch and stating, "Foreign policies fashioned in the White House exclusively cannot be a bipartisan policy."[63] While Aiken was making his speech, the White House received a call from Saigon reporting, with dismay, that two Senate investigators, Richard Moose and James Lowenstein (the latter was appointed Deputy Assistant Secretary of State by Kissinger in 1974), were in Saigon and proceeding to Phnom Penh, where they were reported to be in the process of building the strongest possible case against giving any further assistance to both Vietnam and Cambodia. Partially in response to this, the White House approved Abshire's recommendation to send Undersecretary of State John Irwin to brief the Foreign Relations Committee the following day.

On November 25, Secretaries Rogers and Laird testified before the House Foreign Affairs Committee on the Supplemental. The House committee was cooperating fully by scheduling hearings so quickly after the bill arrived on the Hill. On the Senate side, Senator Fulbright introduced his own version that would require the authorization of such aid on a country-by-country basis.[64]

On November 30 and December 1, the House Foreign Affairs Committee continued its speedy consideration of the bill, hearing Assistant Secretary of State Marshall Green and Lt. General Robert H. Warren, the Deputy Assistant Secretary of Defense for Security Assistance.[65]

Abshire held one of his morning breakfast briefings with Senators McGee, John Sparkman, and Charles Percy on December 2. Assistant Secretary of State Marshall Green and Deputy Director George Pickering were the principal briefers. After the presentation the Senators seemed favorably disposed, but Percy in particular suggested that the entire issue would stand or fall on whether the Supplemental was seen as an enlargement of the scope of U.S. involvement. In this respect the issue of the presence of advisers and trainers was central in his mind. McGee pointed out that he had been asked to chair the Senate Appropriations Subcommittee because there was no one on the Byrd subcommittee who would defend the Supplemental. He agreed with both Sparkman and Percy that the issue was whether or not it was seen as a deeper commitment; but he added that that was a much deeper question, that the vote would really be a test between those who wanted the United States to withdraw from the world and those who supported the Nixon Doctrine. He expressed the firm opinion that unless the President was clearly visible in leading the fight, there was no chance of success. McGee also pointed out that Fulbright had introduced his separate bill with line items for each country because he intended to offer an amendment to detach Cambodia. Special attention was given to Sparkman, the second-ranking Democrat on the committee, whose support would carry considerable weight on the floor.

December 3 proved the wisdom of the special cultivation of the House Foreign Affairs Committee, when that body passed the Supplemental Authorization Bill, sending it to the floor with a solid vote of 25-6, with no amendments.[66]

A new front was opened in the legislative battle, however, that same afternoon, when the Senate Appropriations Committee reported out the Defense Appropriations bill (H.R. 19590) with an amendment of section 843 to include the sense of the original Cooper-Church amendment: "In line with the expressed intention of the President of the United States, none of the funds appropriated by this act shall be used to finance the introduction of American ground combat troops into Laos, Thailand, or Cambodia."[67]

Under Abshire's guidance the coordinating group met daily to plan every detail of strategy for the coming "engagements." Two decisive engagements loomed during the second week of December, with Secretaries Rogers and Laird scheduled to testify in public session before the Byrd subcommittee of the Senate Appropriations Committee on December 8, and Rogers scheduled to testify before the Senate Foreign Relations Committee on December 10. Elaborate preparation was based on careful reconnaissance of committee members to ascertain the questions they would be most likely to ask and to develop answers for Laird and Rogers that would most appeal to the target Senators. Warm-up sessions to drill the Secretaries were scheduled before each appearance, and detailed back-up briefing books and question and answers were provided to the Secretaries and accompanying assistants to study prior to the hearings. The prepared statements to be given at the opening of each hearing were carefully combed to consider the impact of every sentence. Literally thousands of rather high-priced man-hours were devoted to this task; and in comparison with what was going on to prepare the Senators, there was an overwhelming disparity. The staffs of the Senators involved did no more than provide collections of newspaper clippings in advance of the hearings.[68]

In the meantime, on the House side, Abshire gave careful personal attention to members of the Rules Committee, which was expected to take up the Supplemental on December 8 and, if favorably disposed, could get the bill to the House floor by the latter part of that week.

On December 4, the Public Affairs Bureau of the State Department distributed 20,000 copies of a very effective position paper in their "Current Foreign Policy" series to the media, the academic community, and foreign-affairs civic groups around the country.[69]

Two days later, Foreign Relations Committee staff members Richard Moose and James Lowenstein returned from Southeast Asia with a report containing some negative conclusions, according to sources in the press corps who informed the State Department.*

The testimony of Secretaries Laird and Rogers before the Byrd subcommittee of the Senate Appropriations Committee on December 8 went very well. Senator McGee conducted the hearing in a helpful manner, stating that the issue was one of "cut and run or phasing out with responsibility." Questions from Senators Milton Young, Gordon Allott, and John Pastore were also helpful. Senator Pastore urged that the administration make a strong public presentation of the fact that the United States would have continuing and heavy aid burdens in Southeast Asia even after U.S. troops had been withdrawn.

At the breakfast meeting hosted that morning by Undersecretary John Irwin, Senator Hiram Fong expressed his opinion that the administration would have no problem with the Senate Appropriations Committee but had a real challenge in getting an authorization from the Senate Foreign Relations Committee. He recommended that if the Foreign Relations Committee did not report out the authorization, action should be taken on the Senate floor.

Over on the House side, the cultivation of the Rules Committee members bore fruit with the granting by the committee of an "open rule" with two hours' debate for the Supplemental, thus limiting the possibility of delaying tactics by critics and reducing the opportunity for restrictive amendments from the floor. That afternoon the Defense Authorization Bill was passed in the Senate by a vote of 89-0, including the restrictive amendment to section 843. Since there was no such restriction in the House version already passed, this was to become bound up with the final solution to the Supplemental question.[70]

On December 9, Undersecretary Irwin hosted a breakfast for Senators Thomas McIntyre, Ernest Hollings, Philip Hart, and Mike Gravel, at which Gravel strongly indicated his skepticism about the administration's Indochina policy in general and the Supplemental in particular. Hollings was also skeptical,

---

*Actually, the report was a balanced and objective evaluation of the situation in Cambodia that many officials in the executive branch found useful. Unfortunately, the committee chairman did not distribute the report until after the debate was concluded and the Supplemental passed. U.S. Congress, Senate, Committee on Foreign Relations, *Cambodia: December, 1970, A Staff Report* (Washington, D.C.: U.S. Government Printing Office, 1970).

and indicated he would have to be convinced. McIntyre and Hart were unconvinced.

Later that morning Senator Cooper, in his daily meeting with Abshire, informed Abshire that he believed that the Senate was certainly disposed to attach a Cooper-Church amendment to the Supplemental if it were passed, but that he had talked with Senator Church and that Church was amenable to working out a compromise that the administration could sign.

In discussions that afternoon at the White House, it was concluded that this conversation indicated the breakthrough that was needed to spring the legislation from the Foreign Relations Committee. It was the judgment that both Cooper and Church badly wanted an amendment of almost any nature that would have their names attached and would provide some restriction on U.S. policy in Indochina, after all of the futile activity during the major Cooper-Church efforts of the spring.

That afternoon brought much encouragement from the House, when it passed the Supplemental Authorization by a vote of 249-102, with only one amendment by Congressman Peter Rodino, concerning narcotics, and the Appropriations Committee reported out the Supplemental Appropriation as part of its omnibus supplemental appropriations legislation. It voted a total of $990 million, a reduction of only $45 million from the administration request; and this, it was indicated, would be restored in the regular aid bill.[71]

That evening it was learned from sources on the Senate Foreign Relations Committee staff that Fulbright had settled on a strategy of splitting Cambodia and Korea from the rest of the supplemental bill and reporting out only the Middle East portion before recess, and this would include a Cooper-Church-type amendment. Moreover, the committee planned to block any attempt to reinstate Cambodia in floor debate by employing a filibuster. Since Congress was expected to adjourn as early as the following Friday, December 18, the Abshire coordinating group became extremely concerned. A strong recommendation was therefore sent to the President by the National Security Council, on behalf of the coordinating group, urging him to make a very strong endorsement of the measure at a press conference that he was scheduled to have the following day, December 10.

The next day Secretary Rogers appeared in open session before the Foreign Relations Committee for almost four hours. The hearing went reasonably well, with Senators Aiken, Cooper, Harrison Williams, Jacob Javits, and McGee being generally supportive, which greatly heartened Abshire, who—counting Sparkman and Thomas Dodd—believed that there was now a chance to get a majority of the committee to report out the Supplemental.

Senators Cooper and Church, as expected, argued that an amendment designed to forbid ground combat troops and advisers in Cambodia would be necessary, to which Rogers replied that the administration would not favor such an amendment but that it was willing to discuss possible language. Also not unexpectedly, Senators Fulbright, Albert Gore, and Clifford Case argued that there was a historic inevitability to our involvement in Cambodia dictating that this commitment to support would unfailingly grow, regardless of present good intentions. Rogers repeatedly emphasized that the purpose of the assistance was to enable Vietnamization to proceed and to save American lives. Toward the end of the session Fulbright indicated his strategy of preventing further consideration of the assistance until the new Congress, arguing that the President could still use discretionary provisions of old legislation to make do for the rest of the year.[72] Good news came again from the House that afternoon, when it passed the Supplemental Appropriation by a vote of 344-21.[73]

That afternoon, Assistant Budget Director James Schlesinger held a strategy meeting in his office that was attended by National Security Council staff and the White House Liaison Office. It was decided that as a matter of tactics, the fiscal year 1972 aid bill that was ready to be transmitted to Congress would be delayed until the Supplemental was passed either in this session or the new Congress, so that Fulbright would not use it for an excuse to delay action on the Supplemental. A more far-reaching decision was taken on a measure that would be sure to create a storm in Congress. It had been decided by the National Security Council and Budget to take military assistance out of the aid bill and submit it instead as a line item in the defense budget, in order to escape the jurisdiction of the Foreign Relations Committee. The implementation of that decision would be postponed because it would be almost certain to provide Fulbright with a good issue to delay the Supplemental.[74]

That evening during the President's press conference, the only mention of Cambodia came in the following exchange:

> *Mr. Scali*: Mr. President, Secretary Rogers assured the Senate Foreign Relations Committee today that there is no present intention of ever using American ground forces in Cambodia. Can you foresee any circumstances whatever under which we would use ground forces in Cambodia?
>
> *The President*: None whatever.[75]

On December 11, Secretary Laird appeared before the Foreign Relations Committee and gave a very strong presentation based on the theme of the implementation of the Nixon Doctrine.[76]

## VICTORY IN THE COMMITTEE

In his meeting with Senator Cooper on December 12, Abshire got down to specifics as to what the administration might not oppose. Cooper agreed that he would not support an amendment going beyond a limitation on United States ground forces and advisers. He agreed further to work that afternoon to convince Senator Church of that formula. Concern was now growing that with the Senate moving more rapidly to adjournment, the deadline would not be met.

At Abshire's urging, Secretary Rogers telephoned Senator Javits, who was to be in New York for most of the following week, urging him to return to Washington to attempt to vote out the Supplemental on Monday. Javits agreed to support the administration's bill and to oppose any attempts to widen the Cooper-Church amendment beyond the formula already agreed to with Senator Cooper.

Javits returned from New York on Monday morning, and the committee met to consider the bill. At nine-thirty Senator Cooper reported to Abshire that Senator Church had reluctantly agreed to Cooper's version of the Cooper-Church, and that they would both oppose Fulbright and would attempt to vote the bill out that morning.

At one-thirty that afternoon the Foreign Relations Committee voted out the Supplemental by 8-4. Fulbright had lost his own committee, despite being joined by Senators Symington, Mansfield, and Gore in opposing the reporting out. The committee did adopt Fulbright's version of the bill treating each country on a line-item basis and included three amendments: the Cooper-Church amendment secretly worked out with Abshire, forbidding the use of funds under any act to finance U.S. ground combat troops in Cambodia or to provide U.S. advisers to or for Cambodian forces in Cambodia; an amendment offered by Javits providing that no assistance, military or economic, shall be construed as a commitment by the United States to Cambodia for its defense; and an amendment offered by Senator Symington providing that the President could not use the special authorities under previous legislation for Cambodia unless he gave 30 days' advance notice to the Congress.[77]

Later that afternoon the full Senate adopted the Supplemental Appropriations Bill, including the full amount requested by the administration, thus putting its bill $45 million above that already passed by the House. Senator Fulbright objected strenuously in floor debate that authorizing the appropriation before the authorization bill had been acted upon directly undercut the responsibilities of the Senate Foreign Relations Committee. Senators Harry Byrd and Roman Hruska assured Fulbright that they would be faithful in the conference to the principle that the appropriation could become available only upon enactment into law of authorizing legislation.[78]

Senator Mansfield lamented to the press that the Cambodia Supplemental was now likely to pass Congress before recess, and that he had been unable to lose his fear of "another Vietnam involvement...you start these things, they're awfully hard to stop."[79]

December 15 began the final showdown on the Supplemental, which by now had become inextricably bound up with the Defense Appropriations Bill and Defense Authorization Bill. The House-Senate conference finally reached agreement on the Defense Appropriations Bill, with the Senate conferees acceding to the House by deleting the phrase "or Cambodia" from section 843 and substituting the phrase "provided that nothing contained in this section shall be construed to prohibit the President from taking action in said areas designed to promote the safe and orderly withdrawal or disengagement of United States forces from Southeast Asia or to aid in the release of Americans held as prisoners of war." This came to be known in the debate as the "loophole clause." The House also appointed conferees for the Supplemental Appropriations Bill.[80]

On the Senate side, as expected, Senators Fulbright, Symington, and Gravel attempted a filibuster, using as their vehicle an amendment by Gravel to strike from the bill the $155 million for military assistance and economic assistance to Cambodia.[81]

In a tongue-in-cheek attempt to highlight the hypocrisy of some Senators, Senator John Williams of Delaware introduced an amendment to the Cooper-Church amendment in the committee bill to read:

> In line with the expressed intention of the President of the United States, none of the funds authorized or appropriated pursuant to this or any other act may be used to finance the introduction of United States ground combat troops into Cambodia or Israel or to provide United States advisors to or for Cambodian or Israeli military forces in Cambodia or Israel.

Most Senators failed to see the humor in the amendment and rejected it by a vote of 60-20.[82]

## CHURCH-STENNIS COLLOQUY

The most significant action of the day was a colloquy that took place on the floor between Senator Stennis and Senator Church, and provided a definitive legislative history of the intent of the Cooper-Church amendment to the committee bill. Because of Fulbright's attempt to filibuster, Senator Sparkman, the second-ranking Democrat, was managing the bill on the floor. Therefore Senator Stennis addressed his question to Senator Sparkman, asking, "Is that language intended to be a prohibition on the President's going into Cambodia with United States combat troops to meet a situation like the sanctuary battle that we had last June and July...?" To which Sparkman responded, "...the answer is that that would be a Presidential power, that he would be exercising his own powers, and that this language does not prohibit that." Sparkman requested the views of the amendment's sponsor, Senator Church, who answered:

> ...within the framework of past precedent, there is an area of discretionary action open to the President as Commander in Chief... [the present Cooper-Church language] would clearly prevent the deployment for an extended period of time of a substantial number of American troops in Cambodia...[however] if there were a particular concentration just over the border which constituted a serious imminent threat that could be suddenly struck and destroyed, that might fall within the President's powers as Commander in Chief....I could not say, however, that this prohibition in the bill would not preclude an invasion of Cambodia on the scale that took place and for the length of time that occurred last summer. I feel it would.

In giving his view of the intent of the Foreign Relations Committee, Senator George Aiken said, "If an incursion is necessary for the safety of our men, there would be no objection...the committee did make a sharp distinction between an incursion and an invasion."

Senator Stennis then summed up the colloquy in the following terms:

> It seems to me that the colloquy has made it clear that this language does not take any of the responsibility nor the power away from the President of the United States to do what he thinks is reasonably necessary, within reasonable limitations of time, in destroying arsenals, armories, armies, or anything else that is in close proximity to our borders, which we have designated by the general term "sanctuaries," as in the past.

Senator Church then recounted to the chamber the conversation he had had the previous evening with the President at the White House, saying:

> From a conversation I had with the President last evening, it is my understanding now that he no longer takes exception to the limiting language. He feels it conforms with his own policy in Cambodia. He says that he has no intention of sending back troops.[83]

This colloquy proved to be the critical threshold. The hawks had their worst fears about the restrictions of Cooper-Church calmed by Stennis' legislative history, and by the revelation that the President himself had agreed to it, a fact that was verified by White House legislative personnel working out of Senator Scott's office. The doves were, except for the hard core who were undertaking the filibuster, elated over the prospect of finally getting a Cooper-Church, however watered down, enacted.

## SHOWDOWN

Senator Fulbright and his supporters were counting on their filibuster to provide the means to put off final consideration of the Supplemental in order to make way for the appropriation for the SST, a highly contended issue that the House was expected to—and did—pass that same day as part of the conference report on the Department of Transportation bill.[84] Mansfield, however, was pleased at the administration's acceptance of the modified Cooper-Church amendment and was displeased by Gravel's and Fulbright's tactics on the floor, including a specific rejection of a plea from Mansfield to limit their filibuster. Consequently, Mansfield arranged for an agreement that no further business would be taken up until the Supplemental was disposed of, with a vote set for the following day.

Despite the pressures brought to bear by the Democratic leadership on Fulbright and Gravel the day before, when debate reopened on the morning of December 16, it became clear that they intended to keep the filibuster going. Gravel declared, "There hasn't been enough attention to what the President is trying to slip through here at the eleventh hour....I think when enough people realize what's happening it won't pass." Fulbright said that the administration's policy was "very dubious," and that passage of the Supplemental would be the equivalent of adopting "a political instrument like the Gulf of Tonkin Resolution."[85] During the filibuster Fulbright inserted the derogatory report prepared by Moose and Lowenstein on their recently completed "fact-finding visit" to Vietnam and Cambodia.[86]

It began to look as if the Democratic leadership might have to concede after all, and call up the conference report on the Department of Transportation appropriation, when Senator James Allen of Alabama unexpectedly made a move.

Senator Allen had achieved the honor of being considered the undisputed master of the filibuster, and at noon he used his mastery of Senate rules to undo Fulbright and Gravel by obtaining a ruling from the chair that both Gravel and Fulbright were ineligible to speak further on the Gravel amendment since each had already spoken twice on the subject in the same legislative day. Since it became clear that they had lost the general support of the Senate, Fulbright and Gravel finally had to give up, and at two-thirty the Gravel amendment was voted upon losing by a vote of 61-33. Then a final vote was taken on the Supplemental authorization, and it passed by the margin of 72-22.[87] The final version, as passed, authorized the full amounts requested by the executive branch and included a modified Cooper-Church:

> Section 7 (a) In line with the expressed intention of the President of the United States, none of the funds authorized or appropriated pursuant to this or any other act may be used to finance the introduction of United States ground troops into Cambodia, or to provide United States advisors to or for Cambodian military forces in Cambodia; (b) military and economic assistance provided by the United States to Cambodia and authorized or appropriated pursuant to this or any other act shall not be construed as a commitment by the United States to Cambodia for its defense.[88]

At the same time, in the House, the defense appropriations conference report including the "Presidential loophole" on Cambodia was passed by an overwhelming vote of 328-30.[89]

Needless to say, there was much elation at the White House. Four weeks before, the prospects of getting the Senate to authorize such a sizable commitment to Cambodia had seemed almost impossible; and now it had been done, without having to accept restrictions that would interfere with the policy set by the executive branch.

The President's press secretary was given the following guidance to respond to questions on the passage of the Supplemental:

Q. Comment on the Senate's passage of the Supplemental today.

A. The President was gratified by the prompt and responsible action of the Senate in passing this legislation.

Q. Does the administration endorse the Cooper-Church amendment attached to the Supplemental by the Senate?

A. Examination of the legislative record in the Senate confirms that the Cooper-Church amendment attached to the supplemental bill is in harmony with the policy and intentions of this administration.

Q. How is this consistent with the administration's opposition to the Cooper-Church amendment attached to the FMS [Foreign Military Sales] Bill last spring?

A. There is a great difference both in intent and detail between the amendment to the Supplemental and the old Cooper-Church amendment. The Cooper-Church amendment of last spring remains unacceptable.

## CONFERENCE BATTLE BEGINS

On December 17, it became clear that Senator Fulbright had not quite given up. Through procedural devices he did not proceed to the naming of conferees to meet with the already appointed House conferees to fashion a final bill. That evening Abshire met with Senators Cooper and Sparkman to devise means of bringing pressure upon Fulbright. The next day, Chairman Thomas Morgan of the House Foreign Affairs Committee attempted to persuade Fulbright to schedule a conference, but Fulbright refused. Abshire telephoned Senator Church to ask his advice on how to get the conference moving. Church indicated that a letter to him affirming that the administration would conduct Cambodian policy in conformity with the Cooper-Church provision in the authorization bill would give him the leverage he would need to move the conference forward despite Fulbright's opposition. Abshire responded that he thought such a letter might be possible. That afternoon Abshire worked with the NSC staff, drafting a letter to be signed by Secretary Rogers that would tread the careful line between what would be insufficient to satisfy Church and what would go too far in specifying what U.S. contingencies would be foresworn.

The next morning the NSC staff explained the state of affairs with the bill and recommended that the President approve the draft language worked out the day before to be sent to Church by Rogers. The President's staff was very reluctant to put such a commitment in writing, but it was pointed out that the "Presidential loophole" that had been put in the Defense Appropriations Bill had given rise to fears, among those on the Foreign Relations Committee who supported the Supplemental, that the administration would attempt to use that loophole to get around the policy embodied in the Cooper-Church amendment. Further, it was shown that because of this, it was impossible to move the Supplemental to conference; and it could well then be carried over into the new Congress, with a delay of several months. It was further demonstrated that the language of the letter went no further than what the President had already committed to Church. The President approved the letter.

That afternoon Abshire carried the letter to Senator Church, which read simply:

Dear Senator Church:

Confirming Assistant Secretary Abshire's conversation with you, I should like to reaffirm that the administration's programs, policies, and intentions in Cambodia in no way conflict with section 6 of H.R. 19911, or with the concerns expressed in the colloquy on the floor of the Senate on fifteenth December.

William Rogers

Both Cooper and Church were pleased with the text of the message and said that they could now move the conference forward.

Later that afternoon Congressman George Mahon, chairman of the House Appropriations Committee, telephoned one of the President's advisers to ask whether he believed it wise for Mahon to agree to the deletion of the "Presidential loophole" in order to get the Supplemental passed. The adviser told him that while the administration would rather have the language, in order to get the Supplemental through, he should go ahead and accept the deletion. Mahon thereafter informed the House and Senate conferees that he was willing to drop the entire amendment, including the "Presidential loophole." The next day, however, Mahon came under considerable fire from his committee colleagues who wanted to "hang tough." He therefore had second thoughts on his "deal."

In the meantime, the Foreign Relations Committee conferees met with the House conferees and agreed to the authorization bill including the Cooper-Church amendment. On December 21, the House passed the conference report, leaving only Senate floor action on it to send the authorization to the President for his signature.[90]

There were still many loose ends, and some of them began to appear to be unraveling. There were indications from Senator Allen Ellender of Louisiana, the chairman of the Senate Appropriations Committee, that he would not move forward on the Supplemental Appropriations Bill. The House version had been passed earlier in the day. Because of the danger of another filibuster against final approval of the authorization bill conference report in the Senate, and because of the danger of Ellender's holding up the appropriations, an emergency meeting was held in the White House to manage the crisis. The NSC staff chaired the meeting of the members of the Abshire coordinating group. It was decided that the defense appropriations problem should not be interfered with; that Mahon would have to work that out himself; and that, in any case, with the conference report already passed in the House, the main effort should be exerted on the Senate leadership to get the calendar cleared.

At this point many Senators were beginning to panic, since they now faced the prospect not only of being "in" until Christmas Eve, but also of having to return to work round the clock right up until the new Congress would be seated. There might be filibusters on at least five major bills still on the calendar. Mansfield had announced double sessions for the remainder of the year, and he was considering seeking debate-limiting motions to block some of the talkathons so as to avoid disaster.[91]

That afternoon Senator Fulbright refused to bring the conference report to the Senate floor, arguing that until the question of defense appropriations language was resolved, he would not budge. Abshire met with Senators Cooper and Church, and found that Church was sympathetic with Fulbright. Using all his persuasive powers, he convinced Senator Cooper that it was his responsibility to bring Senator Church around; and Cooper finally did so later that afternoon.

By December 22, everything had ground to a halt. The House was refusing to pass the authorization conference report until the Senate acted, and the Senate was refusing to move on the conference report until the defense appropriations language issue was settled. The House conferees, refusing to delete the "Presidential loophole," passed the conference report, and considered the matter closed. Senator Ellender, however, refused to call the conference report to a vote as long as the "Presidential loophole" clause was retained.

The Supplemental Appropriations Conference was deadlocked, because the House refused to accept the clause requiring that the authorization bill be passed before any money was appropriated. This was due primarily to Congressman Otto Passman, who for many years had harbored the desire to establish the precedent of passing appropriations without authorization.

But the Senate conferees, led by Senator McGee, refused to budge. In addition, the appropriation bill for foreign assistance for fiscal year 1971 had become bound up in the impasse, with the Senate refusing to vote on the conference report over the issue of $200 million for foreign military sales authorities. It was now obvious that Congress could not begin its Christmas recess on December 22.

## BREAKTHROUGH

Throughout the day there was feverish intriguing and maneuvering, with all of the legislative liaison forces of the executive branch deployed through the corridors of the Capitol. Finally, late in the afternoon, the knot was cut, with Mansfield and Republican Leader Scott finally forcing the Supplemental Authorization Conference Report to the floor, where it promptly passed by a vote of 41-20. The House shortly thereafter passed the conference report by voice vote, and the bill at last was sent "downtown."

This breakthrough started a chain reaction, clearing the conference on the Supplemental Appropriations Bill, which then reached agreement and was sent to each house. The House immediately passed the conference report, and then both houses went home for Christmas.[92]

The reaction at the White House could only be described as jubilation, with the President giving special praise to the brilliant leadership of his "field marshal" Assistant Secretary Abshire.[93]

Only the Foreign Aid Bill and the Defense Appropriations Bill remained to be resolved. On December 28, Congress returned to its mass of remaining work. The Supplemental Appropriations Conference Report was finally adopted by the Senate. The Defense Appropriations Bill, however, got into deeper trouble when Senator Ellender offered a motion to table the report (in effect rejecting it), which passed by a voice vote, thus sending it back to conference.[94]

During the renewed conference, several of the conferees called the NSC for its view. House Republican Leader Gerald Ford called the White House to urge that a clear signal be given to the House conferees, since there was much confusion over what the executive branch really required.

A call was placed to Congressman John Rhodes during the conference to tell him that it was thought very important to keep Cambodia out of section 843 and to keep the phrase "required to insure the withdrawal of United States forces" in section 838. It was the NSC belief that this loophole was necessary for its use in negotiations, to point out to the North Vietnamese that they could not exclude the possibility of further U.S. action in Cambodia. Senator Stennis pledged to stand firm in the conference.

This situation was quickly turned around when the conferees agreed upon a slight modification of the language of one of the two sections by changing section 838 to read:

> Provided further, that nothing contained in this section shall be construed to prohibit support of actions required to insure [rather than "support of free world or local forces in actions designed to promote"] the safe and orderly withdrawal or disengagement of United States forces from Southeast Asia, or to aid in the release of Americans held as prisoners of war.

They then readopted the compromise worked out in the first conference that amended section 843 to read:

> In line with the expressed intention of the President of the United States none of the funds appropriated by this act shall be used to finance the introduction of American ground combat troops into Laos or Thailand, provided that nothing in this section shall be construed to prohibit the President from taking action in said areas designed to promote the safe and orderly withdrawal or disengagement of United States forces from Southeast Asia or to aid in the release of Americans held as prisoners of war.

The second conference report was immediately sent back to each house, where it passed the Senate by a vote of 70-2 and the House by 234-18. It was finally signed into law on January 11, 1971, as Public Law 91-668 (Title VIII, secs. 838, 843).[95] The text of the Rogers letter figured prominently in debate on the bill in both houses. During the conference there were almost as many executive branch legislative personnel hovering around the meeting room as there were members of Congress.

Later that afternoon the Foreign Aid Appropriation Bill for fiscal year 1971, the conference report, was adopted by the House.[96] On December 30 the Senate adopted it by a vote of 60-12.[97]

Since the Cambodia problem had largely been settled with the passage of the Supplemental and the Cooper-Church amendment, the nine-month deadlock on the Foreign Military Sales Bill was the old Cooper-Church amendment in it seemed pointless. In an effort to clear this up, Senator Mansfield attempted to have a conference called on the morning of December 30. Senator McGee, however, who supported the administration's position on legislation, not only the old Cooper-Church amendment but also the sections 9 and 10 that the administration also opposed (see Chapter 3), conveniently lost the appropriate papers when he realized that all of the members who were supporters of the administration position were absent. The conference therefore had to be postponed until the following day. That afternoon Senator Mansfield called the White House to attempt to work out an acceptable compromise in order to get the Foreign Military Sales Bill out of the conference. The National Security Council remained adamant that sections 9 and 10 must be modified and the Cooper-Church amendment must have sections 3 and 4 dropped, so that it would go no further than the Cooper-Church amendment already in the Supplemental bill.

The conference finally met on the Foreign Military Sales Bill on December 31; and after much bargaining the conferees agreed to reduce section 9 to a figure of $100 million, which the National Security Council had indicated would be acceptable. Section 10 was dropped after Senator Sparkman intervened to say that since he offered it, he had the right to withdraw it. The conference deleted the Cooper-Church amendment entirely. It finally reported out an agreed bill, which was immediately sent to each house. Both passed the conference report the same afternoon in a voice vote as Public Law 91-672 (January 12, 1971).

On January 6, 1971, the President signed the Supplemental Foreign Assistance Act; and as a capstone to the accomplishment, he issued a signing statement drafted by the NSC staff and Abshire that read:

I heartily welcome the prompt and decisive action of the Congress in passing H.R. 19911. The additional foreign assistance funds which I requested only a little over a month ago are vital to the security of the United States and to the success of our foreign policy. They are critical to the success of the Nixon Doctrine, and to our efforts to achieve a peaceful solution in the Middle East.

The funds made available by this bill represent major support by the United States for our friends and allies who are assuming greater responsibility in the building of the peaceful and stable world we all seek in the 1970's. They enable us to provide the assistance required by nations which, with our encouragement, are assuming a greater burden for their own defense, and thereby enabling us to reduce our direct overseas involvement.

I am particularly pleased by the consultation and accommodation between Congress and the administration demonstrated in the legislative history of this bill. America's world leadership depends upon our being able to put aside partisan differences when the national interest is at stake, and to band together to demonstrate the unity of purpose so vital to the success of our foreign policy. We have done so on this legislation.[98]

Press Secretary Ronald Ziegler further amplified the signing statement in his press briefing that morning, saying:

This particular authorization does contain provisions regarding involvement in Cambodia, which is totally consistent, as we have said before, with the administration's intent....I should say that the President is gratified that the Senate and House...rejected what was considered at one stage of the debate to be dangerous, restrictive language in both the Defense Bill and the Foreign Assistance Supplemental Bill, and the extensive legislative history as the debate unfolded on this matter gives full recognition to the President's right to take actions required to safeguard the nation's security.

Thus, on January 6, the administration had accepted some clear restrictions on its freedom of action regarding policy in Cambodia; and the Congress of the United States, through the authorization and appropriations process, had participated with the Executive—indeed, it had given its authorization for the launching of a new policy with unknown ramifications in Southeast Asia.

## CONCLUSIONS

The executive branch request in November 1970 for $255 million in military and economic assistance for Cambodia was granted after months of internal debate and vacillation. To be sure, some military supplies and equipment had been provided since April. In fact, by the time the Supplemental was finally passed, nearly $100 million had been borrowed from other accounts and used to supply the Lon Nol government. Some had pointed to this transfer as a demonstration that Congressional action was irrelevant, that the Executive had already committed the nation to Cambodia. This in fact was not the case. In the Executive, while many recommended such a commitment, all assumed that it could be accomplished only through Congressional appropriation of the supplies necessary. It was not until mid-autumn that the President decided to opt for such a commitment by requesting the money.

Executive officials would have agreed fully with Senator Fulbright's assessment, given after passage, "that providing money to finance the war in Cambodia was in fact a commitment whether we called it that or not." He might well
have added that it was a national commitment made in partnership by Congress
and the Executive. He dismissed as silly the phrase added to the appropriation
by the Senate, asserting that the aid "shall not be construed as a commitment,"
saying that in effect it merely said, "This commitment shall not be construed as
a commitment."[99]

The prospects for success in obtaining the "commitment" were seen by
all as very slim. The bitterness of the spring and summer Indochina debates and
the ABM battle had left everyone tired and disillusioned. That Congress and the
public abhorred anything that might widen or prolong the war was overwhelmingly clear. Adding a further element of hopelessness was the necessity to begin
the struggle at the burnt-out end of a frustrated Congress called back to the first
lame-duck session in many years.

The interaction on the Supplemental as analyzed in this chapter constituted the most intensive period of consultation and debate between the branches
on foreign policy since the Marshall Plan. Unlike the Cooper-Church debate outlined in Chapter 3, the Supplemental involved real give and take on both sides
with minds that were not closed. At the conclusion of the process, the Executive
had its commitment for Cambodia; but Congress had decisively molded the
policy regarding that commitment. The most obvious accomplishment of Congress was final passage of a version of the Cooper-Church amendment.*

The practical effect was to eliminate the possibility of the Executive's
sending U.S. forces back into Cambodia on the scale of the previous spring.
This was certainly understood—and regretted—at the White House. The NSC
regretted losing not the option but the deterrent value of the threat. But Senator
Church himself had conceded that limited strikes across the border by U.S.
forces against enemy concentrations constituting "a grave and imminent threat"
would still fall within the powers of the Commander in Chief to order.[100]

---

*Actually it was the Senate alone. The House had a solid majority against even the
modified Cooper-Church. As Representative Samuel Stratton of New York, one of the
House conferees, put it, it was "slipped through in a conference committee as, frankly, a
ransom to the Senate for getting their approval of the supplemental." Detroit *News*, January
26, 1971, p. 28.

The final version signed by the President was as follows:

Section 7(a). In line with the expressed intention of the President of
the United States, none of the funds authorized or appropriated pursuant to
this or any other act may be used to finance the introduction of United States
ground combat troops into Cambodia or to provide United States advisers to
or for Cambodian military forces in Cambodia.

Perhaps a more meaningful effect was the prohibition of U.S. advisers in Cambodia—more meaningful because an influential segment of senior executive officials strongly advocated that course. As a result of this restriction, and a subsequently enacted ceiling, U.S. personnel were to be kept to fewer than 200 persons who were allowed to process delivery of materiel but forbidden to advise.

It was the subsequent judgment of responsible U.S. officials in Cambodia that this restriction wasted U.S. resources and was a crippling obstacle to the building of a viable Cambodian defense force in consonance with the Nixon Doctrine.[101]

The Executive, however, had one ironic gain. Since the Cooper-Church debate, it had refrained from providing direct air support to Cambodian forces except where there was a connection with the North Vietnamese supply system. The President himself had disavowed such support in his July interview.[102]

In the course of interplay, debate, and compromise, however, the prohibition on direct air support that passed as part of the Cooper-Church amendment on the Foreign Military Sales Bill was specifically dropped. This was taken by executive supporters in the Senate, by the House leadership, and by the White House to be an implicit authorization of such air support.[103] U.S. close air support to Cambodian forces began in earnest shortly after Cooper-Church became law.

Another intangible price that was paid by the Senate was a kind of exhaustion that settled over its activities for the next six months. The war critics were deeply depressed by the passage of the Supplemental "commitment." Senator Gravel, for instance, after he had been defeated, not by the hawks but at the hands of Cooper, Church, Javits, and others, said:

> If the victory of the Cooper-Church amendment—and that victory let me say is the interpretation of a remark at a Christmas party—if the price for that victory is the legalization and the undertaking of the Cambodian affair, the expansion of the war in Southeast Asia, and our agreeing to that as a part of national policy—that price, to my mind, is too much to pay.[104]

Fulbright was very bitter:

> You just can't generate this kind of enthusiasm up here again. People become injured and feel they are tilting at windmills. They'd rather go after pollution or a number of other things. I feel a sense of futility.[105]

After considering the complex interaction between the branches, and between and among the authorizing and appropriating committees in dealing with the tangle of six separate bills, the judgment of another participant seems a better view. "Congress," said John Stennis, Chairman of the Senate Armed Services Committee and ex officio members of the Appropriations Committee, "still retains almost absolute power in practically all areas, if it desires to exercise it, by controlling appropriations and by limiting the expenditure of appropriated funds."[106]

## NOTES

1. Joseph Harris, *Congressional Control of Administration* (Washington, D.C.: Brookings Institution, 1964), p. 46; Edward Corwin, *The Constitution and What It Means Today* (New York: Atheneum, 1967), p. 30.

2. Corwin, *The Constitution*, p. 26.

3. Ibid., pp. 71-72.

4. Ibid., pp. 80-81.

5. "Federalist No. 58," *The Federalist Papers* (New York: New American Library, 1961), p. 359.

6. "Federalist No. 24," ibid., p. 158.

7. "Federalist No. 26," ibid., p. 171.

8. E.A. Kolodziej, *The Uncommon Defense and Congress* (Columbus: Ohio State University Press, 1966), p. 436.

9. Louis Fisher, *The President and Congress* (New York: Free Press, 1972), p. 110.

10. Ibid., p. 111.

11. For a detailed review of this struggle see Wilfred Binkley, *President and Congress* (3rd ed; New York: Vintage, 1961), pp. 33-82.

12. Cited in Fisher, *President and Congress*, p. 111.

13. Ibid., p. 127.

14. Ibid., p. 129.

15. *Guide to the U.S. Congress* (Washington, D.C.: Congressional Quarterly, 1971), p. 188.

16. Harris, *Congressional Control*, p. 52.

17. *Guide to Congress*, p. 39.

18. Fisher, *President and Congress*, p. 128.

19. Corwin, *The Constitution*, p. 81.

20. *Guide to Congress*, p. 40. Also see D.S. Alexander, *History and Procedure of the House of Representatives* (Boston: Houghton Mifflin, 1916).

21. Harris, *Congressional Control*, p. 54.

22. Ibid., pp. 55-56; Binkley, *President and Congress*, pp. 205-20.

23. Cited in Arthur Schlesinger, Jr., *The Imperial Presidency* (Boston: Houghton Mifflin, 1973), p. 398.

24. Harris, *Congressional Control*, p. 56.

25. *Guide to Congress*, p. 44. Also see Richard F. Fenno, *The Power of the Purse: Appropriations Politics in Congress* (Boston: Little, Brown, 1966).

26. George R. Brown, as cited in Binkley, *President and Congress*, pp. 270-71.

27. Francis Wilcox, *Congress, the Executive, and Foreign Policy* (New York: Harper and Row, 1971), p. 74.

28. Ibid., p. 81; *Guide to Congress*, p. 53.

29. Cited in Harris, *Congressional Control*, p. 69.

30. Cited in Wilcox, *Congress, the Executive, and Foreign Policy*, p. 90.

31. Cited in Schlesinger, *The Imperial Presidency*, p. 207.

32. John Stennis and J.W. Fulbright, *The Role of Congress in Foreign Policy* (Washington, D.C.: American Enterprise Institute For Public Policy Research, 1971), pp. 24-25.

33. Ibid., pp. 25-26; Kolodziej, *Uncommon Defense*, p. 445.

34. Elias Huzar, *The Purse and the Sword: Control of the Army by Congress Through Military Appropriations* (Ithaca, N.Y.: Cornell University Press, 1950), pp. vi, 132.

35. U.S. Congress, House, Armed Services Committee, *Military Procurement Authorization Fiscal Year 1964* (Washington, D.C.: U.S. Government Printing Office, 1963), pp. 3-4.

36. William Elliott, *United States Foreign Policy* (New York: Columbia University Press, 1952), p. 66. For a conflicting view see Stanley Falk and Theodore Bauer, *National Security Management* (Washington, D.C.: Industrial College of the Armed Forces, 1972), p. 92.

37. John Norton Moore, *Law and the Indochina War* (Princeton: Princeton University Press, 1972), p. 629.

38. See discussion and citations for these cases in Chapter 3 and in Schlesinger, *The Imperial Presidency*, pp. 290-94.

39. Ibid., p. 292.

40. Ibid., p. 293.

41. Richard E. Neustadt, *Alliance Politics* (New York: Columbia University Press, 1970), p. 11.

42. Schlesinger, *A Thousand Days*, p. 556.

43. Elliott, *United States Foreign Policy*, p. 48.

44. Harris, *Congressional Control*, p. 87.

45. Ibid., p. 92.

46. Falk and Bauer, *National Security Management*, p. 88.

47. Harris, *Congressional Control*, p. 101.

48. Fisher, *President and Congress*, p. 113.

49. Cited ibid., p. 129.

50. Schlesinger, *Imperial Presidency*, p. 236.

51. Cited in Fisher, *President and Congress*, p. 124.

52. Internal memorandum cited by Schlesinger, *Imperial Presidency*, p. 237.

53. Fisher, *President and Congress*, p. 113.

54. John Rothchild, "Cooing Down the War: The Senate's Lame Doves," *Washington Monthly*, August 1971, p. 13.

55. Emmet Hughes, *The Living Presidency* (New York: Coward, McCann and Geoghegan, 1972), p. 222.

56. Rothchild, "Cooing Down the War," p. 13.

57. Fisher, *President and Congress*, p. 112.

58. Ibid.

59. Burton Sapin, *The Making of United States Foreign Policy* (New York: Praeger, 1966), p. 39; Elliott, *United States Foreign Policy*, pp. 114-18.

60. Washington *Post*, April 28, 1970, pp. 1, 11.

61. United States President. *Public Papers of the Presidents* (Washington, D.C.: Office of the Federal Register, 1972), Richard M. Nixon, 1970, p. 405.

62. New York *Times*, November 22, 1970, p. 4.

63. U.S. Congress, Senate, 91st Cong., 2nd sess., November 24, 1970, *Congressional Record*, p. S18781.

64. Ibid., November 25, 1970; H.R. 19845; S. 4542; S. 4543. Also see U.S. Congress, House, Committee on Foreign Affairs, *To Amend the Foreign Assistance Act of 1961* (Washington, D.C.: U.S. Government Printing Office, 1970), pp. 44-80.

65. U.S. Congress, House, Committee on Foreign Affairs, *To Amend the Foreign Assistance Act of 1961*, pp. 81-200.

66. U.S. Congress, House, 91st Cong., 2nd sess., December 3, 1970, *Congressional Record*. The committee defeated an amendment by Congressman Paul Findley to prohibit funds from being used for advisers or military personnel in Cambodia by a vote of 18-9.

67. Ibid.

68. Based on interview with a member of the Senate Foreign Relations Committee staff, October 1971.

69. U.S. Department of State, Publication 8559, "Current Foreign Policy" series 250, December 1970.

70. U.S. Congress, House, 91st Cong., 2nd sess., December 8, 1970, *Congressional Record*; H.R. 195901 et seq.

71. U.S. Congress, Senate, Committee on Foreign Relations, *Legislative History of the Senate Committee on Foreign Relations, January 3, 1969 to January 2, 1971* (Washington, D.C.: U.S. Government Printing Office, 1972), p. 27.

72. U.S. Congress, Senate, Committee on Foreign Relations, *Supplemental Foreign Assistance Authorization, 1970* (Washington, D.C.: U.S. Government Printing Office, 1970), pp. 3-83.

73. U.S. Congress, House, 91st Cong., 2nd sess., December 10, 1970, *Congressional Record*, 116: 40944.

74. Based on an interview with Assistant Budget Director James Schlesinger, December 1970.

75. U.S. President, *Public Papers of the Presidents*, Richard M. Nixon, 1970, p. 1101.

76. U.S. Congress, Senate, Committee on Foreign Relations, *Supplemental*, pp. 84-133.

77. U.S. Congress, Senate, Committee on Foreign Relations, *Legislative History*, pp. 23-27.

78. U.S. Congress, Senate, 91st Cong., 2nd sess., December 15, 1970, *Congressional Record*, p. S20109.

79. Washington *Star*, December 14, 1970, p. 3.

80. U.S. Congress, House, 91st Cong., 2nd sess., December 15, 1970, *Congressional Record*, p. H11762.

81. Ibid., p. S20236.

82. Ibid., p. S20234.

83. Ibid., pp. S20185, 20186.

84. U.S. Congress, House, 91st Cong., 2nd sess., December 15, 1970, *Congressional Record*, 116: 41494.

85. Washington *Star*, December 16, 1970, p. 1.

86. U.s. Congress, Senate, Committee on Foreign Relations, *Cambodia*.

87. U.S. Congress, Senate, 91st Cong., 2nd sess., December 16, 1970, *Congressional Record*, 116: 41732.

88. Public Law 91-652, January 5, 1971.

89. U.S. Congress, House, 91st Cong., 2nd sess., December 16, 1970, *Congressional Record*, 116: 41946.

90. U.S. Congress, Senate, Committee on Foreign Relations, *Legislative History*, p. 27.

91. Washington *Post*, December 17, 1970, p. 1.

92. U.S. Congress, House, 91st Cong., 2nd sess., December 22, 1970, *Congressional Record*, 116: 43342.

93. Based on interview with Bryce N. Harlow, December 1970.

94. Ibid., December 28, 1970, 43702.

95. Ibid., December 29, 1970, p. S21371.

96. Ibid. 116: 43813.

97. Ibid., 44114.

98. U.S. President, *Public Papers of the Presidents of the United States*, Richard M. Nixon, 1971, p. 26.

99. U.S. Congress, Senate, 92nd Cong., 1st sess., February 5, 1971, *Congressional Record*, p. S5888.

100. Washington *Post*, January 1, 1971, p. 4.

101. Interviews with senior United States Embassy officials at Phnom Penh.

102. See Fisher, *The President and Congress*, p. 110.

103. Interviews with senior members of the Senate Armed Services Committee and senior members of the bipartisan leadership of the House, January 1971.

104. Rothchild, "Cooing Down the War," p. 16.

105. Nick Thimmesch, "A Feeling of Defeat—Fulbright," Los Angeles *Times* Syndicate, February 13, 1971.

106. Stennis and Fulbright, *The Role of Congress*, p. 2.

# 7

## CONCLUSIONS

It would not be unreasonable, after pondering the nearly 200 years of contention between the branches, of opportunities missed, of peace eluded and hopes proved false, for the student of U.S. foreign policy to find merit in de Tocqueville's observation that effective conduct of foreign affairs demands not the qualities peculiar to a democracy but, "on the contrary, the perfect use of almost all those in which it is deficient."[1] De Tocqueville saw this fact as a strong argument for concentration of power in the Executive. Many Presidents since that time have in one form or another paraphrased Theodore Roosevelt's simple urge, "Oh, if I could only be both President and Congress for just ten minutes."

Effective foreign policy, however, was not high among the priorities of the founding fathers; and the dispersion and sharing of powers was arranged to safeguard other values. As was seen in Chapter 1, the Constitution did not specify how the foreign affairs powers would be distributed and shared by Congress and the Executive. The balance was left for events to decide, in part intentionally and in part because the contending views of the founding fathers were never really reconciled. Any attempt to divine the "intention of the framers" as a means to prescribe reforms to the current constitutional balance is an essentially futile exercise.

History, we have seen, has proved to be only marginally better in establishing the distribution of powers through precedent and practice, settling some in traditional usage, shifting and uprooting others from one Congress to the next. There are, in short, no frameworks, no cookbooks, no valid models, and no "golden ages" of administrations past to which we might refer in judging a "proper" distribution of powers or even "constitutional" relationship between branches. The student of these affairs must therefore resign himself to continuing paradox, to insoluble contradiction, even to an element of sustained mystery.

The Nixon administration was the first in 120 years in which both houses of Congress were controlled by the opposition party. The Senate ratio was 43-57 and the House 192-243. Partisan political considerations could therefore be expected to have more influence on the relationship between the branches than might otherwise be the case.

Of more importance, however, the entire political atmosphere was colored by deep concern over the unsuccessful conflict still proceeding in the area of foreign affairs. There were two bitter disputes over funding for ballistic missile defense in 1969 and 1970, a continuing debate over war-powers legislation, disputes over renewal of the draft, MIRV deployment, USIA polling, Radio Free Europe, the rights of access of the General Accounting Office, controversial ambassadorial nominations, end-the-war amendments such as Hatfield-McGovern, POW resolutions, and of course the annual defense, foreign assistance, and international banks bills.

Since World War II, with the practice of requiring annual authorizing legislation for defense appropriations, foreign assistance, and State Department funding, Congress has become much more involved in the foreign policy process.

A partial reversal of this trend occurred for a time with the reorganization of the National Security Council in January 1969. The hierarchical system of review and interdepartmental groups brought a great centralization to the policy process in the executive branch. Decision-making of the kind formerly diffused through the State and Defense Departments was drawn into the White House. Substantial power was placed in the hands of the Assistant to the President for National Security Affairs and his staff. As was observed in Chapters 3-6, both long-term strategy and day-to-day legislative tactics were set by the NSC/White House, not in the departments. Nothing of consequence was permitted to be done by State or Defense without clearance from the NSC.

Thus, while Congress had finally obtained a pervasive grip on State and Defense through the investigative, authorization, and appropriations processes, the locus of executive power had largely left the departments and was thriving in the White House. With increasing frustration, the committees and members of Congress realized they had no effective way to "get at" Kissinger and his staff.

Kissinger himself actually desired to testify before Congressional committees, but was prevented from doing so by the administration's interpretation of executive privilege. As a substitute, a series of informal briefings of the committees was begun in late 1969. At these meetings, Kissinger was remarkably open in informing the committees of the most sensitive matters under way, and soliciting their advice. To his surprise, there never was a leak of information from one of these sessions.

This method of interaction, however, was completely one-sided, providing only the most superficial influence, and that only to the committee members who would express a policy concern to Kissinger—which they did only in the most deferential tones.

Clearly, if more substantial methods of interacting were not developed by Congress in order to adjust to the redistribution of power in the Executive, then a shift in the balance of shared powers was inevitable. The issue was made partially moot by the confirmation of Kissinger as Secretary of State, which in effect restored Congress' hold on the center of executive power in foreign policy. This, however, was a subjective, not an institutional, fix, for the reorganized machinery centering power in the NSC remained in place. Congress' grip was dependent upon the Secretary of State's including in his person the role of effective head of the NSC. The removal of the second hat in November 1975 once again placed the NSC beyond Congressional reach.

The new NSC system has proved so effective that unless the next President is uninterested in directing foreign policy, the shift of the real levers of power from the departments to the NSC is likely to be permanent. Congress must sooner or later arrange itself to deal effectively with that system.

It has been traditional to end any study on this subject with a chapter proposing sweeping reforms. In the 1930s and 1940s the academic bookstalls groaned under learned calls to reorganize and strengthen the Executive, to redress constitutional imbalance, or to reorganize and restrict the recalcitrant and mossback Congress. In the 1950s, and again in the 1970s, the shelves groan under equally learned calls to even more sweeping reform to lasso the runaway Executive, or to strengthen and further empower a somehow enlightened Congress.

There are several ideas that reappear cycle after cycle. To improve the presidency, for instance, there is the item-veto to end the tiresome problem of riders and restrictions, or an expanded right to impound appropriated funds. The office, some urge, should be divided in two, one part to perform as head of state and the other as prime minister. Others urge giving Cabinet officers access to the floors of Congress, the better to lobby executive policies or, conversely, to require their presence on those floors periodically to answer to Congress.

Lately the reforms most favored are variations of the parliamentary supremacy models, such as making leading Senators full Cabinet members or full members of the NSC with independent staff, or drastic imposition of a party whip, so that the party controlling Congress may be a cohesive force.[2] ·

Most commonly heard are the perennial, eminently sensible, and highly unlikely proposals to rationalize the internal workings of Congress through reform of the seniority system. The reforms of early 1975 were the first serious attempt to that end, restructuring the competing and overlapping committee system, and establishing a joint committee on national security affairs. The latter would consist of the chairmen and ranking minority members of the Foreign Affairs, Armed Services, and Appropriations Committees, and the majority and minority leaders of both houses. This committee would have oversight over the NSC and the full range of national security issues. The Nixon administration expressed no objection to several pieces of legislation designed to carry this out;

and the NSC actually favored it, foreseeing in it the possibility of a practical and secure method of dealing with Congress. It has never gotten very far, however, because of the unwillingness of present standing committees to yield parts of their suzerainty to the proposed committee.[3]

## THE STRUGGLE FOR CONTROL

The research of this inquiry suggests that the "struggle for control of foreign policy" written into the Constitution is proceeding vigorously, with neither branch having achieved the kind of dominance that would make institutional reform necessary. It is not, after all, the growth of power of the Executive or of Congress that matters. What would matter would be the growth of the net power of one branch over the other, and that has not taken place.

All too often scholars and commentators seem to assume that some ideal constitutional balance exists, in the manner of a table of organization for a large corporation, which, if discovered and enacted into law, will forever guarantee the formulation and conduct of wise and just foreign policy. The present balance is there, well-developed and functioning. It is to that reality that analytic attention should be addressed.

The issue of executive dominance is illustrative. As noted, its existence has been an assumption of this study, derived from the very natures of the two branches. It is meaningless to decry it, to say it shouldn't be or wasn't intended to be so—it *is* so. It is far from meaningless, however, to examine its substance and the paths of its operation, for these may yield areas of improvement—the attitude of the judicial branch toward dominating action, for instance. We have noted throughout the present study that "Whereas exercises of extraordinary power are involved, the Court restrains itself and not the President." This is a matter of judicial attitude that may have been carried to excess. The courts should be performing the valuable function of checking excessive Presidential dominance in foreign policy, in Corwin's words, "by acting as a symbol of restraint, a moral force, and a constant reminder of established principle." But they also should be adjudicating cases where serious questions arise, which they shrank from doing in the case of air strikes in Cambodia after March 1973.

But this is only an example of degree. The Executive will continue to be the mover of events, capable of focusing, making, or unmaking issues; of determining the subject of all Congressional attention; of granting national stature to a member by a private breakfast with the Secretary of State, a cruise on the *Sequoia*, or a Presidential letter released at the White House—in short, all of the vast levers and trinkets of power reviewed in Chapter 2 that *must* inhere in the Executive.

Congress by its nature is set up to be—and expects to be—dominated, if for no other reason than that its members will always (except in aberrational periods such as Watergate) feel considerably more solidarity with a President of their own party than with their colleagues of the other party. Thus, in each of the cases examined, the command post of the Executive in its legislative battles was located not in the White House basement but in the back office of the Senate Minority Leader. Further, in Chapter 3 it was seen that a President disposed to compromise on Cooper-Church was persuaded not to do so by the Congressional leaders of his party. It was they who organized and carried out a seven-week filibuster. Some students of the presidency, however, have pointed out that the Republican inheritance of Whig distrust of Presidential leadership has meant that Republicans in the White House suffer considerably less support from Congress than do Democrats.

But the issue of dominance itself is not that important, unless it becomes domination. Though the coxswain sets the course, it is not he who determines whether, how, or at what speed the shell is rowed.

It is the natural tendency of members of every legislature to make themselves conspicuous, to make their mark, to make their will felt upon public affairs. As Walter Bagehot noted:

> All these mixed motives urge them to oppose the Executive. They are embodying the purposes of others if they aid; they are advancing their own opinions if they defeat; they are first if they vanquich; they are auxiliaries if they support.[4]

There is, then, an inherent legislative dynamic to oppose the Executive. It is magnified in the United States by the facts that no Congressional elections are won by supporting foreign policy "giveaways" and that the important interest groups in any member's constituency nearly always include one or more opposed to any given foreign policy issue. The member is far more likely to please these important interests by opposing the Executive than he is by supporting. Thus conflict, far from being the deplorable breakdown in relations between the branches that politicians at both ends of Pennsylvania Avenue ritually lament, is in fact the more natural and proper state of affairs.

There is a tendency within the executive branch to view this compulsion to oppose as mere grandstanding or as uninformed and irresponsible gadflyism. While there is often justice in the change, the body of members, having daily contact with the people, provide a constant folkish challenge to the policies of detached experts, developed in the "secrecy, energy and dispatch" of the executive branch. Many an ill-informed, embarrassingly naive question, posed by a posturing and perhaps irresponsible member, has made the Executive blush to admit there was no adequate answer. There is great value in assuring that some men of stature who do not owe their jobs to the President have a ready forum to raise the kinds of questions publicly that the President might not hear from his close advisers. The New York *Times*, in reporting the President's speech of April 30, 1970, on Cambodia, perhaps not unintentionally included the following misprint: "After full consultation with the National Security Council, Ambassador Bunker, General Abrams and my other *admirers*,..."[5]

## THE VALUE OF CONFLICT

In each of the four interaction patterns identified and examined earlier, conflict and struggle are to be an essential part of the process—the crucible, as it were, in which all joint policy is made. The more directly traceable results of each of those conflicts have been examined, but the deeper-reaching effects and feedbacks can only be the subject of speculation. As Arthur Schlesinger described the aftermath of the bitter conflict between the Kennedy administration and the House over composition of the Rules Committee: "It was a close and bitter business, and the memory of this fight laid a restraining hand on the administration's legislative priorities for some time to come."[6]

Conflict—friction, tensions, disputation—while essential, can all too easily become excessive, and thus dysfunctional. In relations between the branches it has often degenerated to that point since Washington first stormed out of the Senate Chamber never to return. It once resulted in a civil war, broke Wilson's health, added a new word for contempt to the dictionary with McCarthyism, and drove President Johnson from office.*

While none of the four cases reviewed in this study reached that depth of conflict, the Cooper-Church amendment and the Symington subcommittee hearings involved very deep and excessive bitterness, particularly between the White House and some members of the Senate Foreign Relations Committee. There was no dialogue, no compromise, no real interaction between the two

---

*Conflict may fairly be said to have gone a bit too far in the following interchange:

...my faithful enemy, Senator Wherry, began badgering me from directly across a narrow table, finally leaning over it and shaking a menacing finger in my face. I have a reputation for " not suffering fools gladly." However—the adverb aside—until that moment I had suffered as many fools patiently as any man. But quite suddenly I had had enough of Kenneth Wherry and was on my feet admonishing him in tones and language far from diplomatic not to shake his "dirty finger in my face." He bellowed that he would, and he did. My answering haymaker was interrupted by my friend and colleague...." Dean Acheson, *Present at the Creation* (New York: W.W. Norton, 1969), p. 439.

antagonist groups. It was all-out, bitter conflict, which was in the interest of neither branch and certainly not in the public interest. Yet the process creaked and groaned on, and matters were eventually resolved; there was no paralysis, no breakdown. And what was the alternative in a situation where there was no consensus, no common ground possible on the policy issues? All-out conflict became an operational substitute for consensus politics.

## CHECKS AND BALANCES

The Executive may indeed be dominant; but there are many ways and means by which Congress can, and does, check and challenge executive thought and deed. The U.S. Congress is the only democratic legislature that sets the tenure and service, the pay and benefits of every executive employee; enlarges, cuts, and twists the executive budget; dictates administrative action by line-item appropriation; and organizes, empowers, and delimits the very agencies of the Executive. And much of this is not even done by formal act or statute. The greatest exercise is through committee action, telephone admonition, and bourbon in the back room.

One facet of Congressional interaction with the Executive given scant attention in the literature is the symbiotic relationship enjoyed by the media and Congress. The one regularly makes the other an instrument of its dirty work. If a reporter or commentator fails to get what he wants from the State or Defense Department, he simply goes to his friendly Congressman or committee staff to make it a Congressional request. In return, the member or staffer is provided a regular supply of inside information gleaned from the bureaucracy or spoon-fed at "off-the-record" breakfast meetings with the Secretary of State. These latter tidbits are generally of the sort calculated by the journalist to goad and gall the Congressman. Of such stuff are stories made. By its nature the media is a powerful catalyst of conflict between the branches, and never of harmony.

Nor is television, as a phenomenon apart from press conferences, a benefit to Presidential power (as the common wisdom holds). The critics, the evidence countering executive assertions, the concrete results of policy decisions, and the proceedings of Congressional investigations are checks to executive power that receive considerably more air time than do the speeches of the President or the arguments of his principal foreign policy advisers.

But as we have seen in our case studies, while the operation of these myriad checks is essential, and conflict is a fundamental element of the relationship, they are also the enemy of free communication. More than any other aspect of the relationship, communication and consultation are most capable of improvement. Congress does actively participate and does make important judgments affecting foreign policy at many levels. It will make them without increased information from the Executive—or with it.

## COMMUNICATION

A conclusion of the present study is that the Executive must do more to meet its responsibility to establish an informal consensus in Congress, and it can do this only through a general rule of openness. Congressional judgments must be made on a fuller explanation of both facts and policy implications.*

Formal and written presentations include the State of the Union Address and State of the World Message, the annual budget message, specific legislative requests, and the annual Defense Posture Statement. It includes the many thousands of hours of testimony by executive officials before Congressional committees.† It includes also the massive volume of corroborating studies, analyses, compilations, and working papers requested from or proffered by the executive branch.

The formal written flow of information is the source of the executive privilege issue. It is an assumption of this study that the privilege exists, that it has been practiced by virtually every President, and, regarding policy issues only, it can cover whatever the President decides to withhold. It can never protect information concerning not policy, but questions of malfeasance or wrongdoing. The attempt by the White House in March 1973 to broaden it to cover Watergate accusations was spurious and has injected a confusion into the issue. Equally spurious are the recent polemical treatments of executive privilege attempting to prove that it does not exist at all, and that Congress has an unlimited right to every document in the executive branch.

Formal written presentations provide the basic grist for the Congressional mill, and their quality can be greatly improved. All too often, important

---

*After his years of combat with Congress, Dean Acheson felt that real consultation and openness were impossible: "We were learning again—although we hardly needed to—what everyone in the executive branch since President Washington's day had learned, that to advise and consult with the Congress is next to impossible. One can learn its uninformed opinion or one can try to inform the opinion of a few key members by long, patient, secret talks, as Lovett had done with Vandenburg leading up to the Vandenburg Resolution of 1948; but to devise a joint approach to a complicated and delicate matter of foreign policy is not within the range of normally available time and people. Here the separation of powers really separates." *Present at the Creation* (New York: W.W. Norton, 1969), p. 318.

†Acheson estimated that while he was Secretary of State he never devoted less than one-sixth of his time to this function, and during some periods it took all of his time. *A Citizen Looks at Congress* (New York: Harper and Bros., 1957), pp. 64-70.

Dean Rusk estimated that he spent nearly 50 percent of his time working with Congress. During his first five years he appeared in 129 formal committee meetings in the House and Senate, and 319 informal working sessions. Cited in Francis Wilcox, *Congress, the Executive and Foreign Policy* (New York: Harper and Row, 1971), p. 66.

articulations of executive proposals are given in hearings with one member present, and he dozing. Those members who do attend usually have done no preparation, cannot grasp the issues, and ask largely irrelevant questions. This sloppiness provides little incentive for the Executive to put out maximum effort.

Formal consultations are most typically the meetings between the Republican Congressional leaders and the President, held every other Tuesday, and the less frequent bipartisan leadership meetings. There are also regularly scheduled Democratic and Republican policy luncheons at which a high executive official often is a featured participant. At the staff level, both State and Defense conduct a regular program of luncheon briefings. In all of these, especially the leadership meetings with the President, there is some genuine two-way consultation; and Congressional participants often do make important inputs to policy in the formative stages—as was noted, for instance, in the May 1970 leadership meeting (Chapter 3).

Perhaps the golden age of "consultation" was the postwar era of bipartisanship in which the Marshall Plan, Bretton Woods, the U.N., NATO, SEATO, and the Japanese Treaty were formulated and carried out with "intimate collaboration" between Congressional leaders and the Executive.

Formal consultation during crisis situations, however, is another matter. Most typically, Congressional leaders are summoned to the White House one or two hours before action is to be taken. They are then informed of the situation and what the President proposes to do about it. Members' comments are solicited, but only in the rarest cases can they have any real effect. "The distinction between solicitation of advice in advance of a decision and the provision of information in the wake of a decision would seem to be a significant one," the Senate Foreign Relations Committee observed of the process.[7] In Chapter 3 it was observed that in the case of the Cambodia incursion, such meetings were held only after the public announcement. President Nixon explained why on July 1, 1970:

> ...in ordering that kind of an action, why didn't I go to the Senate, for example, and the House and ask for their approval?
>
> Well, now let us suppose we had done that. It took them seven weeks for Cooper-Church. Let's suppose it had taken seven weeks. What would have happened? Well, first, all of this year's supply of ammunition that we have acquired would have been gone out of the sanctuaries, or even worse, what might have happened is that the rather fearsome defensive barricades that they had in these sanctuaries would have been ready for us, and we would have lost not just 330 men—that is too many to lose in two months, and that is all we lost in Cambodia—we would have lost 3,000 or 4,000.[8]

Actually, key leaders were notified by telephone several hours before the President went on the air on April 30. This came to be the pattern in the cases of

Lam Son 719 in January 1971, and the May 8, 1972, and December 18, 1972, decisions to resume bombing of North Vietnam. When the controversial decision to use B-52 strikes against the Cambodia sanctuaries was taken in 1969, Senator Richard Russell and Representative Mendel Rivers, Chairmen of the Armed Services Committees, were consulted before action was taken. They concurred in the decision and strongly recommended that no other members should be consulted because of the danger of a leak.

Practice was only slightly better in preceding administrations. In the Middle East war in 1967, little if any consultation took place prior to the outbreak.[9] In the Dominican Republic intervention and in the Cuban missile crisis, leaders were informed only hours before the decisions were carried out.[10] According to Senator John Stennis, however, there had been extensive Congressional consultation prior to the Berlin crises of 1961 and 1959, the Quemoy-Matsu crisis in 1958, and the Lebanon intervention in 1958.[11] Congressional consultations apparently were instrumental in 1954 in dissuading the Executive from intervening in Indochina.[12] According to one observer, the Eisenhower administration sought prior consultations not because it believed Congress had any such right, but because the consultations "...by involving Congress in the take-off, would incriminate it in a crash landing."[13]

In fact, the kinds of consultation described above are really the tiniest fraction of the total. Of major importance are the thousands upon thousands of impromptu or social contacts ranging from a drink with the President aboard "Air Force One" on the way to dedicate a dam, to the many chance meetings between executive officials and members of Congress on elevators, the Eastern Airlines shuttle, and so on. There are also the much-labored diplomatic cocktail and Georgetown dinner-party circuits. A quite useful cross between the formal and spontaneous was hit upon to bridge the gap between Congressional demands to have Kissinger testify, and his inability to do so because of his position. The off-the-record cocktail party/briefings were extremely useful in informing the committees[14] and provided Kissinger with a means both of defusing the executive privilege issue and of accutarely gauging the concerns of the two committees.

## INVISIBLE CONSULTATION

It is this latter dimension of consultation that is usually overlooked in the learned treatments of the subject. Assessing the fears, concerns, prejudices, and tolerances of Congress—gauging the mood—is the most important product of consultation. In each of the four cases examined, that mood was an essential—even if unspoken—factor in executive deliberations. In this sense Congress is ever-present in the Situation Room and at every step of the executive policy process. In a very real sense the executive perception of Congressional concerns, and the strength with which they are held, sets the parameters of policy and the range of practical options. The greater the volume and the higher the quality of consultation in all its forms, the more useful and creative Congressional influence at formulative stages of policy making will be.

It is of course not sufficient to consult only with the leadership. Two members, regardless of how powerful, cannot speak for Congress. There are 535 members who must be given at least the opportunity to hear their concerns answered and executive thinking articulated. Consultation below the leadership level unfortunately is sparse and haphazard. Full consultation on any issue is of course impossible, and therefore making use of strong figures to represent their many lesser brothers is essential.

## LOBBYING

The third category of communication between the branches is lobbying. All executive agencies have personnel assigned full-time to work with Congress in a liaison function. These people are not only for the purpose of lobbying for executive policy and agency budgets; they spend the greater part of their time representing the special requests and interests of members of Congress to their own bureaucracies, rather like ombudsmen.

The Pentagon has by far the largest legislative liaison operation in the government. Depending on whom you count, there are between 300 and 500 people working full-time on one aspect or another of Congressional relations for the Pentagon. Each of the services maintains a large staff and has an office in the House and in the Senate office buildings. The overwhelming majority of the work of these people is in servicing Congressional requests and constituency inquiries. A healthy minority of their man-hours, however, is spent in lobbying for the weapons and administrative programs of their particular service. Unfortunately, this function has always involved undercutting the programs of other services that are competing for scarce Defense funds.

It was persistently vexing to the White House during the more difficult legislative struggles on such matters as ABM, the aircraft carriers, the Trident missile submarine, and the B-1 bomber to find that the very best position papers against aircraft carriers circulating on the Hill, for instance, were traced back to the Air Force. The best position papers against proceeding with the B-1 bomber were prepared by the Navy. In an attempt to get control of this fratricide, the position of Assistant Secretary of Defense for Congressional Relations was established in 1973, over the strong opposition of the military services.

The State Department has a much smaller legislative liaison office, consisting of an Assistant Secretary, two Deputy Assistant Secretaries, and a staff of about 15 people. The position of Assistant Secretary dates back to the first Hoover Commission on the organization of the federal government, which recommended the creation of that position, making it the oldest such in the government.

The White House first became involved in lobbying below the level of the President during the Eisenhower administration, with the establishment by President Eisenhower of the first office within the White House formally charged with Congressional affairs; Bryce Harlow was its first incumbent. Eisenhower reportedly set up this office not because of his excessive concern that members be well serviced with an institutional channel of communication, but because of his distaste for dealing with members of Congress.[15]

This office has come to be the focal point of executive lobbying with Congress. It was never more than two or three persons in size during the Eisenhower, Kennedy, and Johnson years: and even under the Nixon administration it never had more than seven professional staff members. In the Nixon administration, however, the office was given a formal mandate to supervise all of the Assistant Secretaries and Legislative Affairs Officers in the entire executive branch.[16] As was observed in each of the four case studies, it was the White House ad hoc groups that quarterbacked all of the legislative strategy.

The White House liaison and the NSC had evolved a formidable array of tools for actively participating in Congressional consideration and debate of national security issues. We saw in Chapter 3 the powerful impact of a letter from the President or from a senior NSC official directed to a member of Congress at a crucial point in debate. In addition to letters, the skillful application of telephone calls from such an official or from the President at the right moment, especially if it could be accompanied by such dramatics as having the Senator called off the Senate floor to take a call in the cloakroom, proved time and again to be invaluable tools. There was also a well-developed method of drafting tightly reasoned and persuasive "talking papers" of one or two pages, directed at refuting an opposition argument or making the best possible case for a disputed point. These "talking papers" were then distributed by the White House liaison personnel to the appropriate Congressmen. At times such broadsides were distributed through the Republican leaders, or a friendly Democratic member, to every member of Congress preceding floor consideration of an issue. All of these devices were also used with effect during closed committee sessions and markups of important bills.

The volume of work for the White House legislative office during the Ninety-first Congress showed a tremendous increase over that of any previous administration.[17] Estimates based on the records of that office reveal the following interesting statistics:

—The legislative liaison office answered 160,000 incoming telephone
    calls from all sources (roughly 300 per day)
—placed 300,000 outgoing calls (about 575 per day)

—processed 120,000 pieces of paper, including correspondence, memoranda, reports, and studies (approximately 230 a day)

—attended 1,400 structured meetings excluding internal staff meetings (about three meetings per day)

—made over 1,600 trips to Capitol Hill (roughly three round trips per day)

—prepared over 450 draft speeches for record inserts for members of Congress (averaged more than one per day).[18]

Consultation as a process, however, requires as much active involvement on the part of Congress as on the part of the Executive. Failure to consult is a constant complaint from Congress, but the fault quite often lies with the members of Congress rather than the Executive. During the period 1969-73, for instance, the National Security Council had a standing offer to brief any member of Congress on whatever foreign policy issue he desired. The ground rules for such briefings were to provide the fullest and most highly classified information on the issue, but to allow no transcript and to provide no documents. According to the records of the NSC, this offer was taken up only three times in five years. The very sparse attendance at committee hearings has already been noted, and it is always difficult to round up an audience of any number on Capitol Hill to hear executive branch officials brief on a policy unless it is the crisis topic of the day.

It is of course a fact that members of Congress represent their individual constituencies, where the interests and horizons are, of course, much more parochial than what might be labeled the broader national interest. A proposal, for instance, to close a navy base in Brooklyn is certain to excite far more Congressional interest than, say, building one in Cam Rahn Bay.[19]

Senator Fulbright was perhaps a bit overly harsh when he said, "With their excessively parochial orientation, congressmen are acutely sensitive to the influence of private pressure and to the excesses and inadequacies of a public opinion that is all too often ignorant of the needs, the dangers, and the opportunities in our foreign relations." Of his own committee Senator Fulbright observed, "This is the kind of committee that senators like to be on, but they don't like to do anything."[20]

He might also have added that elections are not won by service to national security affairs. He learned this, to his cost, by being defeated in his own Democratic primary on May 28, 1974, after holding the chair of the Foreign Relations Committee longer than any other man in history. Through his defeat he joined his distinguished predecessors Senator Tom Connally of Texas and Senator Walter George of Georgia, each of whom retired from the Senate while serving as chairman of the Foreign Relations Committee rather than face defeat at the polls.[21]

Thus a Congressman, to avoid diselection, must devote the vast majority of his time and energies to the relatively peripheral and parochial activities that fall under the heading "constituent service," and reserve service to international affairs as a kind of twice-weekly afternoon relaxation. This, in any case, seems to be the lesson that many Congressmen draw.

## THE ORGANIZATION OF CONGRESS

The dysfunctional organization of Congress for the effective and thorough consideration of foreign policy and national security matters was treated in Chapter 2. The committee system is perhaps the most glaring example of where improvement would seem to be easy. The hobbling effect of jurisdictional overlap and redundancy, coupled with the great proliferation in numbers of committees dealing with foreign policy, would not seem to defy efforts at simplification.

Foreign aid, for example, is handled at one stage or another by nearly three dozen Congressional committees and subcommittees. The administration of the State Department involves ten different committees, for instance.[22]

To take the statistics of one Congress, the Eighty-eighth, each Senator averaged 2.81 full committee assignments; 9.19 subcommittee assignments; 1.07 assignments to joint committees; and 19.49 assignments overall, including committees, conferences, boards, and commissions.[23]

In the Ninety-first Congress, Senator John Sparkman of Alabama, then the second-ranking Democrat on the Foreign Relations Committee, also served on four other full committees and was chairman of two of them. Senator Jacob Javits served on five other committees and Senator John Sherman Cooper on four.[24]

The dysfunctional organization and procedure within Congress predisposes it, as an institution, to pigeonhole, obstruct, deadlock, stalemate, or emasculate coherent policy ideas originating within the institution itself. It makes it an institution that by its nature is suited to opposition rather than policy creation, and this need not necessarily be so.

Organizational weaknesses are exacerbated by the completely inadequate system for staffing the committees and members of Congress. There are no real incentives provided to keep very capable, energetic personnel in career staff positions in Congress. Moreover, while the number of staff positions has steadily increased over the years, the size of committee staffs and of members' staffs is far too small to give adequate attention to the magnitude and number of policy issues with which they must deal. The system of recruiting and retaining Congressional staff has been described as "helter-skelter and haphazard."[25]

It has been concluded by some that this state of affairs is the result of a conscious desire by the leadership of Congress not to involve themselves systematically in national security affairs and thereby assume a share of the burden of responsibility for their day-to-day success. As Dean Acheson put it, "to be indignant at either inclusion or exclusion—at either 'putting Congress on the spot' or 'bypassing' it—is a congressional prerogative, highly prized."[26]

All of these problems are worthy of attention because Congress should be required to bring to bear upon foreign policy issues an independent judgment based on its close contacts with the people, and it should reach this judgment on the basis of full information after a process of open discussion. Only Congress as an institution is capable of ventilating all sides and all implications of opposing policy positions. Only it can provide, in simple understandable terms, a public understanding of political objectives in diplomatic and military policies, along with their probable consequences. Only Congress can provide the vital link between the Executive and the people in establishing the level of costs and risks of both lives and treasure that the public is willing to undertake in the great issues of national security policy. To say that Congress cannot play an equal role because of its dysfunctional organization, the failure of its members to do adequate homework, and the great superiority of executive energy and dispatch is to say only that Congress will be involved in the process in different ways than will the Executive. But it *will* be involved.

When all is said and done, and all of the virtues and vices of both institutions are reviewed, it remains that Congressmen and Senators, unlike the officials—all save one—of the executive branch have a unique legitimacy and independent political authority that can come only from an independent political base. This, as Senator Fulbright has reminded us, gives members of Congress alone the invaluable position from which, when necessary, they are able "to tell the President to go soak his head." They thus have the capability, even if one rarely taken advantage of, to bring into the open risks that the President's "admirers" may have overlooked. It substitutes the experience of the many for the expertise of the one. Above all, the role of Congress is indispensable if a consensus is to be established concerning the goals and direction of American foreign policy.


## CONSENSUS


The word "consensus" is the most overworked and ill-defined term in the current political lexicon. It has even taken on a distinct negative ring in modern political dialogue, carrying overtones of complacency, mediocrity, and the stifling of dissent. It is the central conclusion of this study that the loss of consensus on policy goals in Congress and among the people constitutes the fundamental cause of the problems and dysfunctions in the sharing of foreign policy powers between the branches. The elimination of these problems and dysfunctions can be accomplished only through the restoration of a consensus. The use of the term "consensus" here is limited to the acceptance by most members of Congress, the Executive, and, most important, the American people of a common conceptual framework for their understanding of the world and the place of the United States in that world. Only by the development of such a common conceptual framework, and a wide agreement on its validity, can the Niagara of daily events be given the kind of ordering necessary for coherent policy.

Prior to World War II, it was sufficient to deal with policy issues on a fragmentary and individual basis; the functional involvement of the United States in world affairs was so low as to make no difference. World War II marked the involvement of the United States in global affairs on a massive and permanent scale, involving vast amounts of American resources and directly influencing the lives of all of its people to such a degree that ad hoc and fragmented policy was no longer possible.

It was fortuitous that events in the period after World War II were of a simplicity and scale readily grasped by the American people and by their representatives in Congress. The postwar period was marked by the existence of an almost universally accepted conceptual framework for world events—the Cold War. The concept was simple and easily understood: There was a large segment of the world under the control of a revolutionary and aggressive power; and there was another section of the world known as the "free world," whose high calling it was to "contain" the aggressive designs of the revolutionary power upon both the free world and the remaining portion of the world, which was then known as the "underdeveloped world." The specter of world Communism preached was a phenomenon no one questioned. The free world response of "containment" was questioned only by those arguing to carry it one step further, to "roll back" Communism. In this universally accepted biopolar view of the world, the process of sharing foreign policy powers functioned with unprecedented smoothness.

Under the banner of "bipartisanship," the Executive and Congress proceeded to conclude the U.N. Charter and the U.N. Participation Act in 1945; the Rio Treaty in 1947; the Truman Doctrine and aid to Greece and Turkey in 1947; the Marshall Plan in 1948; the formation of NATO; the Vandenburg Resolution and the Mutual Defense Assistant Act in 1948 and 1949; the Allied action to break the Berlin Blockade in 1948; the Foreign Economic Assistance Act and the launching of the Point Four Program in 1950; the United States-United Nations action to defend South Korea in 1950; the Japanese Peace Treaty in 1952; U.S. assistance to Indochina from 1949 to 1964; West German rearmament in the early 1950s; mutual defense treaties with the Philippines, New Zealand, and Australia in 1952; the ratification of the Korean armistice in 1954; the OAS Caracas Declaration of Solidarity in 1954; the Manila Conference and the SEATO Treaty in 1955; the U.S. and Republic of China Mutual Security Treaty in 1955; the Austrian State Treaty in 1955; the Panama Treaty in 1955; the

Eisenhower Doctrine and the U.S. intervention in Lebanon in 1957 and 1958; the Berlin crisis of 1958-59; the Mutual Defense Assistance Programs for Pakistan and Iran; the U.S. support of the formation of the CENTO Alliance from 1955 to 1958; the U.S. action in the Congo from 1960 to 1964; the United States-Japan Mutual Security Pact of 1960; the 1961 Berlin crisis; and thousands of lesser joint legislative-executive actions.

The validity of these criticisms is not relevant to the subject of this inquiry. During this period the conduct of foreign policy proceeded with remarkable smoothness and efficiency because the executive branch and Congress shared a common conceptual framework, thus permitting a high level of dialogue along roughly parallel lines that focused on the means for carrying out policy based on goals that were not the subject of dispute. There was, moreover, considerably more conflict between the branches than both admirers and detractors of bipartisanship care to remember. The "great debate" over sending troops to Europe, and the bitterness between the branches throughout Dean Acheson's tenure (especially during the Korean War), provide clear reminders that all was not harmony. The literature of the period reminds us also that many of the ideas resulting in policy during that period originated in Congress, such as the Surplus Agriculture Commodities Program, the International Development Association, and the Arms Control and Disarmament Agency.[27]

One possible reason for the success and longevity of this period of executive-legislative partnership was that the events of the world seemed to respond to American actions so as to confirm the validity of the conceptual structure of the Cold War, thus legitimizing it and accelerating further action along the same lines.

The structure of the world, however, was in flux. Sometime between the late 1950s and the mid-1960s the conceptual framework of the Cold War lost its functional conformity to the real world. American actions in the world no longer seemed to be met by the response predicted by the framework. Unfortunately, the policy leaders in both branches of government were considerably behind reality in perceiving the changing world structure. As a result, there was no modified or new structure put forward as a framework for policy. Policy formulation and decisions proceeded according to the established norms. In Cuba, the Dominican Republic, Guatemala, Chile, the Congo, Tanzania, and Indochina, American foreign policy proceeded in established channels that had less and less conformity with the real world structure.

By 1965, the weakness of the old conceptual framework was blatantly evident, yet no replacement came forward. The policy consensus between Congress and the Executive, and between the people and their government, collapsed. The executive branch had completely lost faith in the old concept, but having no new one to put forward, and having a heavy vested interest in the momentum of established policy, gritted its teeth and forged ahead. Congress had no new concept, but many voices decrying the old. The result was policy chaos in the late 1960s and early 1970s.

With the accession of the Nixon administration in 1969, a new conceptual framework was for the first time put forward. Underlying the slogans of the Nixon Doctrine, Vietnamization, "the U.S. will no longer be the world's police-man," and "era of negotiation not confrontation," was a coherent and compre-hensive conceptual framework being articulated by Henry Kissinger. Instead of the simple bipolar model of containment, the world was seen to conform to a model of diffuse power centers wherein American interests must be pursued by adjusting policy to the power realities. Overtures to mainland China, calling on allies to shoulder the burden of their own defense, and pursuing negotiations with the Soviet Union based solely on mutual interest exhibited an internal logic that became evident to growing numbers of people. Congress naturally took a great deal longer to grasp this conceptual framework than did the unified execu-tive branch. It is tragic that just as this consensus began to emerge, it was obliter-ated by the devastation of the Executive as a result of Watergate.

At the present writing it is still not possible to say whether a generally accepted conceptual framework shared by Congress, the Executive, and the people can be forged in the wake of the tumultuous events of 1974-75.

## NOTES

1. Alexis de Tocqueville, *Democracy in America* (New York: Doubleday, 1969), Ch. XIII.

2. See variations on this theme in Jacob Javits, "The Congressional Presence in Foreign Policy," *Foreign Affairs* 49 (January 1970): passim; William Elliott. *United States Foreign Policy* (New York: Columbia University Press, 1952), pp. 115-17; Francis Wilcox, *Congress, the Executive, and Foreign Policy* (New York: Harper and Row, 1971), p. 93.

3. Stanley Falk and Theodore Bauer, *National Security Management* (Washington, D.C.: Industrial College of the Armed Forces, 1972), p. 83; Wilcox, *Congress, the Executive and Foreign Policy*, p. 81.

4. Walter Bagehot, *The English Constitution* (London: Fontana Library, 1963), p. 75.

5. Cited in Emmet Hughes, *The Living Presidency* (New York: Coward, McCann and Geoghegan, 1972), p. 144.

6. Arthur Schlesinger, Jr., *A Thousand Days* (London: Mayflower Books, 1967), p.557.

7. Cited in Arthur Schlesinger, Jr., "Congress and the Making of American Foreign Policy," *Foreign Affairs Quarterly* 51, No. 1 (1972): 100.

8. U.S. President, *Public Papers of the Presidents* (Washington, D.C.: Office of the Federal Register, 1971), Richard M. Nixon, 1970, p. 543.

9. Wilcox, *Congress, the Executive and Foreign Policy*, p. 42.

10. Schlesinger, "Making of Foreign Policy," p. 100; Wilcox, *Congress, the Executive and Foreign Policy*, pp. 43-45.

11. John Stennis and J.W. Fulbright, *The Role of Congress in Foreign Policy* (Washington, D.C.: American Enterprise Institute For Public Policy Research, 1971), p. 70.

12. See Schlesinger, "Making of Foreign Policy," p. 99.

13. Ibid., p. 98.

14. Based on interview with Senator William Spong of Virginia, March 1973.

15. Hughes, *Living Presidency*, p. 210.

16. Interview with William Timmons, January 1973.

17. Timmons interview, March 1971.

18. Ibid.

19. Wilcox, *Congress, the Executive and Foreign Policy*, p. 84; Burton Sapin, *The Making of United States Foreign Policy* (New York: Praeger, 1966), p. 54.

20. Washington *Star*, May 4, 1970, p. 15.

21. Wilcox, *Congress, the Executive and Foreign Policy*, p. 98.

22. Falk and Bauer, *National Security Management*, p. 82.

23. Randall B. Ripley, *Power in the Senate* (New York: St. Martin's, 1969), p. 139.

24. Wilcox, *Congress, the Executive and Foreign Policy*, p. 72.

25. Sapin, *The Making of United States Foreign Policy*, p. 46.

26. Dean Acheson, *Present at the Creation* (New York: W.W. Norton, 1969), p. 72; Wilcox, *Congress, the Executive and Foreign Policy*, p. 88.

27. Wilcox, *Congress, the Executive and Foreign Policy*, p. 14.

Acheson, Dean. *A Citizen Looks at Congress*. New York: Harper & Bros., 1957.

———. *Present at the Creation—My Years in the State Department*. New York: W.W. Norton, 1969.

Alexander, D.S. *History and Procedure of the House of Representatives*. Boston: Houghton Mifflin, 1916.

Andrews, Wayne, ed. *The Autobiography of Theodore Roosevelt*. New York: Scribner's, 1958.

Bagehot, Walter. *The English Constitution*. London: Fontana Library, 1963.

Berger, Raoul. *Executive Privilege: A Constitutional Myth*. Cambridge, Massachusetts: Harvard University Press, 1974.

Binkley, Wilfred E. *President and Congress*. Third edition. New York: Vintage, 1962.

Brierly, J.L. *The Law of Nations*. Edited by Sir Humphrey Waldock. Oxford: Oxford University Press, 1963.

Burns, James MacGregor. *Presidential Government: The Crucible of Leadership*. Boston: Houghton Mifflin, 1965.

Congressional Quarterly, Inc. *Guide to the United States Congress*. Washington, D.C.: Congressional Quarterly, Inc., 1971.

Corwin, Edward S. *The President, Office, and Powers 1787-1957*. New York: New York University Press, 1957.

———. *The Constitution and What It Means Today*. New York: Atheneum, 1967.

Dicey, A.V. *An Introduction to the Study of the Law of the Constitution*. London: Macmillan, 1965.

Dvorin, Eugene P. *The Senate's War Powers*. New York: University Press, 1971.

Eisenhower, Dwight D. *The White House Years: Waging Peace 1956-1961*. Garden City, New York: Doubleday, 1965.

Elliott, William Yandell. *United States Foreign Policy: Its Organization and Control*. New York: Columbia University Press, 1952.

Fenno, Richard F. *The Power of the Purse: Appropriations Politics in Congress*. Boston: Little, Brown, 1966.

Fisher, Louis. *President and Congress: Power and Policy*. New York: Free Press, 1972.

Fulbright, J. William. *The Crippled Giant*. New York: Vintage, 1972.

Gallagher, Hugh. *Advise and Obstruct*. New York: Delacorte, 1969.

Halberstam, David. *The Best and the Brightest*. New York: Fawcett, 1972.

Hamilton, Alexander; Madison, James; and Jay, John. *The Federalist Papers*. New York: New American Library, 1961.

Harris, Joseph P. *Congressional Control of Administration*. Washington, D.C.: Brookings Institution, 1964.

Henkin, Louis. *Foreign Affairs and the Constitution*. Mineola, New York: Foundation Press, 1972.

Hirschfield, Robert S. *The Power of the Presidency—Concepts and Controversy*. New York: Atherton Press, 1968.

Hughes, Emmet John. *The Ordeal of Power*. New York: Atheneum, 1963.

———. *The Living Presidency: The Resources and Dilemmas of the American Presidential Office*. New York: Coward, McCann and Geoghegan, 1972.

Huntington, Samuel P. *The Common Defense*. New York: Columbia University Press, 1961.

Huzar, Elias. *The Purse and the Sword: Control of the Army by Congress Through Military Appropriations*. Ithaca, New York: Cornell University Press, 1950.

Hyman, Sidney. *The American President*. New York: Harper, 1954.

Jennings, Sir Ivor. *The Law and the Constitution*. London: University of London Press, 1959.

———. *The British Constitution*. London: University of London Press, 1959.

Johnson, Lyndon Baines. *The Vantage Point: Perspectives of the Presidency, 1963-1969*. New York: Holt, Rinehart and Winston, 1971.

Kennan, George. *American Diplomacy 1900-1950*. Chicago: University of Chicago Press, 1951.

Koenig, Louis. *The Presidency and the Crisis*. New York: King's Crown Press, 1944.

Kolodziej, E.A. *The Uncommon Defense and Congress*. Columbus: Ohio State University Press, 1966.

McGeary, Nelson M. *The Development of Congressional Investigative Power*. New York: Columbia University Press, 1940.

Moore, John Norton. *Law and the Indochina War*. Princeton: Princeton University Press, 1972.

Neustadt, Richard E. *Presidential Power: The Politics of Leadership*. New York: John Wiley, 1960.

———. *Alliance Politics*. New York: Columbia University Press, 1970.

Nicolay, John, and Jay, John, eds. *The Complete Works of Abraham Lincoln*. New York: Francis D. Tandy, 1894. Vol. 10.

Reedy, George E. *The Twilight of the Presidency*. New York: World Publishing, 1970.

Ripley, Randall B. *Power in the Senate*. New York: St. Martin's, 1969.

Robinson, James A. *The Monroney Resolution: Congressional Initiative in Foreign Policy*. New York: Holt, 1959.

———. *Congress and Foreign Policy: A Study in Legislative Influence and Initiative*. Revised edition. Homewood, Illinois: Dorsey Press, 1969.

Rossiter, Clinton. *The Supreme Court and the Commander in Chief*. Ithaca, New York: Cornell University Press, 1951.

———. *The American Presidency*. New York: Mentor, 1956.

Sabine, George H. *A History of Political Theory*. Third edition. New York: Holt, Rinehart & Winston, 1961.

Sapin, Burton M. *The Making of United States Foreign Policy*. New York: Published for the Brookings Institution by Frederick A. Praeger, 1966.

Schlesinger, Arthur M., Jr. *A Thousand Days: John F. Kennedy in the White House*. London: Mayflower Books, 1967.

———. *The Imperial Presidency*. Boston: Houghton Mifflin, 1973.

Stennis, John C., and Fulbright, J. William. *The Role of Congress in Foreign Policy*. Washington, D.C.: American Enterprise Institute for Public Policy Research, 1971.

Tocqueville, Alexis de. *Democracy in America*. New York: Doubleday, 1969.

Truman, David B. *The Congress and America's Future*. Englewood Cliffs, New Jersey: Prentice-Hall, 1965.

Waltz, Kenneth N. *Foreign Policy and Democratic Politics: The American and British Experience*. Boston: Little, Brown, 1967.

Whalen, Richard J. *Catch the Falling Flag*. Boston: Houghton Mifflin, 1972.

Wilcox, Francis O. *Congress, the Executive, and Foreign Policy*. New York: Harper and Row, 1971.

Williams, Harry T. *Lincoln and the Radicals*. Madison: University of Wisconsin Press, 1941.

Williams, Raymond, ed. *Political Ideas*. The New Thinker's Library. London: C.A. Watts, 1966.

Wilson, Woodrow. *Constitutional Government in the United States*. New York: Columbia University Press, 1908.

———. *Congressional Government*. Boston: Houghton Mifflin, 1913.

JOHN LEHMAN, deputy director of the U.S. Arms Control and Disarmament Agency, first entered government service in January 1969. Initially appointed staff member to the National Security Council, he was made special counsel and senior staff member in 1971. In July 1974, he was named a delegate to the Mutual and Balanced Force Reductions Talks (MBFR) in Vienna. He served in that capacity until his nomination by the President to his present post. Prior to his government service, Dr. Lehman was a staff member of the Foreign Policy Research Institute at the University of Pennsylvania.

Dr. Lehman graduated from St. Joseph's College and holds B.A. and M.A. degrees in International Law and Diplomacy from Cambridge University. He earned his M.A. and Ph.D. in International Relations from the University of Pennsylvania. He is the author and co-editor of several publications on foreign policy and arms control. He is an officer in the U.S. Naval Reserve.